THE HUMAN DRAMA

THE
HUMAN
DRAMA

World History:
from 500 to 1450 C.E.

Jean Elliott Johnson
and Donald James Johnson

Markus Wiener Publishers
Princeton

Dedicated to our three grandchildren,
Jack, Rob and Grace, who once requested,
"Tell us a true story about the past
and make it interesting."

Second printing, 2006.
Copyright © 2002 by Jean Elliott Johnson and Donald James Johnson

For information write to:
Markus Wiener Publishers
231 Nassau Street, Princeton, NJ 08542
www.markuswiener.com

ISBN-13: 978-1-55876-220-6
ISBN-10: 1-55876-220-5

Book design by Cheryl Mirkin

Markus Wiener Publishers books are printed in the
United States of America on acid-free paper, and meet the guidelines for
permanence and durability of the Committee on Production Guidelines
for Book Longevity of the Council on Library Resources.

CONTENTS

ACKNOWLEDGEMENTS

As with all human endeavors, historians build on the experiences and accomplishments of those who have gone before. We particularly acknowledge the cutting-edge world historians who have had a profound influence on our own historical worldview. We are greatly indebted to William McNeill, who first inspired our continuing search for a unified world history, and to Ross Dunn, Jerry Bentley, Kenneth Pomeranz, and John Voll for their enduring efforts to expand the cause of world history with both new and exciting scholarship and with their tireless efforts to infuse world history into the curriculum at all levels of teaching. We also acknowledge the generous scholarly advice from Morris Rossabi, Columbia University, Moss Roberts, New York University, and Yong Jin Kim Choi, Director, Korean Studies Society, The Korea Society.

We wish to make special mention of several scholars who critically read the manuscript prior to publication. Richard Hull, New York University, critiqued the sections on Africa and shared many insights and Steve Gosch, University of Wisconsin, critiqued the entire manuscript and provided many ideas for improving it.

Master history teachers who made significant contributions to Volume I have continued to give us advice on this volume. Among the many exemplary teachers who offered critical evaluations were Michele Forman, President of the World History Association and a teacher at Middlebury Union High School, Vermont, Deborah Johnston, Lexington High School, Lexington, MA, Lorne Swarthout, Berkeley Carroll School, NY, and Jennifer Laden, Fox Lane High School, Bedford, NY. Mary Rossabi, The Fieldston School, NYC, was most helpful with the discussion of the Kievian Rus, and Jack Betterly, The Emma Willard School, Troy, NY, offered many suggestion which have improved the quality of this volume.

The authors are greatly indebted to several of the teachers who are using The Human Drama in their classes who have passed on student reactions to the text and offered both criticisms and encouragement. Among this group are Susan Meeker and Joan Kenyon, Hunter College High School, NY, Karen Jernigan and Bram Hubbell, Friends Seminary, NY, Patience Berkman, Newton Country Day School of the Sacred Heart, MA, and Ben Leeming, The Rivers School. We also thank David Burzillo, The Rivers School, who organized a panel on *The Human Drama* at the Northeastern Conference on World History in March, 2004.

We owe a debt of gratitude to Jessica Keefe, of Octo Studies, who not only created most of the maps for this volume but also offered expert aid about other technical details, and to Cheryl Mirkin and Susie Van Doren who have contributed their considerable editorial and layout expertise.

We also thank our publisher, Markus Wiener, for his continued faith in this project and his efforts to promote the text. Finally, we owe more than we can say to our son Keith Johnson: without his unflagging patience and constant technical support and encouragement this text would not have been completed.

SETTING THE STAGE

The human drama opened hundreds of thousands of years ago on the East African stage when our oldest common ancestors gradually emerged as human beings. These earliest human actors and actresses were scavenger/gatherers and then hunters, spending much of their time searching for berries, roots, and animals, both dead and alive. From their first homeland in East Africa, they spread out over the globe, creating settlements across Eurasia and the Americas. By learning to cooperate, to speak and create categories and symbols, to make tools, to share their knowledge, and to support the very young and old, they survived and multiplied.

By forty thousand years ago humans had developed large brains and had essentially the same intellectual capacity as people have today. The cast of characters in the drama used their intelligence to make many different choices, depending on the area in which they settled and the values they shared. They developed different languages, unique ways of adjusting to their environment, distinctive spiritual beliefs and artistic expressions: in brief, they created many diverse cultures.

Around twelve thousand years ago, as some ingenious people in several parts of the world figured out how to raise crops and breed animals, the drama grew more complex. Three distinct lifestyles developed: hunter-gatherers, semi-nomadic herders, and settled farmers. Most of those playing the roles of settled people became farmers, revered the land and cows as their sources of sustenance, and they prayed to mother goddesses for protection, fertility, and prosperity. Those who lived on the grasslands, which were too arid to support agriculture, herded sheep and cattle. Military might was important for them, and their warrior sky gods empowered them as they moved from place to place, seeking grass for their herds. Once they tamed the horse—which provided speed, status, food, and security—many became fully nomadic. Hunter-gatherers, meanwhile, continued to forage for survival in their small bands.

Improved farming tools and techniques enabled farmers to produce surplus food so not everyone had to farm, and the drama grew still more complex. Surplus led to specialization, and some actors took on starring roles as kings or large landholding aristocrats. Others were given supporting roles playing peasants and artisans, and some, like slaves, served only as stagehands. Some talented actors got choice roles such as priestesses and priests, artists, bureaucrats, and writers. Women seldom got important parts and almost always played small supporting roles or had jobs making costumes and serving food to the stars. Despite unequal roles, specialization enabled the human cast to build villages, towns, and eventually large cities.

Nomadic Migrations and Invasions

Every exciting drama needs conflict, and the human drama seldom had a shortage of competition and strife. One of the longest-running feuds was the often-troubled relationship between nomads and settled people. When prevented from trading for the goods they needed to survive, nomadic groups often plundered settled communities. Settled people constantly feared that nomads would come thundering into their midst, destroying what had taken centuries to build.

An extended period of nomadic expansion into the settled world occurred during the early centuries of the second millennium B.C.E. Wave after wave of Semitic nomads from the Arabian Peninsula, as well as Indo-European nomads who had come originally from Inner Asia, stormed into the urban societies, with far-reaching consequences for everyone. Climactic changes, disease, inadequate food supplies, increases in population, new technology, wars, and political, social, and economic weakness in neighboring areas all may have pushed these nomads from the steppes. Certainly, the fresh opportunities and the possibility for getting rich that cities seemed to offer as well as the desire to acquire new land helped pull many to leave their homelands.

Nomads took on new roles in cities, which were hardly an appropriate place for raising herds of sheep and cattle. They learned to eat grain along with their traditional meaty meals and told stories about how their sky gods married local goddesses. Settled people became more militaristic as they tried to meet the challenges the newcomers presented. Cities grew and merchants struggled to have more say in their societies' political and cultural life.

The Axial Age

Interaction between nomads and settled people created some distressing scenes. Urban life was insecure, the old gods and goddesses no longer seemed able to answer prayers, and the actors and actresses, especially those playing roles in cities, questioned their beliefs and values. As a result, from the seventh to the fourth century B.C.E. philosophers and teachers from Greece to China came on stage, offering ways to tame the warriors and help people deal with the insecurities of urban life. They included Thales and Pythagoras in Greece, prophets such as Amos and Jeremiah in Israel, Zoroaster in Persia, the Buddha and Mahavira in India, and Confucius and the Daoists in China. They probed the nature of divinity, examined the basis of moral action, tried to suggest standards to guide the way people treat one another, and searched for the ultimate meaning of life. They also suggested ways to bring about social justice and harmony and create societies where people treated one another with dignity and respect. This period has been called the Axial Age because its thinkers began traditions that continue to this day.

Empires

All this theorizing and ethical discussions were well and good, but how could most men and women live up to such lofty ideals, especially as conflict in the drama also intensified? Some actors grew discontent with their roles as leaders of small territories; they aspired to be superstars. Toward that end they attacked other leaders, conquered new land, and turned their city-states into kingdoms and empires. The most impressive and long-lasting were the Achaemenid (Persian) in Iran (550–331 B.C.E.), the Mauryan in India (320 B.C.E.–185 B.C.E.), the Han in China (220 B.C.E.–220 C.E.), and the Roman (31 B.C.E.–476 C.E.). These empires were composed of many diverse peoples, and some, such as the Achaemenid and Roman, tolerated a great deal of cultural pluralism, while others, such as the Han, created a common philosophy. Rulers had to find ways of establishing their legitimacy, keeping the peace, protecting their borders, keeping others—especially wealthy landlords—from trying to depose them, and making their subjects obey the rules, pay taxes, and serve in the military. These goals proved difficult to achieve, and bad-acting emperors and choruses of over-taxed peasants and unemployed workers contributed to the end of each empire.

Cross-Cultural Interaction

Two expanding stages, one in the western hemisphere and the other vastly larger territory that stretched from England to Japan, grew crowded as actors and actresses from different areas came into contact with one another. Towns, cities, and empires cannot survive without trade, and extensive exchanges over both land and sea developed. Men and women with very diverse ways of looking at the world shared all manner of things such as ideas, goods, technology, beliefs, germs, and gossip, which resulted in many changes.

From 200 B.C.E. to 300 C.E., the Silk Roads—going east and west between Europe and China, and north and south into the Eurasian steppe and India—facilitated interaction across Eurasia. In addition, ships in the Mediterranean Sea and Indian Ocean carried heavy items, such as raw materials, food grains, and manufactured goods. Ships and camels began to knit the entire Afro-Eurasian land-mass into a single trading system and communication zone, making possible the exchange not only of goods but of science and technology, new foods, styles, diseases, and religious and philosophic concepts.

What's Ahead?

As we pick up the human drama, we will first visit the Western Hemisphere and focus on early civilizations in Mesoamerica. We will then turn to the Eastern Hemisphere at about 500 C.E., and examine first the development and spread of religions that were open to everyone and then the flowering of empires and the emergence of new states across Eurasia. We will constantly be addressing the importance of cross-cultural contact and exchanges.

Numerous questions emerge as we ponder what is going to happen. How will increasing trade and contact change people's beliefs and lifestyles? Will the agriculturally-based urbanized empires continue as the norm in many parts of the world; if not, what new kinds of states will emerge? What new technology will develop? What effects will it have not only on people but on the environment? Will new inventions enable people to live happier lives or will the innovations be used to kill and enslave others? How will improved transportation and communication facilitate the sharing of knowledge for human development? Who will benefit from such things as better roads, bridges, canals, postal systems and an increasing storehouse of written records?

How will the Axial Age messages of peace, justice, harmony, and humaneness play out in the drama ahead? How will these impressive teachings affect the lives of peasants, artisans, scholars, businessmen, church leaders, and average men and women, both rich and poor? Will kings and emperors, merchants and landlords, harness these ideas to control those they rule and justify their own wealth and power? Will people find ways to "turn their swords into plowshares," or will cruelty increase and violence in the name of religious faith become fully justified and morally acceptable? How will men and women build on the insights from the past?

All these questions and many more lead us to ask whether history moves forward and whether there is such a thing as "progress" or whether gains in some areas are offset by setbacks in others. If control over nature and better technology is the measure of progress, then perhaps it exists, but if we evaluate societies by their compassion and community, then we might question the idea of historical progress.

We can also look for the "engine" that moves history. What causes change? What role does new technology play? Do ideas of change originate first in the human mind? Does it occur when people encounter and adapt or resist new ideas? Does change result when people move to new areas and face new challenges? Is change a result of a combination of causes? Or is it mostly accidental?

As we enter the human drama in the coming epoch, keep these questions in mind. Human history is an unfolding drama, and events are not predetermined. At each point, men and women have options and make choices which affected what happens next. Be on the lookout for the options people had and the choices they made. Join with us as we consider what will happen in the acts ahead.

Complex Societies Develop in the Americas

In the centuries between 25,000 and 14,000 B.C.E., nomads from Central Asia began following caribou and other animals across the land bridge that connected northern Siberia to mainland North America. Others probably came by boat, following the Alaskan shore down the west coast of the Americas. Over the next millennia these scavengers and hunters slowly worked southward to present-day Chile and eastward across North America. Fourteen thousand years ago human settlements were scattered along the western coast of the Western Hemisphere; 11,500 years ago they were in the lower Hudson Valley; and by 10,000 years ago, people inhabited the eastern seaboard of the continent as well.

Because the distinctive stone points the early settlers had made were first discovered near the town of Clovis, New Mexico, scholars called the people in the area "Clovis" people and suggested that the entire Native American population, including Eskimos and other groups, had descended from these Asiatic wanderers. However, new archaeological evidence proves that humans had reached southern Chile a millennium before the Clovis people did. In fact, they may have arrived thousands or even tens of thousands of years earlier, coming in different waves and traveling a number of routes.

7

Some probably migrated in hide-covered boats, hugging the southern shore of the Bering land bridge or perhaps making a more southerly landfall and continuing down the west coast of North America. They may have sailed past North America and landed initially along the southern coast. Fifty thousand years ago people in Australia had boats that could sail on the open sea, so some may have come from Australia or even Southeast Asia. A recent archaeological discovery of the nose and jaw of a young woman has added to the debate. She probably lived in the savanna of what is now south-central Brazil about 11,500 years ago, and her features look Negroid, not Mongoloid. Scholars wonder if her ancestors might have come across the Atlantic from Africa's northwest coast, and they are trying to fit this discovery into the larger picture of American settlement.

On the other hand, archaeological evidence has proven that Norsemen from Scandinavia called Vikings reached North America at the end of the first millennium C.E. They had already raided and then settled areas along the north coast of the British Isles, and later they sailed farther west into the Irish Sea. By 874 they had colonized Iceland. In about 985, when he was banished from Ireland, Eric "the Red" took a small group and settled on the southern tip of the next island. He named it Greenland, hoping the name might induce others

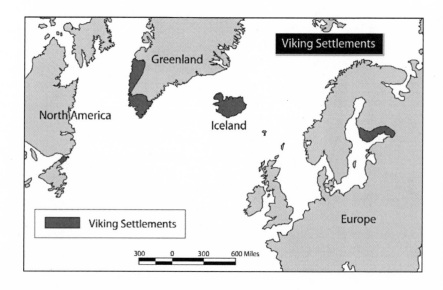

to join his group there. Traveling from settlement to settlement took only two or three days in good weather, and soon there was regular contact among Norway, the British Isles, Iceland, and Greenland. In 1000, Leif Erikson (Eric's son) explored the coasts of Newfoundland and Labrador, and established European settlement in the Americas. The colony in Newfoundland lasted for about a hundred years.

People in several areas of the Americas, stretching from present-day Peru to the southwestern portion of what is now the United States, learned to raise crops and breed animals about eight thousand years ago. Farmers gradually developed successful farming techniques even without large animals or wheeled vehicles and cultivated plants unknown in Eurasia. Their major crops included maize (corn), potatoes, beans, and squash, and they were the first to grow tomatoes and capsicum peppers. Corn and potatoes were unknown in any other part of the world until after 1492. Maize and beans produced more calories per acre than rice farming in Asia or wheat and barley crops in West Asia and Europe. Protein came from dogs, turkeys, fish, turtles, and birds, including geese that migrated from North America. Surplus food made urban life and complex societies possible.

Type of Cities

Urbanization is a major theme in human history. The men and women who developed cities in the Tigris-Euphrates, Nile, and Indus river valleys created the first complex societies, with cities composed of many diverse people living close together and performing different jobs.

We can identify at least four distinct types of cities: a sacred city, a cosmic city, a city that serves as the society's political center, and a city with a major focus on trade. Sacred cities are founded at places people consider holy, such as a sacred spring, mountain, or the site of some special event. People make pilgrimages to these places and traders come to sell their goods to the pilgrims. Gradually a village develops, and then a town, and finally a city. (Maybe one day Graceland, in Tennessee, will become a city.)

Cosmic cities are carefully designed. The city's plan represents the vision people have of the universe or cosmos. The size and location of streets and monuments reflect what the community values most as well as its keen desire to control forces in the universe. Streets and buildings are often laid out in a regular pattern and consciously aligned with the movement of the sun or stars. Cosmic cities can be constructed anywhere. Of course, a cosmic city that is built at a sacred site has even more importance and power.

Cities are often political centers where the ruler and government reside. Government buildings and the ruler's palace often dominate the landscape and symbolize the ruler's power and legitimacy. Washington, D.C. is an example of a political city. So are Brasilia, the capital of Brazil, and Ankara, Turkey.

Finally, a city can be a major commercial center. Trading centers often originate at crossroads or near rivers or large bodies of water where people meet to exchange their goods and traders and animals rest before the next lap of the journey. People supporting the merchants, such as farmers with food to sell and others on the lookout for bargains, often settle near those crossroads, and gradually a town and then an urban center develops. New York and London are two examples of cities in which trade is important.

The layout of many cities often becomes a model of the community's shared past and common faith as well as a model of those values for future generations. Many early towns in the United States had a shared open space called a common, originally used for grazing animals, that centered the community. Statues of local heroes and commemorative plaques prominently displayed in town squares reminded the community of its shared faith and how individuals had sacrificed for the public good.

As we studied early history, we noted examples of these different types of cities. People in India believe that Varanasi is the birthplace of the god Shiva. Jerusalem is sacred to Jews, Christians, and Muslims. Ancient Greeks considered Delphi the "navel of the universe." The Han capital was laid out as a cosmic city. Because economic and political control are often closely related, important cities frequently serve as both political and economic centers. Constantinople was both a major trading center and the seat of political power of the Eastern Roman Empire. Changan under the Han was not only a carefully planned cosmic city but a political and commercial center as well.

Characteristics of a City-State

Some cities are the centers of small states, and the city-state provides some form of central control and political leadership. Many of us associate city-states with the Greek polis and the direct democracy that citizens in Athens developed, but there are many other examples. Singapore is a well-known contemporary city-state.

The city is the city-state's well-defined center. It is usually surrounded by walls or water. City-states are most often ruled by a group of elite citizens who are usually large landholders. Family background (lineage) often determines who leads, but sometimes very rich traders and merchants are able to become part of the ruling oligarchy. Because city-states are small, their leaders can govern directly rather than through the several layers of delegated authority common in larger states and empires.

A city-state, like any other state, is sovereign, which means it has the final authority over its territory. Residents of a city state, like citizens of most modern nations, share a common language and often believe that they share a common history as well. Its leaders try to preserve the independence of the city-state from outside threats. Because they are relatively small, city-states often have to make alliances, hire mercenary armies, and try to weaken their potential enemies by following a divide-and-rule political strategy. Even so, the life span of even the most successful city-states is usually no more than four to five hundred years.

Besides sovereignty and political independence, city-states want to be economically self-sufficient. However, most depend on resources from the surrounding agricultural lands and from trade. In addition, city-states, such as those in Sumer and Greece, shared a common heritage with other city-states in the same area.

The history of Mesoamerica in the first millennium C.E. is largely a story of numerous different urban centers. Many were city-states with impressive religious structures. Several combined cosmic and sacred characteristics. We shall be on the lookout for the characteristics and common elements that developed in Mesoamerica as we examine their complex societies.

SCENE
ONE

THE OLMECS

Setting the Stage

Mesoamerica refers to the geographic area that includes present-day southern Mexico, Guatemala, Honduras, Belize, El Salvador, and part of Costa Rica. Although its climate, topography, and ecology are very diverse, it has two main regions. The tropical lowlands are located near the Pacific Ocean and the Caribbean Sea and consist mainly of tropical rainforests. The highlands include mountains and fertile valleys, especially the valley of Mexico, the Oaxaca valley, and the plain of present-day Guatemala.

By about 1500 B.C.E. a group known as the Olmecs had settled in the hot coastal plain near the Gulf of Mexico and developed communities along riverbanks. The Caribbean Sea formed the area's northern boundary; to the south were mountains. Many small lakes created natural borders to the east and west. Although there are no written

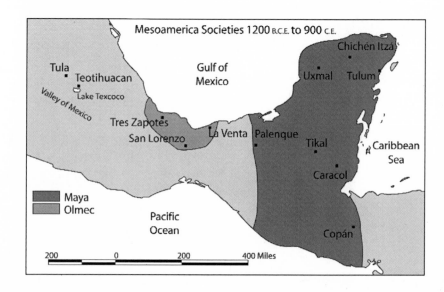

Mesoamerica Societies 1200 B.C.E. to 900 C.E.

records that tell us about Olmec society, much intriguing evidence remains, particularly spectacular stone carvings and impressive earthen mounds. Scholars must infer how the Olmec people lived and what they believed from these mute objects.

Who Were the Olmecs?

Historians are not sure who the Olmecs were, where they came from, or what they called themselves. Later groups referred to them as the rubber people, perhaps because rubber trees grew in that area. Old poems speak of a legendary land:

> in a certain area
> which no one can reckon
> which no one can remember. . .
> there was a government for a long time.

Olmec society probably developed for many of the same reasons that societies along the banks of other rivers had emerged: abundant resources, such as fish and birds, ease of transportation, and, most important, periodic flooding that kept the land fertile and allowed the same area to be farmed for long periods. Like Egyptian civilization, which has been called the "Gift of the Nile," San Lorenzo, the first important Olmec settlement, was a "gift" of the Coatzacoalcos River and its tributaries. The coastal area had ample rain, and people worked to clear forests, drain swamps, check the threat of flooding, and control the amount of water getting to the crops, much as settlers had done in earlier river valley civilizations. This was especially difficult because the water table was very high and the area tended to become swampy, especially following heavy rainfall.

San Lorenzo and La Venta

San Lorenzo was probably an important Mesoamerican settlement from around 1500 to at least 1200 B.C.E. Laborers, carrying baskets of dirt, constructed a plateau about 150 feet above the lowlands on which the city was built. Archaeological evidence suggests that religious, political, and economic activities took place in the city's center. A large population supported it. The society's hierarchy may have developed as people competed for the best farmland near the river and for commercial opportunities.

La Venta, another important Olmec site, was built between 1150 and 800 B.C.E. on swampy land near the coast, and it was important until about 400 B.C.E. It must have been impressive. The people constructed a 110-foot-high volcano-shaped pyramid of clay, the largest that had been built in Mesoamerica up to that time. La Venta also contained a large ceremonial plaza, courts with columns, splendidly carved stone altars, and enormous stone slabs, called stelae, covered with sculptured reliefs. The plaza was only a small part of the extensive site. Farming that supported the city was done on levees built along the shore; some of the levees were about twelve feet high. Archaeologists have discovered several other impressive Olmec sites but no evidence of any centralized power. The centers were probably independent rather than politically united.

Art Provides Clues About Olmec Life

Judging from Olmec art, religion may have focused on the jaguar or a half-man, half-jaguar being. In their magical world, the jaguar symbolized earth, night, and possibly fertility. Many of the figures are fat, sexless infants, with downcast mouths that make them look as if they are either crying or snarling.

A jaguar spirit

One interpretation suggests the faces might represent toads. One species of toad that thrives in these wet coastal lowlands sheds its own skin periodically, like a snake, and then eats it. What some art historians describe as fangs on a jaguar-type figure may actually be a toad eating its own skin. This action may have suggested rejuvenation or some kind of conquest over death. Toads were perhaps associated with the primal waters of the underworld, where rejuvenation was believed to take place. Many images have a cleft in the forehead, and from some of the clefts a tree emerges. This also suggests renewal.

The Olmecs created an amazing number of outstanding jade objects, including masks, human figurines, cylindrical beads, pendants, and even a hollow canoe which, when turned upside down, is a human hand. Jade, a very hard stone, was difficult to carve and was found only in isolated ravines and riverbeds. Even after Olmec artisans began working with gold and silver, they seem to have prized jade above those metals and may have considered it sacred.

Statues of human beings indicate Olmec society had a definite hierarchy. Social status is revealed in the types of clothing and ornaments the figures wore. Males were depicted with short skirts held up by belts and tunics, while females wore little capes or short tunics in addition to skirts and belts. Priests also wore elaborate headdresses. Nudity was associated with low status. Some figures were dressed in long cloaks that probably signified high status. Men and women wore lots of jewelry, particularly ornaments made of jade and other colored stones.

What Is the Significance of the Colossal Heads?

Archaeologists have discovered at least seventeen colossal heads, some six feet high and each weighing from sixteen to eighteen tons. These basalt and granite heads are probably the most impressive artwork the Olmecs created. Each head appears to have been a complete work of art, without a body attached to it. The faces have thick heavy lips, full cheeks, broad noses, and somewhat swollen eyelids, and each wears a close-fitting helmet, similar to those worn by players in Mesoamerican ball games. The faces are expressionless, but they were probably portraits of individuals. If they are portraits of leaders, they may por-

Olmec head

tray hereditary kings.

Clearly the heads and the people they represented were important. The stone was quarried miles from where the heads were found, so transporting it took a great deal of time and effort. Because some of the features seem to be Negroid or Australoid, the heads caused some speculation over whether there might have been contact between Africans and/or Pacific Islanders and Mesoamericans in these early centuries.

Writing and a Calendar

Scholars have difficulty dating Olmec events. Archaeologists have found a stele that contains both Olmec writing and a calendar. The Olmecs used a Calendar Round that meshed a 260-day year with the 365-day solar year. A day from the 260-day year coincided with a day in the solar year once every 52 years. But the Calendar Round did not indicate in which 52-year cycle an event had occurred, so it did not indicate how long ago an event had taken place. For that the Olmecs used the Long Count, counting forward from a single date.

Jade, obsidian, iron ore for mirrors, and cacao beans for making chocolate have all been excavated from Olmec sites. Because these items were not available locally, the Olmecs must have had extensive contacts outside their communities and an effective system for exchanging goods and ideas. The Zapotecs, who lived in the valley of Oaxaca, were in contact with the Olmecs and also used the Calendar Round. In fact, there was probably extensive interaction among various groups as early as the second millennium B.C.E.; they shared innovations in writing and marking time as well as other aspects of their culture.

Unanswered Questions

Scholars have concluded that the Olmecs had strong centralized governments that may have been run by a hereditary elite. But there are many unanswered questions about this society. Who organized and supervised the making and moving of those colossal heads or the building of the mounds and pyramids? Who kept the ceremonial centers in good repair? How were exchanges carried out? What kind of relationship did the Olmecs have with people in the highlands and other regions?

And what caused the Olmec decline? In both San Lorenzo and La Venta, many of the large sculptures were mutilated. Some were battered and broken into fragments. Others had entire sections broken off or grooves cut into them, and some images were effaced. Many statues were decapitated, and then their heads were buried in carefully aligned rows. Initially scholars thought either invaders had smashed the sculptures or disillusioned farmers and other poor subjects had become so angry with the rulers that they had revolted and destroyed the ritual centers. But if that is what happened, why would they take the time to bury the damaged sculptures so carefully? If the statues represented leaders or other individuals with supernatural power, perhaps the Olmecs believed that their power became dangerous once they had died and could no longer control it. Perhaps mutilating the statues was a way to neutralize that power. Many questions remain.

Archaeological records clearly reveal that the Olmecs developed a complex civilization with specialization, stratification, centralized control, a shared system of beliefs, and trade. Efforts to understand their civilization are important because it may have influenced later groups in Mesoamerica. As we consider Teotihuacan and the Maya, we can look for possible Olmec legacies as well examine their examples of urban life.

COSMOPOLITAN TEOTIHUACAN

Setting the Stage

After the Olmecs and their neighbors disappeared, other communities developed in Mesoamerica during the first millennium B.C.E. They also produced surpluses and specialized occupations, monumental buildings, some type of centralized control, and evidence of shared meanings. Monte Alban was probably a planned city founded by an alliance of groups in the Valley of Oaxaca. It was built on high, neutral ground that was easy to defend. Its impressive arrow-shaped building was aligned to enable astronomers to observe the planets and stars. But the main purpose of that building seems to have been to display forty stone slabs illustrating military victories. In addition, some three hundred twenty carved reliefs have been found that illustrate nude (and therefore humiliated), tortured, and executed prisoners of war. These images were probably made to intimidate any group that might consider getting out of line.

Teotihuacan, another very impressive city-state that developed during the period after 150 B.C.E., dominated the central highland of Mesoamerica. Teotihuacan is located in the Valley of Mexico about thirty miles from present-day Mexico City. The valley—700 feet above sea level—is surrounded by even higher mountains.

Why Was Teotihuacan So Sacred?

Teotihuacan was built on a spot that was considered holy from very early times. It is situated at the foot of a sacred volcanic mountain whose name meant Mother of Waters, the source of life-giving springs. In addition, there is a sacred cave at the site. Caves were important in Mesoamerican religion and myth. People thought they were entrances to the underworld and the fertile womb of the earth. The cave at Teotihuacan was believed to be the place where the world began, where time started and the gods were born. Two of the gods gathered there in the primordial darkness sacrificed themselves and became the sun and the moon.

Men and women began to make pilgrimages to this sacred site early in the first millennium B.C.E, performing ceremonies with both fire and water. It probably served as a pilgrimage center for centuries. By 200 B.C.E. perhaps as many as two thousand people had settled near the sacred mountain and cave.

What Makes Teotihuacan a Cosmic City?

Religion seems to have been the driving force behind the establishment of Teotihuacan. In the first century of the common era, priest-architects made a plan for the city that represented their idea of the cosmos. It was a grid pattern of wide boulevards and streets that met at right angles. Two major boulevards, the north-south Street of the Dead and an east-west avenue, divided the city into quarters. The Citadel (most probably the political center) and the Great Compound (a market area of about forty acres) were situated in the center of the

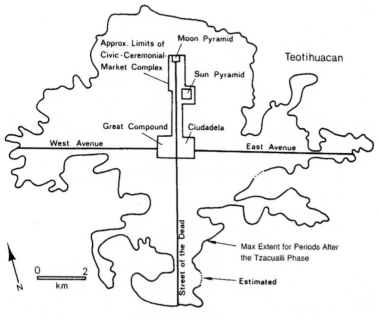

Plan of Teotihuacan

Pyramid of the Moon and Pyramid of the Sun

city where the two boulevards crossed. Homes for the city's most important residents and more than twenty temple complexes lined the Street of the Dead, including the imposing Pyramid of the Sun.

The Pyramid of the Sun was built beside the Street of the Dead and directly over the sacred cave, the birthplace of the gods. One scholar, who has made extensive excavations at the site, remarked that the pyramid's "very existence is unmistakable evidence of the vigor and power of the city as a sacred and ritual center." There was no natural spring under the pyramid, but drains built inside the cave suggest that priests piped in water for ritual purposes. The sides of this impressive pyramid are about two and a half football fields long and it was about 215 feet high. There were probably two small temples on top, one to the Goddess and the other to the Storm God.

The Pyramid of the Moon stands at the northern end of the Street of the Dead. It may have represented the sacred mountain in the distance that frames it. The Street of the Dead rises almost a hundred feet as it runs from the Citadel to the Pyramid of the Moon. Ritual possessions may have symbolically transported worshipers from the earth to the heavens or offered a comparable spiritual experience. The whole carefully planned, magnificent complex suggests that the architects made a conscious effort to overwhelm viewers by the sheer size and grandeur of both the avenue and the pyramids and temples beside it.

Gods and the Goddess

Teotihuacan's major deity was the Great Goddess. She nourished life but also had a terrifying aspect, indicated by human hearts on her headdress. She was associated primarily with water but also with mountains, caves, and all that the earth produces. She was often represented as a woman wearing a nose bar with a pendant hanging from it. She was also portrayed with gifts cascading from her outstretched hands, although those hands are sometimes claws, symbolizing her destructive power and reminding devotees that sacrifice is essential to maintaining the cosmos. Human figures, pictured serving her, were almost always much smaller and shown in profile.

The Storm God was another important deity. Historians conclude he was associated with war and power because his emblem appeared on warriors' shields. Headdresses were a common symbol of authority in Teotihuacan art, and in one mural the Storm God is shown carrying a headdress on a platter. In another mural he carries corn, suggesting he brings prosperity as well. The Great Goddess and the Storm God may have represented a male-female dual divinity.

A third deity was Quetzalcoatl, the feathered serpent who was linked to royal power. Serpents shed their skins, suggesting renewal or rebirth, and Quetzalcoatl was also associated with fertility. Birds are associated with the sky. Quetzalcoatl combined the germinating power of the earth with the creative powers of the heavens and transcended seeming opposites such as earth and the heavens, life and death, and humans and the gods.

A pyramid dedicated to the feathered serpent was part of the Citadel, which also contained residences for the ruler or ruling elite. Constructed about 150 C.E., the pyramid has a low relief of the feathered serpent's body. Per-

Quetzalcoatl, the Feathered Serpent

haps the leaders were trying to link themselves to Quetzalcoatl's multiple powers in order to enhance their legitimacy. Rulers also decorated their clothes with the quetzal bird's beautiful emerald feathers.

The Political and Commercial Center

The Great Compound appears to have been an enormous market, suggesting that Teotihuacan was a thriving commercial center and that trade was very important. Items made of obsidian, a dark volcanic rock, were among the city's most important exports, and there were over 600 workshops producing obsidian items. The government made sure that the city had a monopoly on their production and trade.

The leadership of Teotihuacan may have sent settlers to other areas, but its strength and influence was probably mainly due to its vast trading network. Military forces may have helped ensure trade with areas that had important minerals or other necessary resources. But without any easy means of transporting troops or supplies, Teotihuacan probably actually controlled only the immediate surrounding area.

The city's population expanded dramatically during the first century C.E., most likely because outsiders swarmed into the city and not because of an internal population explosion. These newcomers included people from different areas who had a variety of beliefs, as well as people performing various occupations. About ninety percent of the total population under the authority of Teotihuacan lived inside the eight-square-mile city.

Some source of authority, whether it was an individual or a group, was able to control and motivate masses of people. Scholars do not know whether people moved into the city and worked on constructing the boulevards and massive pyramids voluntarily, or were forced to do so. Think of the long hours of corvée required to build the pyramids of the Sun and Moon as well as the temples, especially without animals large enough to pull wheeled vehicles. Organizing and carrying out these enormous resettlement and construction projects must have taken impressive administrative skill.

The ruler or rulers probably lived in the Citadel complex, and power symbolically radiated out from the heart of the city. As many as 100,000 people could gather in the large quadrangle that surrounded the Pyramid of the Feathered Serpent. The dedication of the pyramid, around 150 C.E., included a mass burial of weapons and the sacrifice of as many as two hundred soldiers between the ages of eighteen and fifty-five; some of those who were sacrificed had their hands tied behind their backs, and many were facing away from the pyramid as if they were guarding it. Important men and women and perhaps even the ruler were also buried there.

Very soon after the pyramid's dedication, however, the government seems to have changed. For one thing, a platform was erected that partially obscured the Pyramid of the Feathered Serpent, suggesting that the power it represented had decreased. Instead, it appears that a group of leaders took over and governed the city, although there is no evidence of who they might have been. Teotihuacan society was definitely stratified, but no representations of individual leaders or their exploits have been found. In addition, after 250 C.E., there do not seem to have been any buildings commemorating individual kings or priests. The government remained strong and military might was important, but it is unclear exactly who was exerting the power.

Chinampas

Scarcity of water was always a problem, which may be why the Great

Chinampas: source of abundance

Goddess was associated with providing it. One source was the nearby river that ran in a man-made channel through part of the city. People also diverted water from springs to fields and around the *chinampas*.

A chinampa, a raised bed, is a type of garden that appears to float on standing water. It is one of the most productive forms of agriculture ever devised and was probably the major reason Teotihuacan could support so many people. People constructed chinampas by transplanting plants to the swamps and anchoring them against small trees. They put several layers of plants on top of one another until they had created a bed of soil that was higher than the water level, and they planted their crops in these raised beds. The surrounding water seeped into the beds and nourished the roots of the plants. As the weeds f armers threw onto the beds disintegrated, they put nutrients back into the soil.

The raised beds were laid out in a grid pattern, and some were even aligned with the plan of the city. Canals running around them allowed water to circulate. The soil in these beds and the water surrounding them were rich and produced abundant crops and fish. Perhaps as many as 65 percent of the city's residents used them to grow staples: maize, beans, and squash.

Supporting Diversity

About 200 C.E., coinciding with the change in leadership, the people of Teotihuacan began to build residential compounds, one of the city's most distinctive features. By around 250 there were about 2,000 apartment compounds that obviously had been carefully planned. They had drains under the floors and were aligned with the city's major streets. Each housed from sixty to a hundred people and resembled a small community, protected by high, windowless outer walls. Inside each compound were between fifty and a hundred rooms clustered around their own interior courtyard, many of which had a shrine, usually dedicated to deities associated with specific groups. Sometimes a person, perhaps a famous ancestor, was buried under the courtyard floor. Several of the compounds had murals on the walls; most did not. Some were very luxurious, even palatial; most were modest.

Apartment compounds were one way Teotihuacan handled its very diverse population. Each compound probably housed people with

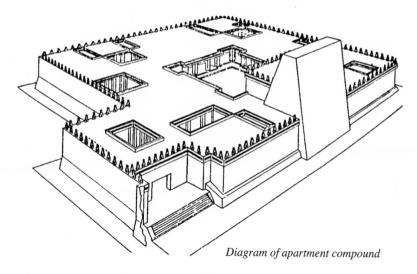

Diagram of apartment compound

common kinship as well as regional or commercial ties. Patios within the building compound made it possible for people to be outdoors yet have some privacy. Some of the compounds were reserved for foreign traders, not unlike diaspora communities created by long-distance traders. Apartments that housed craft groups also served as workshops where artisans produced goods to sell.

Compounds gave people a sense of security and community and promoted group solidarity and identity, sort of like a Little Italy or Chinatown in some U.S. cities. People might have been more willing to settle in Teotihuacan if they could live with their own group and continue to practice their beliefs. Sometimes several apartment compounds were grouped together into barrios or residential wards where people engaged in similar rituals and occupations. The barrios served as the basic political unit between the compounds and the leadership.

Promoting Unity

Besides making it possible for different groups to maintain their own cultures, the leaders of Teotihuacan seem to have made a conscious effort to integrate and unify its very diverse population. The Great Goddess may have helped promote unity. Instead of being associated with a particular group or region, this masked and remote deity transcended all factions and areas. Unlike male divinities that tend to take on individual personalities and become associated with particular groups, she was universal. (Think of images such as Blindfolded Justice or the Statue of Liberty.) The Storm God was most often represented in residential compounds where he guarded specific groups, but the Goddess appeared in public places along the Street of the Dead, granting her bounty to all.

Rituals may have been another way to integrate diverse people. Masks and masked images of divinities are common in Teotihuacan art. Because those performing the rituals wore masks, it was difficult to tell who they were, so they could not be associated with a particular group. Masks also suggest that the community was more important than individuals.

Who Would Want to Harm Teotihuacan?

With 200,000 residents, Teotihuacan was the largest city in the Western Hemisphere in 500 and probably the sixth-largest city in the world. (The other five were Constantinople, Changan, Loyang, Ctesiphon, and Alexandria.) Its monumental religious structures dwarfed buildings in other parts of the region.

However, by about 600 Teotihuacan's power and influence were declining. About a hundred years later some group, perhaps seminomadic tribes from the north or dissatisfied residents, deliberately set fire to the ritual center of the city and destroyed the temples and pyramids but harmed little else. Olmec art had been destroyed in a similar way, and in both cases scholars are not sure why.

The leadership may have become careless or oppressive, causing people to revolt. Ecology may help explain its decline. Preparing limestone for mortar and stucco by burning lime or seashells required lots of firewood, so as the city grew, people cut down the surrounding forests. Deforestation caused soil erosion, drought, and crop failure. During the seventh century, drought caused the amount of water throughout the Valley of Mexico to decrease, adding to the city's water crisis. This also harmed the agricultural production needed to support the city. To appeal to the gods to remove these apparent curses, people may have built more temples, making the shortage even worse. About fifty years after the destruction of the ritual center, some people drifted back to the city, and it continued to be a pilgrimage site, but after the fires, Teotihuacan never regained its prominence.

SCENE THREE

ACHIEVEMENTS OF THE MAYA

Setting the Stage

Maya civilization developed in the tropical forested lowlands of present-day Belize, the volcanic highlands of Guatemala, and the low-lying Yucatan Peninsula with its scant rainfall and poor vegetation. The eastern lowlands, an area of approximately two hundred and fifty thousand square miles (about the size of Texas), stretch from the eastern end of Mexico to Honduras. Except for volcanic mountains in present-day Belize, the hills are not more than 150 feet high, so no natural barriers kept people in that area from interacting with one another.

The Pre-Classic Maya civilization existed from 300 B.C.E. to 250 C.E. and Classic Maya civilization lasted from 300 to 900 C.E. During the first millennium C.E., the Maya drew inspiration from the Olmecs and Teotihuacan.

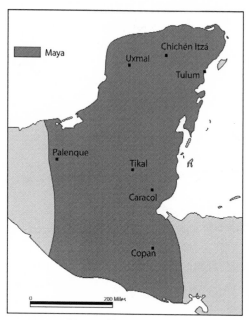

Extent of Maya Terrority

Who Were the Maya?

Recent scholarship suggests that 8,000 years ago, settlers in the tropical lowlands were hunter-gatherers. People settled along rivers and on the Caribbean coast of the Yucatan Peninsula and began to farm sometime between 2500 and

1250 B.C.E. Men and women could move easily from place to place. Artisans in villages scattered throughout the area produced similar types of pottery, and lowland Maya spoke languages as closely related as French is to other Romance languages.

During the period from 1250 to about 400 B.C.E., villagers established interregional trading networks. There is little evidence that these early Maya had a rigid social hierarchy or that they maintained significant boundaries between settlements. Religion was probably a family affair that included rituals to cure disease or celebrate rites of passage. Two large temples, which must have required thousands of people to construct, have been excavated. Leaders must have supervised their construction, and archaeologists have discovered symbols of royal authority.

Agriculture

About 300 B.C.E. the Maya population in the Yucatan began to increase rapidly. Soon the area was dotted with villages, numerous small ritual centers, and five large centers, including Tikal. As with the Olmecs and Teotihuacan, the economic base of Maya culture was agriculture. They used resin for chewing gum and vulcanized rubber for, among other things, the balls for their ritual games. Bees seem to have been especially important in the coastal city of Tulum, and the Maya traded in honey and salt.

By and large the Yucatan was a poor area for farming. The thin layer of topsoil was naturally fertile but easily eroded and exhausted, except along rivers. Heavy rain leached out the nutrients after the Maya slashed and burned, and every few years they had to leave the land fallow so it could replenish itself. Farmers used fertilizer and rotated crops to keep the soil rich. Crop diversity among different areas fostered trade over a relatively large area. In the swampy lowland areas, the Maya farmed on raised beds, similar to chinampas. Although these required a lot of labor, they ensured there would be good soil and adequate water for the crops.

Except for swampy areas or those near rivers, getting enough water was a constant challenge for the lowland Maya, especially during the dry season from February through April. Water collected in *cenotes*, natural openings in the ground connected with groundwater. The

Northern Acropolis of Tikal

Maya also dug large underground reservoirs. In many other early civilizations people worked together to control rivers or build irrigation works and flood-control projects. People in the Maya lowlands had to cooperate to store and distribute water and build raised beds.

The Maya who lived in the highlands developed a different form of farming. They learned to cut terraces into the hills and slopes, and they grew maize on these terraced fields. They planted by pushing kernels of maize into the ground instead of scattering them. Maintaining the terraces required a great deal of labor and cooperation.

The Maya carried goods in a basket supported by a strap around the forehead. They had no wheeled vehicles, although they had wheeled toys for their children. The terrain would have made it difficult to pull wheeled carts, and in any case there were no large domesticated animals to pull them.

Characteristics of the Maya City-States

From 300 to 900 the Maya settled in city-states that dominated the lowlands. During the fifth and sixth centuries, the whole region was dotted with complex, carefully planned city-states. Although they shared a common culture, they were not politically united under a single Maya ruler and there was no Maya empire. In fact, there seems to have been intense competition and even warfare among the city-states, although they also maintained extensive trading networks and shared similar religious beliefs. The population reached at least ten million and may have been three times that number.

During the period from about 600 to 900 there may have been as many as forty Maya city-states. Each had a center that included religious buildings. Using calculations of the movement of the stars and sun, Maya engineers lined buildings up with certain astronomical events, such as the position of the sun at equinoxes or solstices.

Some Maya cities had their own version of suburbia. Recent excavations at Caracol, one of the largest Maya cities, have unearthed a variety of different neighborhoods and industrial zones on the outskirts of the city as well as both poor and relatively well-to-do communities, not unlike what some contemporary urban planners call edge cities. In addition, there were terraced fields, reservoirs, markets, and government buildings suggestive of today's strip malls. Causeways connected these areas to the center so people could get around even during the rainy season. Some roads ended in plazas. Smaller roads led to high-status residences, to nonresidential buildings, and to older communities that had been incorporated into the city.

The pyramids, which may have represented the mythological primal mountain, linked the community and its leaders to the cosmos as well as to the death and renewal of the agricultural cycle. Pyramids may also have served as burial mounds. Rulers were buried within the pyramids in the hope that they would join their ancestors in the afterlife. A ruler who wanted to show his exalted status had to have a grander monument than former rulers had had, so he ordered a larger pyramid built over an earlier one.

Tikal was one of the most impressive Maya city-states. By about 500 it had become the largest one. It exerted hegemony over perhaps one-fifth of the lowland region, in large part because it appears to have received political and military support from Teotihuacan. At its height in 750, the city was home to 80,000 people and included five major 20-story pyramids, 350 lesser ones, and 3,000 houses. Its major pyramid marked the point where the sun at the summer solstice could be seen over the nearby mountain. It was also an important commercial center.

Copan was also a significant Maya city-state. An expanding population may explain its building projects. Laborers carefully built water channels, terraced hillsides, and flattened out ridge tops so they could grow more crops. The result was more food and a dramatic increase in population in the region. The Maya's architectural accomplishments seem all the more amazing when we realize they had no beasts of burden or metal tools.

How Did Rulers Enhance Their Legitimacy?

Control of both the political and the religious life of smaller communities emanated from the urban centers. Leaders were probably members of a highly educated hereditary group that included mathematicians, astronomers, and scribes. The impressive buildings, large plazas, and spectacular rituals and activities that took place on the plazas in front of the pyramids must have inspired awe and increased the rulers' legitimacy and power.

The Maya was the only literate civilization in early Mesoamerica. Unlike in other early civilizations where writing was used to record

Mutilated scribes

economic activities, writing in Maya society served ritual and royal purposes. Scribes, some of whom were members of the royal family, had a very important role in establishing and maintaining the king's legitimacy.

Besides ordering the construction of monumental buildings and sponsoring spectacular rituals, rulers attacked neighboring city-states, not for more land but to gain prominence in their subjects' eyes. To ensure that everyone was impressed with their victories, they would have a monument erected that showed them towering over their defeated enemies. Scribes were responsible for these monuments; they wrote about the ruler's glorious deeds and gave their own interpretation of the events. They also maintained the city-state's library.

When the king was successful, scribes lived well. When the king's forces lost, his scribes suffered. Almost at once they were captured and publicly humiliated, tortured, and killed. Underscoring the importance of their role as court historians and "spin-masters," their fingers were broken and their fingernails were pulled out.

Religion, Ritual Bloodletting, and Sacrifice

The Maya worshiped a large number of gods. The Corn God was particularly important, and others included the god of the underworld and in later times the Feathered Serpent. One ubiquitous deity was the Rain God whose image was often placed at the corners of buildings.

Rituals associated with the new year and those that marked changes in the seasons were significant. Rituals were performed at the spring equinox, at the beginning of the agricultural year, and the first rains. At the fall equinox, the harvest festival marked the beginning of the dry season. Rituals of creation, death, and renewal were closely associated with planting and harvesting corn. Many rituals involved the Corn God. His death and resurrection were ritually linked to the continuity of the rulers and maintenance of the cosmos. With the loss of plants during the dry season or the death of a leader, the community felt threatened, so it performed rituals to ward off any destructive effects.

Human blood was believed to sustain the gods and keep the cosmos orderly. Members of the elite participated in periodic bloodletting rituals. Before the rituals they fasted and took hallucinogens. That, combined with the pain of the ritual, probably brought on trances. Noble woman would draw thorns through their tongues or fingers to make them bleed. Men drew blood from their penises. They may also have bled captives before they sacrificed them. The Maya believed the gods had created the earth and human beings; in return, humans had to sustain the

Ritual Bloodletting

gods by sacrificing their most valuable possession: their blood. They put the blood on a kind of paper and burned it so the blood could reach the gods.

The Ball Game

All Mesoamerican societies played a ritual ball game. It must have had a special place in Maya society because many of the urban centers have ball courts with bleachers. The object of the game was to get a heavy ball through one of the rings attached to the sides of the field, something like modern basketball. However, accomplishing that feat was very difficult because the ball was extremely heavy and players could not touch it with either their hands or feet.

The game may have been a form of sympathetic magic intended to sustain the sun's movement through the heavens.

Hitting the Ball

Players tried to keep the ball that symbolized the sun in motion for as long as possible. Perhaps the game was a reenactment of the cosmic struggle between the powers of darkness and light, revealed in a plant's life, death, and rebirth and in the sun's orbit through the heavens. Murals at Chichen Itza's ball court show the losing players being beheaded. If the losers represented the powers of darkness, then perhaps they were ritually sacrificed in order to ensure that the cycle of life continued. In fact, the sun's victory over the powers of darkness and the agricultural cycle associated with growing corn provided the basis of many of the most important rituals.

Maya Achievements

The Maya maintained an elaborate network of artisans. Major craftsmen included flint and obsidian workers, potters, woodworkers, "dentists" who made decorative inlays for teeth, stoneworkers, monument sculptors, textile weavers, feather and leather workers, manuscript painters, and basket makers. They made especially delicate and intricate flint objects. The demand for luxury items, such as jade, feathers, and cacao for chocolate, also supported large numbers of tradesmen.

The Maya expressed themselves through myth, story, history, and poetry. Their written language had over 800 symbols called *"glyphs."* Some glyphs stand for words, and others for sounds. They wrote on deerskin or on a form of paper made from bark. It is a great tragedy that the Spanish burned all but three of their books. About the only writing that has survived tells about rituals associated with the rulers or dynastic marriages, conquests, and genealogies. Because it may have been used to enhance the legitimacy of the leaders, scholars question the accuracy of these sources.

Maya mathematicians used a base twenty system and invented a concept of zero that functioned as a position holder. Using a bar to represent five and a dot to represent one, they performed mathematical calculations.

The Maya believed time was cyclical, and they wanted to be able to predict reoccurring events such as eclipses. They made exact calendars so they would know when to conduct rituals. They also calculated lucky and unlucky days. Like the Olmecs, they had a Calendar

Round and, to tell how long ago an event happened, they also had a Long Count; it started from a date that corresponds to 3114 B.C.E.

Common Characteristics of Mesoamerican Societies

Several groups in Mesoamerica developed the characteristics of complex societies with specialization, social stratification, central control, and a common worldview. They created city-states governed by several levels of administration, constructed impressive buildings, and maintained capable military forces. In addition, the Maya respected literacy, supported scribes whose records extolled the rulers' achievements, and created accurate calendars.

The urban complexes were home to very diverse groups, some of whom lived in outlying suburban areas. The maize, beans, and squash that farmers grew fed tens of thousands of people who lived and worked in the urban centers. Although the communities were never united under a single power, there is increasing evidence that most people in ancient Mesoamerica shared a common worldview. Similar pyramids have been found in many places, suggesting common beliefs. Ball courts were built in all the major centers. And throughout the region, people appear to have believed that the sun's daily journey, the life cycle of maize, and the process of birth, death, and rebirth were related.

What Happened to Maya Society?

But by the end of the eighth century, the Maya began to revolt, and many Maya deserted the ritual centers. Monuments that had taken centuries to build went up in flames. Disease spread and many were left without enough food to survive. Desperate residents often raided or fought their neighbors to get enough resources to survive.

Although scholars do not agree on the reasons for the collapse of Maya civilization, they suggest several different possible interrelated causes. One major factor may have been the strain on food production that resulted from the steady rise in population in the whole area. Intensive efforts to produce more food led to erosion of the soil. Poor diets, low in animal and vegetable proteins, caused widespread malnutrition. Children's teeth found in excavations indicate long periods of malnutrition. Malnutrition, in turn, heightened the severity of diseases, including malaria, yellow fever, and syphilis. Irrigation canals easily carried germs from one area to another, and standing water, combined with poor sanitation, resulted in much polluted water, all of which contributed to a population decrease of as much as eighty-five percent.

The growing number of aristocrats may have been another cause of decline. Instead of producing food, they demanded luxuries and consumed an excessive amount of the society's resources. In addition, their pride, vanity, and political ambitions often led to conflicts among various communities, further wasting valuable resources.

Other ecological reasons have been suggested. Perhaps there was a dramatic increase in rainfall in the region, leaching the soil and making periodic burning difficult, or maybe there was a long-term drought. Drought would limit food production, leading to a breakdown in social, political, and religious systems.

Whatever the causes, monumental buildings and exhausted farmland reverted to forests. Vaulted roofs collapsed, structures disintegrated, and much of the land was no longer inhabited. Although the lowlands were never completely depopulated, and today twenty-eight different Maya languages are spoken in the Yucatan, Guatemala, and Honduras, the Maya never recovered from this catastrophic collapse or rebuilt their glorious cities.

We shall pick up the story of the other groups who came into Mesoamerica when we return to this area later in the human drama. We now turn to Eurasia after the end of the Han and Roman empires, the very period of Teotihuacan and Maya glory.

ACT ONE – COMPLEX SOCIETIES DEVELOP IN THE AMERICAS

Setting the Stage

1. Outline or color in Mesoamerica on a map.
2. What are the major crops that grew only in the Americas and were unknown in the eastern hemisphere before 1493? Imagine a meal without any of these foods. Imagine a meal with only the foods available in Mesoamerica.
3. What is the difference between a sacred and cosmic city? Think about where you live. Was your community built around a sacred place? Were its streets and monuments planned before construction began? Was it primarily a good place for trade? Is it the capital or a major political center? In what ways does it combine several of these characteristics?
4. Develop a list of sacred, cosmic, political, and economic cities by drawing on your classmates' experience, interviewing people who have lived in different places around the world, or conducting individual research.
5. Take a look around your community or city. In what ways are you and your neighbors reminded of the community's past? Judging by the layout of the community, what is most important? What do statues, plaques, or other commemorative markers reveal about the community's history and values?
6. Diversity and specialization—people performing a variety of jobs—are characteristics of most cities. What kinds of diversity exist in your area? How many different jobs can you identify? Are there people from different parts of the U.S. or the world, different ethnic groups, or members of a variety of religions living in your community? Identify the various groups.

SCENE ONE
The Olmecs: The Foundation of Mesoamerican Civilization

1. Why did the Olmecs settle in a river valley? What advantages did it offer?
2. What evidence is there that Olmec settlements had some kind of central control and that the people cooperated?
3. What information about Olmec life can you infer from the art the Olmecs created? What do you think the scowling figures might symbolize?

4. Describe one of the colossal heads. Who might have been the models for them? Why were they created? What might they symbolize?
5. Develop an explanation for the end of Olmec society. What ecological factors might have weakened their communities? What economic factors might have led to its decline? Why do you think so many statues were disfigured but the heads were carefully buried? Cite your reasons.

SCENE TWO
Cosmopolitan Teotihuacan

1. What characteristics make Teotihuacan a sacred city? A cosmic city? What evidence is there that it was also a center of political and economic power? In what ways does it fit the characteristics of a city-state?
2. What values or concerns of the people are revealed by the attributes and powers of their major deities?
3. What makes historians thinks there was a change in the type of leadership around 250 C.E.? Describe the change in leadership that probably occurred at that time.
4. What are the advantages of using chinampas? Compare this type of agricultural strategy with different types of agricultural practices in other parts of the world.
5. What role did the apartment compounds play in handling the city's diverse population?
6. How did the leaders of the city try to promote unity among the diverse population? What aspects of the city's rituals might have contributed to that effort?
7. What evidence is there that Teotihuacan was involved in trade? What was the city's relationship to other areas in Mesoamerica?
8. Evaluate possible reasons for the destruction of the city's sacred shrines and buildings.

SCENE THREE
Achievements of the Maya

1. Identify the major characteristics of a Maya city-state. In what ways is it similar to or different from Teotihuacan?
2. What strategies did the Maya use to control the supply of water?
3. What is the possible relationship between the lavish rituals and spectacular buildings and the ruler's efforts to establish and maintain his authority and legitimacy?
4. What was the reason for warfare among Maya city-states? What did rulers hope to gain by fighting?
5. What role did scribes play in Maya society? What was their fate if their king was defeated? Why?

6. What were some of the Maya beliefs? What are possible reasons for the bloodletting rituals?
7. What were the purposes of the ball games and what might they have symbolized in Maya society?
8. Identify and research some of the Maya achievements.

Summing Up

1. What are some common elements among these three Mesoamerican societies? What evidence is there that Olmec society influenced later societies in Mesoamerica?
2. Controlling the supply of water, particularly for agriculture, was a challenge for many early societies. What challenges did farmers in Mesoamerica face? How did they handle them? How do their solutions compare to the strategies used in the early river valley civilizations and in early empires?
3. How does Teotihuacan compare with other city-states such as Athens and Sparta? Identify other cosmic and sacred cities or political and economic centers and compare them with Teotihuacan and Maya cities.
4. Discuss possible reasons for changes in population in the Mesoamerican city-states. Consider factors such as agricultural yields, ecological degradation, political and economic strategies, and competition among areas.
5. Identify and evaluate possible reasons for the decline of the Mesoamerican societies. How do these reasons compare with reasons for the decline of societies in other areas of the world?

ACT TWO

The Development and Spread of Universal Religions (200 B.C.E. to 800 C.E.)

Crisis of the Age

To be human is, in part, to seek the meaning of life and our place in the universe. Whether literate or non-literate, rich or poor, powerful or weak, we need to construct our lives and everyday activities within some belief system. Few people are satisfied with just eating and sleeping, raising families, and working and acquiring possessions without being guided by a larger web of values and beliefs.

For much of early history, humans learned and shared their values within small groups. Often each group had its own local gods and goddesses whose power and dominion were restricted to that group. Villages, towns, and cities looked to their local deities for protection and solace. At the same time many nomadic groups tended to believe in a sky god who journeyed with them across the steppes and granted them special protection and favors.

As trade and travel in the Eastern Hemisphere brought more groups into contact with one another, each with its own protective deity, it became increasingly difficult to believe in gods or goddesses whose power was limited to a particular community. The many divinities could not respond to the competing prayers and petitions coming from all their devotees. In addition, as strangers mixed, bloodlines blurred, making it difficult to determine exactly whom the tribal gods were protecting. Further, amid the deepening complexity of everyday life, men and women sought new insights and a more sophisticated understanding of the sacred.

By the mid-first millennium C.E. the Han and Roman empires no longer existed, and there was little or no political stability in those areas. Laws were not enforced, and many criminals went unpunished. People found it increasingly unsafe just to venture out to shop or visit friends. Gods and goddesses seemed indifferent to sacrifices and deaf to prayers. Life was precarious and little seemed dependable. If that was not enough, nomadic tribes that had been kept at bay for centuries were threatening to raid and invade, and governments could not stop them. Everything was changing so fast that long-held values no longer seemed relevant. In these dire times, men and women were desperate for new solutions that might restore a sense of order and bring meaning to their lives.

Characteristics of Universal Religions

Turmoil and insecurity contributed to the adaptation of existing faiths and the development of new religious beliefs and practices. These new beliefs were not limited to particular tribal or political groups nor practiced exclusively by certain ethnic communities; they were valid for all people. These religions are called "universal" religions because anyone could join them and receive their benefits regardless of individual circumstances. They explained creation, suffering, good and evil, justice and salvation. They also provided solace and comfort in a seemingly capricious and hostile world.

Universal religions have several common characteristics. Besides the fact that their insights are available to anyone, they tend to focus on a single all-powerful divinity that transcends human experience but also cares for each believer and can intervene in everyday life to help individuals. A universal faith promises salvation—usually in the form of life after death. Anyone who offers devotion and obedience to the divine power and follows the directives of the religion may achieve salvation. Universal religions often provide a personal link between divinity and humans, such as a messiah, prophet, or saint who helps devotees in their quest for salvation.

Universal religions offer hope for those whose everyday lives seem helpless or meaningless, and they answer questions about suffering and the presence of evil. The promise of heaven helps make up for seeming injustices, especially the perplexing question of why good people suffer. Although this life seems unfair, believers are promised justice in the life hereafter. And finally, the teachings of universal religions are available in forms and languages average men and women can understand. By incorporating existing practices and popular rituals, the faith is accessible to many different kinds of people.

The three main universal religions that spread in the first millennium of the common era were Mahayana Buddhism, Christianity, and Islam. The transition from belief in a tribal or local god to the radical idea of a single universal divine power ushered in a whole new approach to religion. A god that believers claimed loved and cared for all people, no matter their race, tribe, gender, or social status, was a startling concept. Newly settled nomadic groups, men and women concerned with survival, political leaders seeking forms of legitimacy and strategies for unity, merchants looking for profit and peaceful zones of exchange, and common people desperately searching for explanations for suffering, inequality, and evil—could all find personal reasons for embracing one of these faiths.

Dualism, Monism, and a Harmony of Opposites

A major distinction among the universal religions was their approach to opposites. Most of us in the United States have learned to view things dualistically, i.e., we usually think in pairs of opposites. Something is either this or that: big or little, up or down, new or old, male or female, hot or cold, off or on (even our computers are programmed this way). We tend to believe that someone cannot be both guilty and innocent, not after the Greek philosopher Aristotle identified the excluded middle and taught us that B cannot be both B and not B.

Dualism takes on an ethical dimension when we make a moral judgment about pairs of opposites. A statement becomes either true (good) or false (bad); people are either guilty (bad) or innocent

(good); an idea is either right or wrong, sacred or secular; societies are traditional or modern, developed or underdeveloped, communist or free. Developed is good and underdeveloped is bad. Sacred may be good and secular bad or the other way around, but they cannot be both. We can identify this approach as ethical dualism.

Zoroaster, who lived in Persia in the sixth century B.C.E., was one of the first to teach a form of ethical dualism. He believed that a cosmic battle was raging between the forces of good and the forces of evil, and each person had a responsibility to choose the good and fight to destroy evil. At the time of the final judgment, those who had chosen correctly would be rewarded with paradise. Those on the side of evil would end up in hell. So decisions had cosmic consequences.

Dualism influences how many of us think. How many discussions have you had that ended in either/or debates? How many questions and classes are formulated dualistically: Is this statement true or false? Was colonialism good or bad? No wonder we use true-false tests and jury trials. Applying a dualistic orientation to a universal religion may lead to intolerance. Because the religion is open to all, believers may assume that no other faith is necessary or valid. Some may believe that since my faith is right, yours must be wrong. A dualistic approach may make believers try to convince those outside their faith to accept the real "truth." Sometimes the urge to convert can even become violent and result in rigid intolerance of other beliefs.

Many people in South and East Asia, who were not taught to believe that something cannot be both B and not B, learned to view the world more pluralistically. People who hold pluralist views may think of opposites as a sort of illusion, characteristic of the world we can see, but not ultimately real. In India one important strand of philosophy is monism, from *mono* (one). The world is not made up of opposites dueling but is part of one essence that has fragmented into millions of manifestations. Many Hindus have been taught that if they were ever able to get below surface appearances, they would realize that either/or distinctions vanish. Perception, and to a large extent judgment, depends on where you stand and who you are. Things can be both good and bad, developed in some ways and undeveloped in others.

Mahavira, a contemporary of the Buddha, advocated the Doctrine of Maybe. Our opinions result from what we see and experience, he suggested. He told a story about six blind men who went to see an elephant. Each thought the elephant looked like the part he had touched. Each knew. Each had seen. Even so, each was partly in the right, and all of them were wrong. Mahavira advised: be tolerant because "truth" often depends on our perceptions.

In China the relationship of opposites is illustrated by yin-yang, a balance of opposites. Yin stands for soft, dark, moist, feminine, nonviolent qualities, while yang symbolizes male, aggressive, hard, dry, and active qualities. These two halves move in symbiotic rhythm rather than clashing against one another. Opposites clearly exist and are identified, but they are balanced. One side is not necessarily good and the other evil. One side is not better than the other nor trying to destroy the other. They are in harmony, and both are important.

Many Chinese developed an approach to religion that tended to be compartmentalized with specific spirits and ghosts that represented different functions. Most everyone knew how to appease these forces with sacrifices, chants, and charms. There was no need to offer loyalty to only one belief or spirit. When new understandings came along, they could be added to existing beliefs but did not necessarily have to obliterate existing ones.

We do not want to overdo the distinctions among dualism, monism, and a harmony of opposites. These distinctions do not represent unchanging ways of thinking and acting. Rather they suggest tendencies—moods and motivations that may influence how different cultures view the world. We should also keep in mind the difference between religious ideals and how men and women actually practice their faith in real times and places.

How Do Ideas Spread?

The universal religions spread as a result of increasing cross-cultural contacts. Interaction among different groups is one of the most important sources of innovation and change in history; some historians suggest interaction is the major cause of change. It fosters new ideas and inventions, but it also leads to the loss of some beliefs and cultural features as well as the extinction of some species. Exposure to new ideas and cultural values forces men and women to react, adapting or adopting what they find appealing while ignoring, rejecting, or resisting the rest. Often this kind of interaction makes people modify what they already believe or alter their ways of living. Resistance can result in innovation and change as well.

Professor Jerry Bentley, a well-known world historian, has identified three ways people adapt or adopt new ideas, beliefs, practices, or technology: through voluntary association—when people accept the new ideas readily; as a result of political, social, or economic pressure and coercion; and by assimilation—when groups are gradually absorbed into existing cultures, such as the Hebrew "lost tribes." In addition, Bentley argues, in order for people to be receptive to new ideas, these ideas must resonate with what people are already doing or thinking. He calls that process syncretism.

Syncretism greatly enhances people's willingness to adapt or adopt new ideas. Syncretism helped Christianity spread in the Roman Empire. Certain Christian rituals, such as lights, reverence for trees, communal singing, and a belief in heaven and hell were already familiar to many people. Churches arose on sites of earlier temples. Images of the Virgin Mary nursing the Christ Child looked similar to the Egyptian goddess Isis nursing Horus. Syncretism made it easier for people to adopt the new faith.

There are many examples of voluntary conversion and conversion that resulted from economic and political pressure. For example, at first political and economic pressure worked against Christianity because Roman authorities persecuted early Christians. But Emperor Constantine's Edict of Milan in 313 C.E. that legalized Christianity within the Roman Empire—and the economic advantages he gave Christians—helped the faith spread. So did Emperor Theodosius when he forbade the practice of any other faith within the empire and ordered statues of other gods destroyed.

As ideas spread, they also change. There is often a significant difference between religions that are small and practiced by people with little power, such as early Christianity, and those backed by a state and supported by princes and kings. A religion without powerful backing is more likely to adhere to nonviolent ideals. Once that religion secures the patronage of a king or emperor, it usually becomes highly organized and builds expensive complex institutions. It needs to recruit and train officials to conduct rituals and deal with large numbers of followers. And it may shift from a doctrine of nonviolent behavior to a greater acceptance of violence and harsh punishments, especially if it becomes allied with political powers.

We will try to keep these differences in mind as we examine the spread of universal religions and ponder why these faiths had such a powerful attraction for so many people. We turn first to the spread of Mahayana Buddhism.

SCENE ONE

THE WORLD OF MAHAYANA BUDDHISM

Setting the Stage

The Buddha's original teachings in the sixth century B.C.E. do not seem to fit the characteristics of a universal religion. He taught Four Noble Truths. The first states that life is suffering (*dukka*) because we either want something we do not have or are fearful of losing what we do have. The Second Truth is that suffering is caused by desire:

Scenes from the Buddha's life

clutching or clinging to our possessions and beliefs. However, the Buddha's Third Truth promises there is a way out of suffering if one follows the Fourth Truth— the Eightfold Path that leads to freedom from the illusion of the self, the end of rebirth, and the realization of nirvana. The Eightfold Path offers both ethical and spiritual steps to follow. The first five steps advise seekers to have the right attitude, to be attentive to what they say, to refrain from killing, stealing, lying, being unchaste, and drinking, and to have a job that harms others as little as possible. The last three steps move the believer from this world to the world of inner meditation and an understanding that reality is beyond the pairs of opposites, beyond desire and loathing. Ultimately one can realize nirvana by concentration and disciplined meditation.

While the Buddha offered people a way out of their suffering, he did not speak of a god or deities or promise any intermediary to help them reach nirvana. He advised his devoted disciple to: "Be a lamp unto yourself. Seek your own salvation (nirvana) with diligence." Initially Buddhism had no gods, and no one worshiped the Buddha or made images of him. Early Buddhist art shows people prostrating themselves before Buddha's empty seat, a stupa (sacred mounds that held Buddhist relics), or the wheel that represented his teachings. His message was important, not the messenger.

It was easy to become a Buddhist. The confession of faith was an affirmation of the Three Jewels: the Buddha, the Buddha's teachings (*dhamma*), and the community (*sangha*). Serious disciples took vows that they would not kill, steal, tell lies, be unchaste, or take strong drink. Many lived an acetic, world-denying life, and each hoped to become a "worthy" or saint (*arhat*) who experienced nirvana. Buddhists who did not want to become monks and give up their worldly life could join the Buddhist lay community and remain householders, donating money, food, and other goods to support the sangha.

By the time the Buddha died around 544 B.C.E., he had attracted thousands of monks, nuns, and lay followers. During the rainy seasons in the subcontinent, groups of monks sought shelter together. Gradually, with the support of wealthy merchants, members of Buddhist sanghas built more or less permanent monasteries that often had worship halls, meeting rooms, and stupas.

Emperor Ashoka's Role

Political rulers often play very important roles in the spread of new religions. When kings of Bacteria converted to Zoroastrianism, many people followed their example. Constantine's support of Christianity was vital in spreading that faith. In a similar way, Emperor Ashoka of the Mauryan Empire in India (r. 270–232 B.C.E.) was extremely important in the spread of Buddhism. In his early career Ashoka did not act like a Buddhist. He schemed for power and probably had all his brothers killed so he could become king. But the bloody campaign he launched against Kalinga filled him with remorse and probably contributed to his conversion to Buddhism.

Emperor Ashoka's support helped Buddhism spread, and he used the faith to strengthen his authority. He is said to have ordered Buddhist relics enshrined in 84,000 stupas that he had built all over his kingdom, and he convened the Third Great Buddhist Council. It met in 240 B.C.E. in Pataliputra, his capital, the largest city in the world at the time. He also encouraged Buddhist missionaries to carry their faith to Sri Lanka and mainland Southeast Asia. Some Buddhists may also have gone west to Egypt, North Africa, and Greece. Political support greatly enhanced the spread of Buddhism, and Ashoka did not ask people to totally give up the use of violence. Instead, he embraced the Buddhist principle of trying to hurt others as little as possible.

Theravada and Mahayana Buddhism

The Buddha taught that the path to salvation was based on each person giving up the idea of a permanent self and seeking nirvana. At first people shared his teachings orally, but gradually disciples began to write his message down. After several generations, a split developed. One group, known as Theravada Buddhists, followed the "teaching of the Elders." They believed each person had to seek nirvana on his or her own, and that seekers who could actually stop all desires might become arhats.

The other group was more interested in devotion. They felt it was difficult for individuals to seek their own salvation without some help. For them, the Buddha was a savior who could take away bad karma (the cosmic measure of good and bad deeds) and help a person realize nirvana, and they also developed the concept of the bodhisattva.

Bodhisattvas are saintly individuals who could attain nirvana but choose instead to stay in society and work for the salvation of others. When all beings—animal and human—have attained nirvana, then bodhisattvas will also seek it. Bodhisattvas became personal saviors for those who believed in them. In theory, anyone could become a bodhisattva by being compassionate and good:

> The bodhisattva is endowed with wisdom of a kind whereby he looks on all beings as though victims going to the slaughter and immense compassion grips him. . . . So he pours out his love and compassion upon all those beings, and attains to them, thinking, "I shall become the savior of all beings, and set them free from their sufferings."

The Buddha and bodhisattvas were vehicles for salvation, so this group was called Mahayana Buddhists, which means Great (*maha*) Vehicle (*yana*) Buddhists. In Theravada Buddhism, the older form of Buddhism, no one helped arhats realize nirvana, so some referred to it as Hinayana Buddhism or Lesser Vehicle Buddhism. (Those seeking nirvana in Theravada Buddhism can be compared to a young monkey clinging to its mother, while in Mahayana Buddhism, seekers can be likened to kittens being carried by the mother cat to nirvana.) The emphasis on the bodhisattva ideal rather than on the arhat is one of the major differences between the two forms of Buddhism.

The concept of Buddhahood is another important difference between Mahayana and Theravada Buddhism. Theravadans maintain that the Buddha is a human being, a great teacher, and anyone can follow his example and become an arhat. Mahayana Buddhism accepted many bodhisattvas and added many transcendent Buddhas as well. Further, Mahayana Buddhist communities do not require the strict discipline of Theravada groups and welcome lay believers into their study groups and worship. Serving others became a way to attain nirvana, and they encourage people to follow examples of good people so as to become good themselves. Mahayana Buddhism has a strong ethical and moral commitment to make the world a better place and teaches that anyone can build up personal merit and good karma by practicing moral virtues.

By the start of the common era, Mahayana Buddhists began to think of the Buddha as a personal savior and then as a god. By then, Mahayana Buddhism had developed the characteristics we have identified with universal religions: focusing on a divine being (the Buddha), a promise of salvation (nirvana) for all believers, and intermediaries (bodhisattvas) to help people achieve salvation. Gradually Mahayana Buddhism absorbed other Indian deities and made them Buddhas or bodhisattvas as well. Hellenistic influences also were coming into the subcontinent. Greek and Roman sculptures of gods and goddesses had reached India by the first century B.C.E., and some Indian images of the Buddha began to resemble Greco-Roman deities.

The Kushanas Support Mahayana Buddhism

With the decline of the Mauryan Empire after Ashoka died in 232 B.C.E., a succession of nomadic groups from the northwest—Bactrian Greeks, Sakas, Parthians, and Kushanas—invaded the subcontinent. The Kushanas were descendants of central Asian nomadic peoples who lived northeast of India. They invaded in the first century C.E. after Chinese policy discouraged them from trading with the Han. During the first and second centuries of the common era, the Kushanas established a flourishing kingdom that included northern India and present-day Afghanistan.

The Kushanas were devout supporters of Mahayana Buddhism. Starting around 100 C.E., King Kanishka, who ruled for more than twenty years, converted to Buddhism and actively tried to promote the faith in Central Asia. The wealth and learning of Kanishka's court attracted artists, poets, musicians, monks, and merchants. Traders and monks from his court spread the Buddhist faith, carrying miniature stupas as they traveled along established trade routes to China. Aspects of Buddhist rituals helped stimulate trade between India and China. For example, decorating stupas with silk banners created a demand in India for silk from China.

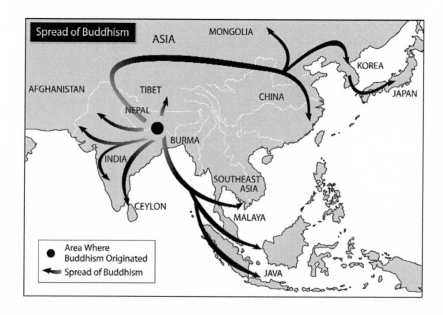

Syncretism Helps Hinduism and Buddhism
Spread in Southeast Asia

During the early centuries of the common era a significant number of traders and Hindu and Buddhist priests and monks sailed from India to Southeast Asia. Indian merchants sought out local chiefs who were willing to trade with them. Chiefs often welcomed these foreigners and hoped to gain an advantage over their rivals by associating with the Indian merchants and adapting Indian rituals and the Indian concept of kingship.

Local rulers were very important in helping Hinduism and Buddhism spread in Southeast Asia during the centuries after Ashoka. They supported these new faiths and found ways to use them to add status and a sense of legitimacy to their rule. Indigenous chiefs enhanced their power and gained prestige by adapting some Indian ideas. As a result, the appeal of both faiths remained largely within the courts and the local people continuted to practice their familiar forms of worship.

Syncretism, when new ideas resonate with what people already believe, helped both Hinduism and Buddhism spread. Similar beliefs helped make it possible for Indian and Southeast Asian ideas to blend

Borobudur

together in a new synthesis. Both Indians and Southeast Asians revered water and snakes (nagas). More important, both believed mountains were sacred. Java, an island that is part of present-day Indonesia, has numerous active volcanoes, and eruptions from them seemed to reveal divine power. The stupa, the sacred Buddhist monument, resembled a mountain. The Javanese built numerous sanctuaries in high places, and many believed that ancestral spirits, responsible for their prosperity, lived on mountaintops.

Borobudur, a unique and beautiful Buddhist monument in the heart of Java, illustrates how the new faith spread and how rulers localized Indian ideas in order to enhance their own authority. Borobudur was built by the Sailendra dynasty that controlled central Java in the eighth and ninth century. This massive stupa resembles a mountain and symbolizes both royal authority and ancestral power. Sailendra means "Lord of the Mountain," and Borobudur stands very near the "Nail of the World," a mountain the Javanese consider sacred.

Visitors to Borobudur must have been impressed by the power and wealth of the Sailendra kings who could supervise the construction of such an impressive monument. Reliefs on the walls illustrate events in the Buddha's life and individuals seeking enlightenment. Walking around the galleries that lead gradually to the top symbolized the search for enlightenment. Men and women who worshiped at the monument must have felt part of something very grand and beautiful, and they were able to add Buddhist insights to what they already believed. The success of Buddhism and Hinduism in Southeast Asia represents an excellent example of syncretism and synthesis.

How Can Asceticism and Filial Piety Be Reconciled?

After the fall of the Han in 220 C.E., China broke up into regional states grouped into first three and then sixteen kingdoms. Nomadic invaders controlled some of these states and Chinese rulers controlled others. In the nomadic kingdoms, Chinese scholars usually served as administrators, and nomads frequently served in the military in the Chinese-ruled kingdoms. The northern border of China was not guarded very well during this period, so nomads continually entered China as did traders and missionaries. Indian traders also traveled to China by sea, and Buddhist missionaries, consciously trying to carry their faith further east, went to Korea and the Japanese archipelago as well as to Sri Lanka and Southeast Asia.

At first glance Buddhism and Chinese values associated with Confucianism would appear to clash, and when Buddhism reached China initially in the first century C.E., it made little impression. The Indian worldview based on spiritual discipline and renunciation stood in stark contrast to the Chinese focus on this-worldly harmony in social relationships. Dropping out of society to seek enlightenment seemed to violate filial piety (reverence for one's parents and ancestors). Who would look after your parents in their old age if you renounced the world and sought personal salvation called nirvana? How could the people of Han possibly be receptive to such an alien faith?

Nomadic leaders who had established several small kingdoms in the northern border of China were more receptive to Buddhism. Clearly, as outsiders, they could not claim they had the right to rule, and they certainly were not continuing any well-established Chinese dynasty. But Buddhism, with its scholarly traditions and sophisticated ideas, backed up by the impressive Indian civilization, could lend luster and legitimacy to their rule. In addition, these non-Chinese rulers liked the fact that Buddhism was a foreign faith: they did not want to assimilate completely to Chinese ways, so endorsing Indian ideas was less onerous for them than adopting Chinese ones. In addition, they considered Buddhist monks more trustworthy than Chinese scholars.

Buddhism Adapts to Chinese Ways

The social and political unrest following the fall of the Han dynasty caused some Chinese to begin to pay attention to Buddhism. Confucian values of moral leadership seemed ineffective in the face of dynastic collapse and warfare. *Li* (proper actions) and *ren* (appropriate feelings) did not alleviate the hunger, sorrow, and insecurity people were facing. Buddhism, on the other hand, taught people to take a radically new attitude toward their plight. Even if they could not change their situations, they could change their attitudes about the problems they faced and become detached from the pain and suffering around them. And Daoism had long offered Chinese people a mystical dimension upon which Buddhism could build.

In an effort to help Chinese men and women understand the Buddha's teaching, scholars tried to present Buddhist concepts in familiar Chinese terms and to equate Buddhist ideas with Chinese beliefs. They translated the Buddha's *dhamma* or message as the Dao, the central concept in Daoism. Nirvana became *wu wei*, the Daoist idea of acting by non-action. Filial piety was used to translate the more general Indian concept of morality.

As Buddhism traveled, it merged with many non-Buddhist ideas that made the new faith more appealing in China. Regional heroes, mythical characters, and local deities became bodhisattvas, allowing people to continue worshiping the same spirits while adding another dimension to their power. In addition, the bodhisattva ideal helped bridge the gulf between Confucian filial piety and Buddhist renunciation, because bodhisattvas helped all living beings along their path to nirvana, including one's parents and other family members. Chinese Buddhists also stressed that the merit a Buddhist monk earned could help his parents reach salvation. Helping one's parents achieve nirvana—life's highest goal—gradually became an acceptable way to fulfill one's filial obligations, even if one's parents did not realize this at first. The new faith added a way of caring for them, rather than making one choose between filial piety or nirvana.

Giving donations to Buddhist communities, especially monasteries, became another way to earn merit for one's family. Rich merchants and aristocrats who hoped to improve their chances for salvation by good works gave money to build stupas, monasteries, and Buddhist temples. As a result, monasteries grew very wealthy. Patrons often commissioned artists to include their own portraits along with images of the Buddha and bodhisattvas.

A story from The Lotus Sutra, which became perhaps the most important Buddhist text in China, illustrates the importance of trying to lead others to nirvana. A rich man's house caught on fire while his three children played inside, unaware of their danger. The father called frantically to them to come outside, promising that three magnificent chariots awaited them. Delighted, the children left their games and raced outside, just ahead of the flames. Life, the Buddhists taught, is like that burning house and we play with its toys like careless children, unaware of our impending doom. Buddhists wanted to

The Lotus Sutra   Escaping a Burning House

free people from their ignorance (playing in the burning house) and bring them to the safety of the Buddha's teaching. The three chariots represented the Three Jewels of Buddhism—the Buddha, his teachings (dhamma), and the sangha—that await believers and can carry them away from the fires of desire.

Although all Buddhists are supposed to believe in nirvana, many Chinese Buddhists were attracted to the idea of a heavenly paradise. Amida (the most widely worshiped form of the Buddha in China) assured his devotees that if they had total faith in him, they would go to the Pure Land of paradise after death. In some forms of Amida worship, devotees had only to say his name once in a lifetime to achieve eternal salvation. Pure Land Buddhism became the most popular form of Buddhism in China.

Traveling Monks

Buddhism helped stimulate contact between China and India. For one thing, Chinese Buddhists used precious stones, called the "seven jewels," prescribed for Buddhist ceremonies, and several of the jewels were only available in India. For another, Chinese Buddhist scholars wanted to go to the source of the faith and find documents that contained the original teachings. Records identify two hundred East Asian monks, nine of them Korean, who traveled from China to India in the first millennium C.E. to learn about Buddhism and collect

Buddhist scriptures. Fa Xian traveled to India in 399 C.E. and on his return he translated the scriptures he had obtained.

Perhaps the most famous pilgrim was Xuanzang who traveled to India and back between 629 and 645. He visited numerous areas and had audiences with a variety of leaders. After he returned to Changan, he translated seventy-four Buddhist works into Chinese. His adventures were later popularized in a classic novel, *The Journey to the West,* which tells how a pig, a horse, and a magical monkey helped the monk obtain the sacred scriptures from India.

Buddhism Helps the Sui Unite China

In 581, the Sui reunited the Chinese empire after 300 years of disunity and established a new dynasty. Emperor Wendi, the first Sui emperor (r. 581–604), sought ways to establish his dynasty's legitimacy. While he supported the study and practice of Confucianism by exempting filial sons from taxation and corvée and by establishing schools and a national college for the study of the Confucian classics, he also used Buddhism to help unify his empire and enhance his authority.

When he first took control of the country, Emperor Wendi ordered the construction of Buddhist monasteries at the foot of China's five sacred mountains, another example of the way Buddhist ideas merged

Great Stupa at Sanchi

with existing beliefs. He was given the title "the Bodhisattva Son of Heaven" and claimed to be a true believer and a patron of the Buddhist community, and he ordered the repair of damaged temples and stupas.

Following Emperor Ashoka's example in India seven centuries earlier, Emperor Wen sent monks to supervise the construction of stupas all over his kingdom. Relics were enshrined on the same day in 111 stupas to symbolize the unity of the country and its support of Buddhism. However, Wendi did not follow Ashoka's commitment to non-violence, and the Sui dynasty was among the most violent in Chinese history. He commissioned Buddhist temples to be built at the sites of his famous battles (a very non-Buddhist idea) and issued the following edict dated 581:

> . . . We regard the weapons of war as having become like the offerings of incense and flowers presented to the Buddha, and the fields of this world as having become forever identical with the Buddhaland.

Chinese Buddhism, like Christianity after Constantine in Rome, had become identified with the political power.

Buddhism in Korea

Confucian ideas and Buddhist influences reached the Korean peninsula by the fourth century C.E. Aristocrats were especially interested in the Chinese writing system, identified with Confucianism, which became the basis for the first written records in Korea.

When Korean monks visited the Sui capital at Changan in the sixth century, they saw how Emperor Wendi was using Buddhism not only to promote unity in China but also to support military expeditions. They brought these insights back to the Korean peninsula, which at that time was divided into three important kingdoms. Monks in the southern kingdom of Silla promoted Five Precepts that reflect early Korean beliefs, including requirements for national defense, and also resonate with Confucian and Buddhist concepts:

First, serve the king with loyalty,
second, serve your parents with filial piety,
third, be faithful to friends,
fourth, do not retreat in battle, and
fifth, do not kill indiscriminately.

The support of both rulers and subjects helped Buddhism spread in the Korean peninsula. Leaders in Silla thought it offered the basis for a broad consensus that could enhance their efforts to unite the country. Identifying the king with the Buddha would reinforce the ruler's legitimacy and strengthen the government. Aristocrats liked the Buddhist idea of karma and rebirth, because these concepts established that their high position in society was the result of their good actions in past lives. Poorer members of society liked the idea that each person could cultivate the Buddha nature and that everyone was equal in the Buddha's sight.

By the ninth century, Pure Land Buddhism came to Korea. Because it provided a way to escape one's karma, it became very popular. So did the idea that good deeds performed for the sake of the dead would lead to rebirth in a better state. In addition, Buddhist monasteries, following the Chinese example, started to serve the poor and became places where the sick and needy could find assistance.

SILLA AND SEOKGURAM

Syncretism aided the process of voluntary conversion to Buddhism in Korea as Buddhist ideas merged with earlier beliefs. For example, there was a widely held and long-standing belief that the Dragon of the East Sea was the guardian spirit of the land. Many Koreans believed it could move between the spirit and human worlds, protecting the country, particularly against pirates, and controlling the waters. As Buddhism spread through the peninsula, people began to associate this new faith with the dragon spirit, and its ability to protect the country merged with the ruler's power and with Buddhist symbolism.

Perhaps the most interesting example of this growing identification of political power and Buddhist ideals concerns King Munmu, who was responsible for unifying the three kingdoms in 668 and who ruled

The Buddha at Seokguram

United Silla until 681. Shortly before he died, King Munmu said he hoped to continue to protect the country even after his death, particularly from threats from the sea. He gave orders to cremate his body and bury his ashes in a tomb in the East Sea. The king expected to be united with the Dragon of the East Sea and to become a guardian spirit that embodied both local beliefs and Buddhism.

The synthesis of the king and the Buddha is vividly illustrated at Seokguram, a grotto constructed in 751. Seokguram resembles an Indian or northern Chinese cave temple as well as a Buddhist stupa, but because there were no rock cliffs into which to carve a cave, it is actually a freestanding temple covered with dirt to make it look like a cave. In its center is a strikingly beautiful image of the Buddha looking east, out to the sea, toward King Munmu's grave, and to the islands of Japan. This exquisite Buddha image, whose rounded form seems inflated with sacred breath, is blessing the grave, protecting the kingdom, and warding off enemies. Buddhism had become a cherished part of life in the United Silla.

Buddhism Travels to Japan

It was largely from Korea that Chinese civilization first came to

Japan. From the sixth to the eighth centuries Korean Buddhist and Confucian scholars carried information about China to Japan. The Japanese must have been impressed by these visitors who came from a more developed culture where people could read and write. The visitors brought impressive scriptures, scholarly philosophical arguments, and awe-inspiring works of art to Japan.

At first only the Japanese aristocracy, hoping to build Japan into a complex civilization, responded to Buddhism. The average peasant farmer, not concerned with building an urban society, found it difficult to accept an outlook that seemed to deny the world. However, most everyone liked the idea of holding services for ancestors because that was a way to honor one's parents. When we look more closely at the development of Japanese society, we shall consider how the Japanese shaped Buddhism to fit their culture.

For a thousand years Buddhism was very popular in India where it had originated, but gradually Indians absorbed much of the Buddha's message into Hinduism. After 500 C.E., Buddhism as a separate religion had practically disappeared in India, but it was growing in importance in the rest of Asia. Kings and princes supported Buddhism, and it became important in several dynasties in China, Korea, and Japan. No wonder John Fairbank, one of the foremost scholars of Chinese history, has suggested that the whole period from the mid-fourth century to the end of the eighth century might be called the Buddhist Age, not just in Chinese history but in Asian history and perhaps in world history. Buddhism influenced more than half the world's population during that time. Buddhist centers were among the leading institutions with the best available knowledge about mathematics, medicine, astronomy and public health.

Both Theravada and Mahayana Buddhism were significantly transformed as they took root in new areas. The original idea of realizing nirvana by one's own efforts gradually gave way to performing good deeds to built up merit that helped one's family. Local deities and heroes entered the Buddhist pantheon as bodhisattvas and traditional rituals and popular beliefs were also incorporated into everyday Buddhist rituals and beliefs. Buddhism grew into a popular faith that offered common people solace in the face of suffering. Perhaps most importantly, by accepting the idea of life after death in paradise through faith alone, Mahayana Buddhism promised justice and comfort for the many who could not find these elusive rewards on earth. As the faith spread, it grew richer and more powerful and had to face the challenges worldly success brings. We shall consider these changes and challenges when we return to the Buddhist world later in the human drama.

SCENE TWO

CHRISTIANITY BECOMES CHRISTENDOM

Setting the Stage

Unlike Buddhism, which gradually developed into a universal religion, Christianity fit the criteria almost from its start. Christianity focused on God, a single divine being. Jesus, the Christ, had died so that all people who believed in him might be saved. Jesus had stressed two commandments—love God with all one's heart and mind and love one's neighbor as oneself—and predicted a final judgment day. The "Good News" that Jesus had risen from the dead and defeated death offered the promise of salvation for anyone. The Christian message of compassion, non-violence, and forgiveness of sins, and its promise of life after death, offered comfort and hope for many struggling to find meaning in the insecurity and hedonism created by the instability of the later Roman Empire.

Jesus responded to the question "Who is my neighbor?" by telling the parable of the Good Samaritan, which suggests that one should treat even those outside one's own ethnic and religious community as neighbors. Paul, the most significant early Christian missionary, was instrumental in taking the message beyond the original Jewish community from which it had sprung, and Paul and other early converts carried the Good News to Gentiles (non-Jews).

Initially Christianity spread slowly among the outcast and dispossessed, and by the end of the first century there were probably no more than 10,000 Christians in the entire Roman Empire. Political and economic pressure worked against the faith because Roman authorities persecuted early Christians. Jesus had told people to "turn the other cheek," and early Christians stressed Christianity's spiritual message and opposed the materialistic values of Roman society and what they considered its rampant immorality. But this changed once political leaders began to support Christianity. After Emperor Constantine issued the Edict of Milan in 313 that made the faith legal in the Roman Empire, and Emperor Theodosius banned all pagan ceremonies, the Roman government helped the faith spread.

Christians Become the Church

The organizational structure of the Church greatly enhanced the spread of Christianity. In its early years, the Church had no clergy (people specially designated for religious work) and many of Jesus' most loyal followers were women. But a more systematic organization was needed, and men began to work full-time as priests (presbyters) and overseers (bishops). As the number of local churches grew, its leaders attempted to copy Emperor Diocletian's organization of the Roman bureaucracy by linking each church into the larger structure. By the fourth century, the Church was becoming an institution with a highly organized hierarchy instead of just informal communities of believers.

The smallest governing body was a diocese that included several churches. All the churches in a diocese elected a bishop. The symbolic and political center of each bishop's authority was his cathedral (from the Latin word for chair). An archbishop had authority over several dioceses. Archbishops in the five most important cities— Rome, Alexandria, Constantinople, Jerusalem, and Antioch—were called metropolitans, and in the fourth century they were given the higher rank of patriarchs (fathers of the Church). There was a clear line of authority from patriarchs down to archbishops, bishops and parish priests, who were in charge of individual churches, and finally to the community of believers. This hierarchical organization enabled the young Church to broaden its appeal to more affluent groups and bring them into its system of governance.

Almost immediately after this organization was established, the patriarchs of the five major cities began competing with one another. The patriarch of Rome demanded special authority, claiming he could trace his succession from the apostle Peter to whom, the Gospels reported, Jesus had said, "Thou art Peter and upon this rock I shall build my church." Gradually, he tried to assert supreme authority, first assuming the title "Roman patriarch," and eventually Pope (from the Latin for father) and Pontiff (meaning one who guards the sacred bridge over the Tiber River). However, many church leaders used the

title "pope" and for many centuries the other patriarchs resisted granting the pope of Rome special authority.

Church Fathers

Christianity spread in part because the Church recruited gifted people
who previously might have served in the Roman government.
Scholars known as "Church Fathers" defined its theology and gave its
teachings intellectual respectability. Jerome (ca. 340–420), one of the
early Church Fathers, compiled a Bible in Latin known as the Vulgate
(Latin for common) version, which remains the official Roman
Catholic Bible to this day. Jerome also sought to bring Greco-Roman
learning into Christian theology, arguing that those ideas would not
necessarily corrupt Christians who studied them. As a believer in
asceticism, he strongly advocated celibacy.

Ambrose (ca. 340–397), an activist, was archbishop of Milan. By
forcing a powerful emperor to perform public penance, he helped
establish the superiority of the Church over the State in spiritual matters, but he strongly believed that Church and State complemented
each other. He stressed the importance of serving others and emphasized the concept of God's grace, the belief that good fortune and personal transformation can come to anyone, at any time, regardless of
his or her actions or deeds.

Perhaps the most gifted Church Father was Augustine of Hippo, in
North Africa, who lived from 354 to 430. Augustine preached about
original sin (when Adam and Eve in the Garden of Eden had disobeyed the Lord by eating an apple from the Tree of Knowledge) as
well as God's grace. Following the dualistic tradition, Augustine
spoke about a field divided between wheat and weeds and predicted
that at the final judgment, God would separate the saints (wheat) from
the sinners (weeds). Believers, said Augustine, must cultivate the spiritual world that was vastly superior to the life of power, money, and
family, but at the same time support human institutions. Augustine
also championed celibacy and in his own life struggled to practice it.

In his major work, *The City of God*, Augustine offered solace to
people devastated by the invasion and sack of Rome. Separating secular life in Rome from the City of God in heaven, Augustine argued
that no human institution could ever truly express God's will. He

offered assurance that faith and love were the best routes to salvation, and his scholarly presentation of grace as a ray of hope in a capricious world comforted average people struggling to find security and maintain their faith.

Debates Over the Nature of Jesus

As Christianity spread, believers disagreed over Church doctrine and argued over who was interpreting the faith correctly. Fearing these disputes might tear the Church apart and make it difficult to spread the faith, Church leaders attempted to determine which interpretation was correct and which were heresies that went against the Church's doctrines. After all, in a dualistic system, there can be only one truth and one interpretation.

One of the major debates focused on the true nature of Jesus: was he man or God, or man and God? Arius (ca. 250–336), a priest in Alexandria, argued that Jesus was neither human nor divine but a demigod somewhere between God and humans. Arius' chief opponent, Athanasius (293–373), said that Christ was the same substance as God, coequal and coeternal. He advanced the idea of the holy Trinity: God the Father, God the Son, and God the Holy Ghost. In an effort to decide the issue once and for all, Emperor Constantine convened a Council of Bishops in Nicea in 325; they condemned Arius and affirmed the Holy Trinity, which has been a foundation of Christianity ever since.

The dispute over the nature of Jesus broke out again in the fifth century when Nestorius, patriarch of Constantinople, argued that Jesus had two distinct and separate aspects, one human and one divine. God was the source of his divine nature, and Mary, his mother, of his human nature. Mary, the Nestorians argued, was not the mother of God, since she had only given birth to his human part. In 431 the Pope of Rome assembled the Council of Ephesus, and, with Nestorius' supporters locked out, voted unanimously to condemn Nestorius as a heretic.

Even so, followers of Nestorius continued to flourish in Egypt and Syria and made significant inroads in Central Asia, where they were welcomed because they had no political ties to Constantinople or Rome. Throughout the vast expanse of Asia, Nestorians were the most numerous Christians until the 13th century. Most Chinese thought that Christianity and Nestorianism were synonymous.

Desert Fathers and Mothers, Monks, and Monasteries

Tension also arose between those who focused on the world and those who emphasized the more spiritual aspect of religious life. Church Fathers such as Jerome and Augustine insisted that the Church emphasize the spiritual aspect, while priests working in their local parishes were more concerned with the daily problems average people faced. Some early Christians despaired of living a Christian life in the midst of what they saw as a corrupt and degenerate world. They dropped out of society entirely and lived alone in the desert, earning the name hermits (from the Greek word for desert). The first hermits were Christian laymen who wanted to live a simple life free of possessions, sex, and concern for social status. Some even practiced self-mutilation because they believed that pain could help them concentrate on spiritual matters.

The urge to drop out was not new. Jewish groups such as the Essenes had been practicing a monastic type of life for generations, and asceticism was a common feature of Hinduism and Buddhism in India, where a person might "go to the forest" to meditate, especially in the second half of life. Moreover, the ascetic

"You seem troubled, Brother Timothy. Is anything worrying you? I mean besides the sins of the world, the vanities of mankind, and that sort of thing."

life was an important feature of several major rivals to Christianity such as the Gnostics and Manicheans, who believed it was possible for individuals to make personal contact with God once they purified themselves.

Early Christian ascetics in Egypt and Palestine were later identified as "desert fathers." There were also "desert mothers" who withdrew from society to lead spiritual lives. Members of both groups, both monks and nuns, established communal societies. As a result, two types of clergy developed. The regular clergy included monks and nuns who lived in monasteries and nunneries. The secular clergy was composed of men who worked in local parishes.

In addition, countless believers tried to live Christian lives in society. Melanie the Elder belonged to one of the richest families in Rome. She was a very pious Christian who spent 27 years in Palestine caring for pilgrims and reading and praying. She also gave money to found a monastery on the Mount of Olives where Jesus had been crucified. When she returned to Rome in 399 she was famous throughout the Christian world for her piety and generosity.

Her granddaughter, Melanie the Younger, was the only heir to the family's palace in Rome and its extensive estates in Iberia, Africa, Britain, and Gaul. She decided to sell all the property, free the family's 8,000 slaves, and use the proceeds to buy land and build monasteries and nunneries for monks and virgins and give them generous stipends of gold.

Basil (330–379) created guidelines for monastic life. He encouraged his fellow monks to give up self-mutilation and instead to take vows of poverty, chastity, and humility, and devote their energies to useful work. An Italian patrician named Benedict brought the monastic ideal to Europe in 529 and founded a community for monks that stressed obedience, labor, and devotion. Benedictine monks played a major role in spreading Christianity in Europe and established the norms and procedures for most of the monastic orders that followed. Nuns living in nunneries ran hospitals, orphanages, and other public service institutions and concentrated many of their efforts on service and caring for others. After the fourth century, priests were increasingly expected to be celibate, although many were not. By the eleventh century, all priests were required to be celibate.

How Does Asceticism Affect the Status of Women?

Women were major supporters of both Buddhism and Christianity. Christianity stressed the importance of fidelity in marriage, condemned adultery as a sin, and opposed divorce, all values that enhanced a woman's security. Life expectancy was only about 35 for women, which means many married women were probably pregnant for much of their married life. A religious vocation provided an alternative to the traditional roles of wife and mother. Besides being able to choose to remain celibate and not marry, they could travel to the Holy Land, join nunneries, learn Latin and Hebrew, and form friendships with men outside their families. The Virgin Mary emerged as an important figure of worship. In contrast to Eve, who embodied women's sinfulness and ability to corrupt others, the Virgin epitomized women's purity and obedience.

Even so, Christian teaching seemed to exalt and denigrate women at the same time. The faith taught that women had souls and were spiritually equal to men, and many early Christians were women. However, women were excluded from leadership positions and St. Paul instructed them to be "silent in church." Anxiety over women's sexuality permeated Christian doctrine. Many men feared that women were temptresses who would prevent devout men from focusing on spiritual matters. Believing the end of the world was at hand, St. Paul had taught that a man should marry only if he were "burning." Sex was to be limited to marriage, and its sole purpose was for procreation. Women were expected to be virgins at the time of marriage and totally

Feeding beggars

subservient to their husbands.

The monastic value of celibacy clearly celebrated a life free of sexual passion, and Augustine and other church fathers taught that a celibate life was the best path to spiritual development. Strenuous support for virginity accompanied the veneration of Virgin Mary. Given the dualistic outlook, an emphasis on spiritual matters tended to make the physical world and the concerns that occupied married women seem at worst irreligious and unredeemable and at best simply not that important. Celibacy was certainly not a Jewish or Roman ideal, and may have become popular because of Indian influences traveling westward or as a response to the excesses of the Roman era.

Christianity Spreads throughout the Byzantine Empire

Recognizing the diminishing power of the western half of his empire, Constantine had chosen Byzantium, a small Greek town on the Bosporus, as the site on which to build an eastern capital. He renamed it Constantinople (Constantine's city). Much of the empire's wealth was in the eastern provinces, which produced the majority of grain and controlled the major trade routes north and east. Because of the growing imbalance between the two halves of the empire, the most able leaders wanted to serve in Constantinople. The eastern half, which gradually split away from Rome, withstood the invasions of nomadic groups and grew into a powerful state in its own right. It became known as the Byzantine Empire or Byzantium.

Byzantium was a Christian empire, and its emperor was considered to be co-ruler with Christ. Byzantine leaders tried to use Christianity to unite their subjects. They hoped everyone would become an Orthodox Christian, and political support caused many to convert. The government promoted Christianity but did not try to force people to convert because they realized many subjects belonged to other Christian communities and many were not Christians.

Christianity Reaches Axum

While Christianity was becoming the official religion in both the Roman and Byzantine empires, missionaries of the new faith were finding willing converts in other lands. Soon after Jesus' crucifixion, a Christian community sprang up in south India where local tradition claimed St. Thomas had lived his last days and was martyred. (According to the Gospels, Saint Thomas was the apostle who insisted on touching the resurrected Christ's wounds.)

Desert fathers and mothers had sought asylum in Egypt, and other Christians went to Nubia in the first centuries of the common era. Axum, a state in present-day Ethiopia, was growing politically and economically stronger. By the second century it had a brisk trade with Egypt, Syria, Arabia, and India. Ships came to Adulis, its main port on the Red Sea, from both the Mediterranean and India. By 300 the people of Axum were minting coins and manufacturing glass crystals, brass, and copper and also exporting ivory, frankincense, and myrrh. Their monumental structures included solid stone stele carved to look like many-storied houses, the tallest over 100 feet high. Their leaders claimed descent from the Queen of Sheba.

Sometime around 320 C.E. a merchant ship en route to India from Syria was shipwrecked near Adulis. Two brothers, the only survivors, sought asylum in Axum and one of them, Frumentius, became an advisor to its king and served as tutor to the two young princes and taught them Greek. He later traveled to Jerusalem where he met Emperor Constantine's mother. The patriarch in Alexandria consecrated Frumentius Bishop of Axum and sent him back to Axum. He soon publicly baptized the princes and in about 344 King Ezana proclaimed Coptic Christianity the official religion. (Copts believe in the single nature—part human and part divine—of Jesus.)

There are several possible reasons the Axumites accepted Christianity. Certainly the close personal relationship between Frumentius and the royal family was important. So was Axum's vast trading network, and especially its link with Constantinople. Travelers and traders must have brought reports about Emperor Constantine's support of Christianity. Perhaps the rulers reasoned that a similar conversion would enhance trading relations with Constantinople and with its large, prosperous Christian community.

Christianity Spreads to Western Europe

The Germanic groups that had migrated into Europe during the decline of Rome gradually settled down, learned to farm, and began to establish their own complex societies. By the sixth century C.E. the

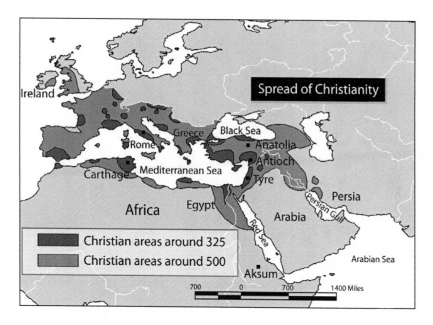

newcomers had consolidated their hold on much of western Europe: the Visigoths in Spain, the Burgundians and Franks in France, the Ostrogoths in southern Germany and eastern Europe, the Lombards in northern Italy, and the Anglo-Saxons in Britain. Further to the east Slavs, including Poles, Czechs, and Bohemians, had also begun to live as settled peoples. Non–Indo-European groups in Central Europe included Finno-Ugric speakers in Hungary (named for the Huns) and Altaic groups in Bulgaria. Finns journeyed along the northern reaches of the steppes and settled in what is now Finland.

At the start of the sixth century most of western Europe was still sparsely settled. The majority of people were illiterate farmers, living in isolated villages, and barely surviving on subsistent agriculture. Their major staples included barley, which they ground into grain and brewed into beer, and pork, provided by the countless pigs that roamed the forests. Small groups of farmers often banded together for mutual protection. Warfare was common as various chieftains and their followers struggled for control of larger groups.

With the decline in Roman power in the fifth century, there was no political structure in western Europe outside of the Church. Priests and bishops performed many of the functions that the Roman govern-

Peasants at home

ment had once fulfilled, including establishing courts, trying accused criminals, controlling elections of city officials, distributing public funds, and providing food and other services for the poor. The Church's message of comfort and the promise of salvation in heaven must have been very appealing; even so, the faith spread very slowly.

Paralleling Buddhism's diffusion among nomads along the Chinese frontier, Christian missionaries sought converts among the nomadic leaders in western Europe. These leaders understood that if they were to gain political power, their subjects would have to give up tribal loyalties. Christianity offered a larger group identity as well as a more orderly and less violent way of life. Being associated with a sophisticated religion like Christianity could confer legitimacy on the emerging leaders and give the people some connection with Rome's former glory.

Popes were particularly interested in sending missionaries among the groups settled north and west of Rome, especially because the eastern wing of the Church seemed to control the urban centers from Constantinople throughout West Asia. Popes realized that when political leaders converted, they usually brought many of their followers with them into the Church. Recognizing the importance of having the support of strong, sympathetic leaders, Church officials learned to make alliances with political chieftains and support "just" wars.

Between the fifth and eighth centuries Celts, Anglo-Saxons, and Franks, as well as West and East Goths and Lombards, were all exposed to Roman Christianity, and many found it attractive. Even so, they did not want to lose their tribal loyalties or be identified with Roman society. As a result, many were attracted to the "Arian" wing of Christianity (followers of Arius who did not believe Jesus was the divine incarnation of God) because it allowed them to avoid being identified with Rome. Church leaders in Rome regarded Arian Christians as heretics.

Christianity Spreads to the Celts

The conversion of the Celtic peoples was a major step in the spread of Roman Christianity. Both early Britons and the Irish were descendents of the Celts who had migrated into West Asia and the British Isles in the first millennium B.C.E. Saint Patrick (ca. 385–461), a Briton credited for bringing Christianity to Ireland, had been enslaved in Ireland for six years when he was a young man. After he escaped and made his way home, he became a priest and decided to try to convert his former captors.

Patrick successfully challenged the *druids*, learned men who advised Celtic leaders in political and religious matters, but he focused most of his attention on converting local kings. He hoped that if they converted, their subjects would follow. Many local leaders associated Christianity with the order and authority of the Roman Empire, and they may also have welcomed a way to reduce the druids' influence.

Syncretism also helped Christianity spread. Earlier beliefs and sacred sites, including wells and springs, became Christian holy places, so the new faith felt familiar to the local people. For example, Brigid, an all-powerful and ever-helpful local goddess, became identified with Saint Bridget, a Christian saint, and her festival was celebrated on the same day as Goddess Brigid's had been celebrated. People did not have to choose between their local beliefs and Christianity, and gradually the two traditions merged.

Monasteries spread quickly in Ireland and became the center of education. Irish education was superior to education in Europe, so students from Europe went to study there, causing monasteries to grow into small towns. Besides teaching Christian texts, the schools also gave instruction in Greek and Roman classics and included mathematics and science in the curriculum. Irish monks spread their message and established monasteries throughout Europe.

The Franks Accept Christianity

The Franks, who occupied much of the territory that is now France and Germany, were by far the most organized and aggressive of the Germanic settlers. The first significant Frankish chieftain was Clovis (481–511), who defeated several of his neighbors and created a small kingdom in present-day France. He had the foresight to try to blend Germanic and Roman elements and encourage intermarriage between the two groups. In about 495, in a dramatic victory for the Roman Church, Clovis converted to Roman Christianity—a severe blow to the expansion of Arianism. As a major political leader among Germanic settlers and as the founder of a successful royal line, Clovis' conversion formed the basis for the development of the Roman Church in much of Europe.

In 768, Charlemagne (Charles the Great) gained control of the Frankish kingdom. Under his rule, which lasted until 814, the kingdom reached its greatest heights. His forces launched more than fifty major military campaigns and absorbed Bavaria and Brittany. He rewarded his most loyal followers, known as counts, by giving them parcels of conquered land and exempting many from paying taxes.

But even at its height, Charlemagne's kingdom was only loosely held together. Instead of establishing a permanent capital, his court traveled constantly. Counts administered the land, called counties, that they had been given. To prevent counts from building up too much power, Charlemagne prohibited them from passing on their titles or land to their sons, and he sent agents from the court to keep an eye on them.

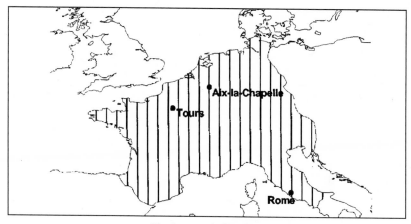

Charlemagne's kingdom

Charlemagne wanted to consolidate his conquests and unite the people within a single culture and administrative system. He tried to introduce a common coinage and language as well as standard weights and measures. Unfortunately, his system of land allocation weakened his authority. Because he had no independent army of his own or money to hire professional soldiers, he was forced to rely on the counts and other nobles for military protection.

Charlemagne, like the vast majority of people in his kingdom, could not read or write. However, he understood the importance of literacy and encouraged the Church to sponsor schools to provide literacy training for priests. In 782 he invited two Irish monks to his court to teach. They opened the Palatine School, which would one day develop into the University of Paris. He also invited scholars trained in Muslim science and mathematics and Greek and Roman philosophy to his court and maintained monasteries in which diligent monks carefully copied major texts, especially the Bible. Despite these early efforts, the level of learning and culture remained very low, and the majority of even the highest aristocrats were illiterate.

Church, State and Christendom

The Roman Church vigorously supported Charlemagne in hopes of

Coronation of Charlemagne

widening the influence of Christianity, and Charlemagne courted Pope Leo III to enhance the legitimacy of his rule. Symbolic of their mutual support, and solidifying the alliance between Church and State, the Pope crowned Charlemagne emperor on Christmas Day, 800. Each leader hoped the gesture would reinforce his own status, and the event established a long tradition of both cooperation and competition between the Church and various political leaders.

The crowning of Charlemagne was only one example of the Church's political power. Besides owning a vast amount of land, bishops were deeply involved in secular affairs. They supervised counts and required believers to tithe (give ten percent of their income to the church), and church officials acted as judges in trials. In return for the legitimacy that came with Church support, Carolingian kings and nobles provided stipends for the clergy, financed the copying of manuscripts, and sponsored monasteries. All this helped shift the center of Roman Christianity to Western Europe, and the whole region, including areas in the Nile Valley and Axum, gradually became part of a general culture called Christendom. Under this common spiritual umbrella, there was only one Church. Those who were not baptized were not full members of society. Those excommunicated by the Church lost other rights as well.

Christianity not only brought a sense of unity to Europe, West Asia, and East Africa, but it also provided the institutional framework for the development of these societies. The schools, libraries, art collections, and the superior knowledge that monks and nuns transmitted all forged a link, however tenuous and weak, between the newcomers' crude ways and the earlier high civilizations of Persia, Greece, and Rome. But Buddhism and Christianity were not the only religions to develop and spread in this period. We now turn to examine the dramatic development and spread of Islam, the third major universal religion.

MUHAMMAD AND THE
SPREAD OF ISLAM

Setting the Stage

As far back as the sixth century B.C.E., West Asia had been under the rule of strong empires, including the Persians, Romans, and Parthians. By the seventh century C.E., the area was divided between two major powers: the Sassanids, heirs to the earlier Persian Empire, who had conquered the Parthians in the early third century, and Byzantium, the eastern or Hellenized portion of the former Roman Empire. Both empires sought to control nomadic groups on their frontiers, often using them as mercenaries, caravan guides, and aids in promoting trade. Both empires carried on prosperous trade to the east along the Silk Roads.

Religion strengthened and helped integrate the diverse subjects into a unified culture in each area. The Sassanids, following the Parthian example, made Zoroastrianism the state religion; Byzantium's faith

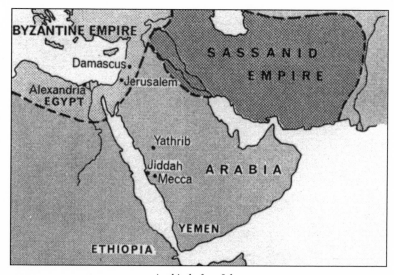

Arabia before Islam

was Christianity. The rulers hoped that a single religion might help them unite their ethnically and linguistically diverse subjects.

These two empires often fought, deploying thousands of soldiers and using the most advanced military technology. In 619 the Sassanids conquered Egypt and were threatening Anatolia, but in a series of massive battles that raged from 623 to 627, Byzantine forces reclaimed those areas. As they exhausted each other in bloody battles, neither the Sassanids nor the Byzantines paid much attention to what was going on in the Arabian Peninsula, an area they regarded as on the fringe of civilization.

Nomadic herdsmen called Bedouins lived in Arabia. They survived by herding flocks of sheep and goats. Most of the peninsula was too dry for agriculture, so periodically they moved their animals from oasis to oasis in search of water. These nomadic herdsman, also known as Arabs, lived in separate tribal groups. Although they shared a common pastoral nomadic lifestyle, members of individual clans and tribes were intensely loyal to their own blood relatives Heated rivalries over grazing areas, access to water, or honor and social superiority frequently led to war.

Arab traders actively engaged in overland and maritime trade. They transported goods going to and from the Indian Ocean via Red Sea and Persian Gulf ports, overland through Palestine to Constantinople, and east to Central Asia and China. Important centers developed around oases where people found ample water and traders exchanged goods.

The Founding of Islam

By the seventh century Mecca was already an important religious site because it housed the Ka'ba, a sacred black meteorite that Abraham, the first Jewish patriarch, was said to have placed there. Pilgrims traveled to worship at the Ka'ba, placing images of their local gods and goddesses around it and paying homage to them. Traders in and around Mecca guaranteed month-long periods of peace in order to encourage pilgrims to visit the shrine. Merchants developed prosperous businesses feeding and lodging these pilgrims, and gradually Mecca became an important long-distance trading center.

Muhammad ("highly praised" in Arabic), the founder of Islam, was born in Mecca in 570. His parents died when he was very young, and a granduncle raised him. After supporting himself with a variety of jobs, Khadija, a prosperous widow, hired him to manage her caravan business. She soon proposed to and married him, and as long as she was alive, Khadija was his only wife.

As Muhammad traveled with Khadija's caravans to and from Syria and Mecca, he met many different Jews, Zoroastrians, and Christians who were followers of centuries-old monotheistic faiths. He also accompanied caravans to urban areas where these faiths were practiced and must have asked people about their beliefs and observed how they lived.

When he was forty Muhammad had a life-changing experience. According to Muslim tradition, while he was sleeping in a cave, the angel Gabriel appeared and told him that he had been selected to receive divine inspiration. There is only Allah, Gabriel told him, one all-powerful, all-knowing, and all-merciful divinity. Allah is the same divinity Jews identify as YHWH and Christians call God.

> Unto Allah belong the East and the West: whithersoever ye turn, there is Allah's countenance. Lo! Allah is All-Embracing, All-Knowing. (Qur'an 2:115)

When Muhammad reported what he had heard, Khadija immediately took the revelations seriously, encouraged him to share them, supported Muhammad when others questioned his revelations, and was the first person to convert to the new religion of Islam. Gabriel said there had been many prophets including Abraham, Moses, and Jesus, and now Muhammad. Over the next twenty-two years, Allah continued to reveal his message to Muhammad, who shared these revelations with others.

Muhammad never claimed any supernatural power. He reminded people that he was an illiterate trader, the empty vessel into which Allah poured inspiration. (Muslims are especially offended when their faith is called Mohammedanism. They do not worship the prophet; they follow Allah's revelations to him.) Gabriel revealed that all people were to submit to Allah's will.

Islam means "submission," and a person who submits to Allah is a

Muslim. Muhammad preached that everyone was equal in Allah's sight and the wealthy should share with the poor. Each person would eventually face a final day of judgment and those who had submitted to Allah would go to heaven, where they were promised gardens with flowing rivers as their eternal home. Those who had not submitted to Allah would be condemned to fiery hell.

Why Is the Hegira So Important?

Because Muhammad's message offended some rich and powerful individuals, and his emphasis on monotheism threatened the brisk pilgrimage trade around the Ka'ba, Meccan aristocrats united against Muhammad and his followers. In 622, when a delegation from Yathrib invited Muhammad to come and try to pacify feuding tribes in that city, he and his followers slipped away from Mecca to Yathrib. This migration, known as the *hegira*, was the origin of the Muslim community. It is so important that Muslims made 622 the first year of their calendar: A.H. (*anno hegira*) 1, and Yathrib became known as Medina, "the city of the prophet."

Impressed with Muhammad's integrity, his business skills, and his ability to negotiate among tribal factions, the people of Medina increasingly looked to him for leadership. As a result, Muhammad became not only a religious prophet but an important political leader as well. He was also a skilled general and his army, which grew to over ten thousand men, subdued and then united many of the tribes of Arabia. In 630 Muhammad and his forces returned to Mecca, took control of the city, destroyed the idols around the Ka'ba, and granted amnesty to his former enemies. The residents of Mecca became Muslims and accepted Muhammad's leadership. Before he died in 632, most of the tribes in the peninsula had either converted to Islam or pledged their loyalty to him.

The Qur'an

In the years after Muhammad's death, his followers tried to write down the revelations Muhammad had received exactly as he had reported them. These revelations make up the Qur'an. They were given in Arabic, the language of the Bedouin tribes, so the Qur'an is written in Arabic. It states:

Read:
in the name of thy Lord
who created. . . .
Read:
And thy Lord is the Most Bounteous,
Who taught by the pen,
Taught man that which he knew not. (Qur'an 96. 1-5)

For Muslims the Qur'an is divine revelation, the closest any human being can come to Allah. Allah's revelations should not be translated because translations distort the original meaning. Anyone who wants to have a true understanding of this holy book should read it in Arabic. In the early years the language united believers and separated the faithful from outsiders.

The Five Pillars

Muhammad taught that there are Five Pillars that every Muslim—regardless of his or her ethnicity, social background, or gender—should accept and observe. The first pillar is the affirmation of faith: "There is no Allah but Allah, and Muhammad is his prophet." If a person makes this statement three times in succession, he or she becomes a Muslim.

The second pillar is to pray five times a day at set times, following a prescribed form. Some prayers are the same for everyone; some are personal prayers. At first everyone was to face Jerusalem when they prayed, but soon they faced the Ka'ba in Mecca instead. Individual Muslims can spread out a prayer rug anywhere and perform the prayers. Muslims try to gather together to perform the noontime prayer on Friday.

Reciting prayers in unison—using the same gestures and rising and falling at precisely the same moment—helped create an emotional bond of unity among Muslims. The public nature of prayer is extremely impressive. Imagine the dramatic effect of ten thousand cavalrymen dismounting, repeatedly prostrating themselves, touching their heads to the earth, and reciting prayers in unison.

The third pillar requires each person to give alms to the poor. In an effort to fulfill one's responsibility to the community, Muslims are

Muslims at prayer

expected to contribute one-fortieth of their wealth each year, not just a percentage of their annual income. From Islam's inception, Muslims were taught to support the "brotherhood of all believers."

The fourth pillar is to observe a month-long fast. From sunrise to sunset during the month of Ramadan, Muslims are to consume neither food nor drink. They break the fast each evening as the sun sets and often eat together during the night. This pillar also enhances the sense of community, both because of the common depravation believers experience and the fellowship of the late-night feasts.

The fifth pillar is to make a pilgrimage to Mecca at least once if at all possible. The annual pilgrimage is called a *hajj*. Muslims from all parts of the world congregate at Mecca, which only they can enter. When they reach the city, they swap their clothing for two white sheets. Wearing identical sheets eliminates evidence of a person's wealth, tribe, or region and symbolizes that all are equal before Allah. Dressing this way is also a humbling experience.

The hajj includes several days of rituals and prayers that culminate in walking around the Ka'ba seven times. In the evenings pilgrims

Ka'ba and Mosque, Mecca

get together, exchanging stories and insights, building friendships, forming alliances, and learning the proper way to practice the faith as well as correct interpretations of Islam's laws.

A person who has made the hajj is known as a *hajji* and gets special respect and status upon returning home. A hajji shares what he or she has learned about the proper interpretations of the law and how the rituals should be performed. In this way the hajj has been an important way of unifying Muslims who live in vastly different areas of the world.

The hajj also stimulated trade. It often took pilgrims several months to reach Mecca, and they needed many rest areas and places to eat and sleep along their way. Pilgrims and merchants exchanged goods, ideas, and inventions, as well as stories. Khadija, Muhammad's first wife, was a prosperous businesswoman, and Muslims, unlike early Christians, had great respect for traders.

Who Should Succeed Muhammad?

Muhammad spoke of Islam as a brotherhood of all believers, and the Five Pillars helped deepen its sense of unity. Uniting the Arab tribes was critical in the early years of Islam, but unity did not come easily. Bedouin tribes, like other tribal groups, tended to challenge one another. If they pledged their loyalty to an individual leader, that bond would end when the leader died. Muhammad attempted to expand the concept of tribal loyalty and said that all those who had pledged their loyalty to him were united in one brotherhood.

When Muhammad died some tribes wanted to break away, claiming his legitimacy came from Allah's revelations, and that he had never named a successor (caliph) or explained how the community should pick the next leader. Almost immediately after his death, factions developed. Some claimed the caliph should be a descendant of Muhammad. Because there were no sons, his daughter's husband, Ali, seemed the obvious candidate. Ali was Muhammad's cousin, the son of the granduncle who had raised Muhammad. When Ali died, they claimed, his sons should succeed him.

But nomadic societies, in which fighting skills are so important, seldom use heredity as the basis for leadership. Sunni Muslims, the vast majority, wanted the caliph to represent strong tribal leadership. Family members are not always good warriors or the most qualified, they argued. In addition, Allah had chosen Muhammad to receive the revelations, so heredity was meaningless. The new leader should be the wisest member of the strongest tribe.

Bypassing Ali, the elders selected Abu Bakr, an early convert to Islam and the Prophet's father-in-law, to be the political and military leader of the community. He concentrated on trying to keep the tribes united. He proclaimed that Muhammad was the last prophet of God and forbade any tribe that was already part of the community from withdrawing. In fact, the first military campaigns were intended to crush revolts and keep the community united.

Stationing troops together in garrisons—fortified settlements—was one way to prevent tribes from breaking away or trying to conquer new territory for themselves. In addition, garrisoned troops could rest after battles, drill, and plan the coming campaigns. Isolating troops also prevented them from mingling with the people they had conquered, especially in cities, which might make the warriors soft and weaken their will to fight.

To prevent hostilities, different tribes lived in separate sections within the garrison towns, and each had its own meeting space and burial area. Wide boulevards separated tribes from one another. There was also an area where the troops could drill as well as one main

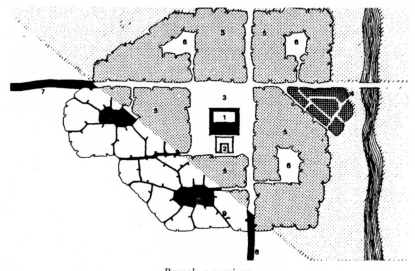

Basrah, a garrison.
1. Mosque 2. Residence of military chief 3. Open space 4. Market
5. Areas for separate tribes 6. Burial areas for each tribe

gathering place, known as a mosque, where everyone could pray together. However, Abu Bakr's efforts to keep the men stationed in garrisons did not ensure unity.

The Community Splits into Sunni and Shi'ite Muslims

After Abu Bakr's death, the elders chose Umar, another one of Muhammad's companions, as the second caliph. Arab military expansion began under Umar's leadership. When he died, a council chose Uthman, a member of the Umayyad clan, as the third caliph. But dissatisfaction with Uthman grew, in part because he restricted the troops to their garrisons and because he favored the Umayyads. A revolt intended to ensure the socioeconomic equality of the community resulted in Uthman's assassination in 656.

Ali was immediately installed as the fourth caliph, but opposition to him was intense. Initially Ali's forces won, but the ensuing clashes proved indecisive. Ali was murdered in 661 and the elders chose a member of the Umayyad clan as caliph. The Umayyads took command and established the Umayyad Caliphate.

To ensure that the Umayyad clan would continue to rule, the leadership transformed the caliphate (the period of rule) into a hereditary monarchy and moved the government to Damascus. Meanwhile, Ali's followers banded together into Ali's Party and in 680 encouraged Husayn, Ali's son, to attack the Umayyads. When Umayyad forces surrounded Husayn's small band of soldiers, none of his supporters came to his aid, and he and his men were slaughtered. From that time forward Shi'ite Muslims, as they came to be called, have continued to look for the divinely inspired Imam (leader) who will lead the faith. As they await the return of the true Imam, whom they believe is in hiding, they have sought

Al-Husayn battles enemies

penance for their betrayal of Husayn. Sunni Muslims, who comprise about ninety percent of the Muslim community today, believe the final authority for the faith rests with the collective wisdom of the community.

The Rapid Expansion of Arab Muslim Control

By the time the Umayyads took over, Muslim Arab forces had already conquered not only Syria and Egypt but had defeated the Sassanids. Their empire had fallen surprisingly quickly, in part because many under Sassanid rule were tired of the fighting between the Byzantines and Sassanids and weary of the heavy taxes levied on them to support the military.

Arab armies then turned their forces against the Byzantine Empire. Many of its subjects also resented being required to fight. Although Constantinople was a center of learning and wealth, many

Christians—including those in the Byzantine Church, Copts, and
Nestorians—as well as Zoroastrians and Manicheans had little affection for Byzantine authority. Resentful of the burdensome taxes levied
to pay for military ventures, some may have viewed the Arabs as liberators from oppressive Byzantine rule. Although the Muslims did not
defeat Byzantium, they captured significant territory in West Asia.
They even established a stronghold in Sind in western India.

Muslim Arab conquests extended far beyond the territories the
Caliphate controlled. Muslim forces also conquered tribal groups in
North Africa known as Berbers (from the Latin word "barbari" for
"barbarian"). Berbers who converted to Islam and crossed the Straits
of Gibraltar and invaded the Iberian peninsula were called Moors. By
719 Moors controlled the peninsula, and a band of Muslims even
crossed the Pyrenees Mountains that separate France and Spain.
However, after losing to the Franks at Tours in 732, the Muslims had
little incentive to try to push farther into sparsely settled northern
Europe. By 750, only 128 years after Muhammad's death, Muslim
Arabs controlled territory from the the Iberian peninsula, across North
Africa and western Asia to Sind in the Indian subcontinent.

It is important to differentiate Muslim political control from conversion to Islam. After the initial conquests in Arabia, conversion was
relatively slow. *Jihad* means self-exertion, and Muslims were

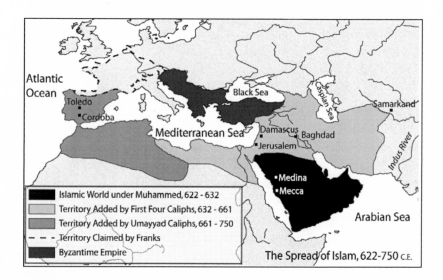

The Spread of Islam, 622-750 C.E.

Legend:
- Islamic World under Muhammed, 622 - 632
- Territory Added by First Four Caliphs, 632 - 661
- Territory Added by Umayyad Caliphs, 661 - 750
- Territory Claimed by Franks
- Byzantine Empire

expected to struggle to follow Allah's will. This included a personal jihad to lead a virtuous life and a more public obligation to try to spread the faith through teaching and preaching. Although Muslims were not to force anyone to convert, they had an obligation to defend fellow Muslims and the faith with the sword, when necessary. The Qur'an states:

> And fight in the way of Allah with those who fight with you, and do not exceed the limits (initiate hostilities), surely Allah does not love those who exceed the limits (are aggressors). (Qur'an 2:190)

Why Were Arab Muslim Armies So Successful?

Many factors contributed to the rapid spread of Muslim Arab political control. The military skill and strength of the armies, composed in large part of nomadic warriors accustomed to fighting, explains many of their early victories. The campaigns were carefully planned and directed from Medina. As the community expanded, it had to find additional sources of food and other resources, which were available in richer areas outside the Arabian Peninsula and along the trade routes. Fighting also provided an outlet for the soldiers' energy, helping to reduce the possibility of tribal tensions.

The importance of an egalitarian community of believers was a very important factor in the Muslims' initial military successes. The promise of the spoils was a strong motivation. Military campaigns resulted in a great deal of plunder. The army was guaranteed four-fifths of the spoils, and generals tried to ensure these goods were divided equally among the soldiers. Sharing the spoils symbolized the ideal of equality and contributed to making that ideal and the brotherhood of all believers a reality.

Initially religion was not a primary motivation for the troops. In the early years, when the victories were most dramatic, most soldiers probably had little knowledge about the specifics of the faith, but they could experience the importance of belonging to a common brotherhood. As one victorious military campaign led to another, the soldiers may have begun to believed Allah was on their side and they were fighting to defend the faith.

The *Sharia*: Rules for the Community

As the Arab Muslim community expanded among diverse peoples, it
needed rules for everyday life. Muslims could no longer turn to
Muhammad for guidance. They had the Qur'an as a source of instruction. They also consulted the *hadith*, which relates what Muhammad
had said and done. The hadith is second only to the Qur'an as a guide
for Muslims.

When people were still not certain what to do in a given situation,
they appealed to learned men who interpreted the Qur'an and hadith
and gave advice to the faithful. They also considered what the community had been doing. These four sources—the Qur'an, the hadith,
insights from the scholars, and the traditions of the community—are
the basis of Islamic law called the *Sharia*, literally "a path to the
watering place." The Sharia provides direction for many aspects of a
Muslim's life. Making laws is usually the prerogative of rulers, but in
Islam rulers were not to legislate; that was the function of religious
scholars who interpreted the text and tradition and determined what
was to be done.

The Mosque

A mosque is a place where believers bow down to Allah, so theoreti-
cally a mosque exists anywhere Muslims pray. The first mosque was
Muhammad's courtyard. Mosques in the early garrison towns were
merely open spaces where the faithful gathered to pray.

Most mosques share certain characteristics. A niche in the wall
called a *mihrab* symbolizes Muhammad's presence and indicates the
direction of Mecca. Mosques have towers (called minarets) attached
to them that point the believer's mind toward the heavens and from
which men call the faithful to prayer. The courtyard has a fountain so
people can perform ritual ablutions before praying. Gradually other
buildings were added, such as schools, hospitals, hostels for travelers,
and places where spiritual and legal scholars studied and taught.

Mosques help Muslims understand important elements of their
faith. For example, the empty space so characteristic of mosques symbolizes that Allah is not found within a building but is present everywhere. The rectangle base represents the earth, and the dome
represents heaven. In order to make it possible for the square base to

carry the weight of the dome, architects first divided the base into an octagon and then into sixteen sides. Later, the transition from square to round was filled by stalactites, a ubiquitous feature of Islamic architecture. It symbolizes the transition from earth to heaven and represents both human longing to reach divinity and divinity's attempt to make contact with believers.

The Appeal of Islam and Islamization

Although Muslim Arab forces rapidly established military and political control over vast areas, conversion to Islam came much more slowly. Initially, most of the people the Muslims conquered kept their own beliefs and were not encouraged to convert. Many Arabs felt that Islam was their special faith and they discouraged non-Arabs from converting. Muslims were especially tolerant of Jews and Christians, whom they called "People of the Book," and Muslims promised to protect them as long as they paid a special tax. Zoroastrians were sometimes also considered members of this "protected" group.

Gradually, as non-Arabs converted, Islam had all the elements of a universal religion. It was strictly monotheistic, worshiping only Allah. It was open to all and promised salvation to all who surrendered to Allah; Muhammad and the revelations in the Qur'an helped believers gain salvation; the rules were few and easy to understand; and the faith addressed many of the issues people were facing. All three universal religions spread most readily in cities rather than in rural settings, and they were shaped by intellectual elites who interpreted the original messages and developed various rules for living.

Many factors explain Islam's appeal. No doubt some people became Muslims for political or financial reasons. Muslims did not pay the protection tax, although they were expected to donate one-fortieth of their wealth to the community. Probably some non-believers, given the choice of paying taxes or converting to Islam, submitted to Allah. Some converted as a result of intermarriage. Some non-Muslim traders or would-be administrators also converted to help their business or to enhance their political fortunes with the ruling Arab elite. The fact that Muslims were not to enslave fellow Muslims may also have motivated some slaves to convert. Few people were forced to do so, although all Arabs were expected to surrender to Allah

Islam's appeal to women was mixed. Muhammad insisted that both men and women were equal before Allah, and the egalitarianism he envisioned included the social equality of women. He prohibited female infanticide, a common practice, and said a dowry belonged to the wife, not her husband's family. A woman can have only one husband while a man can have four wives, if the first wife agrees to the arrangement. All wives are to be treated equally, and husbands are expected to support them. The Qur'an states that men had exclusive authority over their wives and were expected to discipline them. Husbands can divorce a wife just by saying "I divorce you" three times. In addition, some of the images of heaven resemble a utopia for men, not women.

Two of Muhammad's wives were important in the early days of the faith. Khadija, Muhammad's first wife, always supported Muhammad and used her influence and wealth to promote the faith. Aisha, Muhammad's favorite young wife, was the first Muslim woman to wear a veil and be secluded. Muhammad preferred her company to that of other women and died in her arms when she was only eighteen. After his death, she was the source of much of the information about Muhammad in the hadith and took an active role in the conflict over succession.

Islam, like the other universal religions, adapted to new settings as it moved out of Arabia. Muhammad and his fellow Arabs had come from a nomadic society in which many women had significant social authority and even participated in tribal decision-making. Women could initiate marriage and divorce, inherit property, and some even had several husbands. Khadija was a very successful businesswoman. On the other hand, Mesopotamian society tended to restrict women. Assyrian women were expected to wear veils, and women in West Asia generally had few, if any, legal rights. Islam adopted some of these West Asian attitudes and practices as it spread.

No doubt men and women were attracted to Islam because of the Qur'an's essential message. Most people could perform at least four of the five Pillars of the faith. The promise of paradise for those who submitted to Allah must have been very appealing and the desire to escape hell compelling. The community's strong sense of brotherhood and mutual support must have drawn many to the faith.

Even so, by 750 less that ten percent of the people in areas Muslim armies had conquered had converted. It was only after that, especially as a result of urbanization, that the faith spread. Since few peasants could read, they had to learn about the Islam from believers. Village men and women drawn to towns and cities readily found Muslims who spoke and read Arabic and could interpret the Qur'an. As they mixed and socialized with their Muslim neighbors, they gradually copied some of their ways and began to act like the people around them.

This slow process of change is called "Islamization." Instead of one day deciding to convert to Islam, men and women mingled with others in a predominately Muslim community, copied how Muslims spoke, went to their festivals, observed how they prayed, imitated how their bosses acted, obeyed their laws, even married them, and gradually they began not only to act like Muslims and participate in their rituals but to accept and affirm their beliefs. However, Islamization was a very gradual process that did not become widespread until the ninth century.

The Umayyad Caliphate

The Umayyad Caliphate, which covered a vast area of very diverse people, ruled from 661 to 750. Many factors help explain the caliphate's strength and vitality. Muslim armies kept peace in the lands they conquered, and local people were not forced to join the army or convert. Spoils of war paid most of the army's expenses. Those who converted did not have to pay taxes, although the alms Msulims gave to the community amounted to a tax. Umayyad leaders modeled their administration on the efficient Sassanid and Byzantine bureaucratic structure. Local non-Muslim administrators continued to govern the areas and collect the taxes, so conquest caused little disruption to everyday life. Most landowners kept title to their lands.

Just as many successful earlier empires had tolerated diversity, Arab rulers, though devout Muslims, tolerated the cultures of people they had conquered as long as the non-believer obeyed the rules, paid their taxes, and did not try to revolt. Muslims claimed that People of the Book were worshiping the same God. The Qur'an accepts the

major Jewish patriarchs and prophets and Muhammad had taught that
Jesus' message was essentially correct, but that his followers had
made a mistake claiming he was divine.

Trade was very important in Muslim areas. Arabic became the language of administration, business, law, and trade. Islamic power
opened up contact and commercial activities from the Iberian peninsula and Morocco to China. Trade flourished, and through contact in
major trading centers, more than any other factor, people learned
about Islam and were often drawn to the faith.

The three universal religions—Mahayana Buddhism, Christianity, and
Islam—all had doctrines that average people could grasp and appreci-
ate. Each taught how to live a moral life and promised forgiveness
and salvation for all believers. Mahayana Buddhism developed from
earlier Buddhism, which had grown out of still earlier Indian religious
beliefs. Christianity developed from its Jewish roots and offered all
people its Good News. And Islam, expanding both Jewish and
Christian beliefs, identified Allah as the universal divinity and
Muhammad as the Seal of the Prophets.

Arab Muslims quickly took control of many highly urbanized areas
that were heirs to millennia of highly developed civilizations. After
their conquests, they relied on existing bureaucratic structures to govern. Conversion came later. We shall see what problems conversion
will pose for Arab Muslims and what happened as a result when we
return to Islam later in the human drama. We now turn to consider the
Gupta Empire and whether Hinduism should be identified as a universal religion.

ACT TWO – THE DEVELOPMENT AND SPREAD OF UNIVERSAL RELIGIONS

Setting the Stage

1. What are the characteristics of universal religions? What makes them universal? What do they offer their followers?
2. What conditions in society might make individuals and groups receptive to the message of a universal religion? How might the disintegration of the Han and Roman empires have enhanced the spread of one or more of these faiths?
3. Identify the differences among ethical dualism, monism, and a harmony of opposites. Suggest examples that illustrate these differences.
4. What role do you think the introduction of new ideas or technology has had in world history? Cite examples.
5. How does Professor Bentley suggest that ideas spread? What does he mean by conversion by voluntary association? Give some examples. Give some examples of conversion that resulted from pressure or coercion.
6. What does Professor Bentley mean by syncretism? Why is it important for a new idea to resonate with existing ideas? Cite some examples of how syncretism influences the adaptation and adoption of new ideas?

SCENE ONE

The World of Mahayana Buddhism

1. In what ways did Emperor Ashoka contribute to the spread of Buddhism? Why might he have distributed stupas throughout his kingdom?
2. What is an arhat? A bodhisattva? What are the major differences between Theravada and Mahayana Buddhism?
3. What are some of the Southeast Asian beliefs and practices that resonate with Buddhist ones? How does Borobudur illustrate syncretism and synthesis?
4. What Buddhist ideas seemed to be at odds with Confucian values, especially filial piety? How did the Chinese make concepts such as nirvana and the Buddha's teachings appealing to the Chinese?
5. Explain how the idea of merit helped Buddhism spread in China.
6. How did the Emperor Wendi use Buddhism to enhance his power? What ideas did he adapt from Ashoka?

7. What is a stupa? What does it symbolize? What roles did it play in the spread of Buddhism?
8. What was Buddhism's appeal in Korea? How did syncretism help the new faith spread there?
9. In what ways does the grotto at Seokguram illustrate syncretism and synthesis?
10. What seem to have been the major reasons for the spread of Buddhism before 800 C.E.? Cite specific examples.

SCENE TWO

Christianity Becomes Christendom

1. Describe the organization of the early Christian church. How was it influenced by the organization of the Roman Empire under Diocletian? On what basis did the patriarch of Rome claim special authority?
2. What ideas did the Church Fathers stress? How did their teachings help Christianity spread?
3. How did the Church handle the debate over the nature of Jesus? Who were the Nestorians? Why did the Roman Church considered them heretics? How did people in central Asia react to the Nestorians? Why?
4. What were the Desert Fathers and Mothers seeking? What is the difference between the regular and secular clergy? How do their concerns differ?
5. What were some of the reasons women were drawn to Christianity? What about its message might have seemed to denigrate the role and importance of women?
6. What appeal did Christianity have for political leaders in Byzantium and Axum? What were some of the reasons Clovis and Charlemagne supported Roman Christianity? Compare and contrast the ways these leaders reacted to Christianity.
7. Why would Church leaders want to gain the support of powerful political leaders? Why did political leaders want the support of church officials? Who had the most to gain?
8. In what ways did the Christian community change as it moved into Western Europe and more people became Christians? In what ways did Christianity change as a result of support from powerful political leaders?

SCENE THREE

Muhammad and the Spread of Islam

1. Describe Muhammad's early life. What was the source of his revelations? What role did Khadija play in Muhammad's life?

2. Identify the aspects of Islam that fit the definition of a universal religion. What is the reward for submission to Allah? What helps Muslims gain salvation?

3. What is the origin and importance of the Qur'an?

4. Identify the Five Pillars of Islam. How did each Pillar help create a sense of unity among Muslims?

5. Why was determining a successor to Muhammad such a difficult problem for the early Muslim community? What separated the Sunni and Shi'ite Muslims?

6. What territory had Muslim forces conquered by early in the eighth century? Why were Arab Muslim forces so successful?

7. What is the source of the Sharia? What was the relationship between political leadership and Islam?

8. Describe a mosque. What does it symbolize? What role does the mosque play in Islam?

9. Why were there few converts during Islam's first one hundred and fifty years? Why did it spread more quickly in cities than in the countryside?

10. Explain the process of Islamization. How does it differ from a sudden decision to adopt a new faith?

11. What role did trade have in the spread of Islam?

Summing Up

1. Identify possible reasons people might be attracted to the message of the universal religions. Identify one area to which one or more of the faiths spread and discuss how conditions and beliefs there influenced the faith's reception.

2. Why was political support so important in the spread of new ideas? Compare the roles any two or more rulers played in the spread of the universal religions?

3. Compare and contrast the reasons political leaders supported the universal religions.

4. Compare and contrast the appeal the three universal religions had for women.

5. Compare and contrast the attitude of the universal religions toward trade and traders? What role did trade play in the spread of these faiths?

6. Write a dialogue between two or more people who have converted to one or more of these faiths. Have them share and compare their reasons for adopting a new faith.

ACT THREE

The Flowering of Empires (300 to 1250)

The spread of universal religions had a profound effect on the Afro-Eurasian world. Germanic settlers in Europe responded to various interpretations of the Christian message, and many leaders found the Christian worldview attractive and its organization effective. They hoped an alliance with the Roman church would help unite and strengthen their rule. In a similar fashion, nomadic groups who built states in northern China used Buddhism to enhance their status and legitimacy, and leaders in Korea hoped Buddhism would help them unite and protect their country. Muslim Arab control spread quickly, into West Asia, North Africa, and the Mediterranean basin. Muslims created a vital cultural expression that was at once familiar and radically new.

Because anyone could practice these religions, leaders experimented with using them to unite the diverse groups in their kingdoms. Islam, particularly, sought to replace ethnic and blood loyalties with a social identity that stressed the brotherhood of all believers and the commonality of all people within a single faith. Leaders who supported one of the universal religions probably believed it would enable them to expand their territory as well as provide a common system of cultural values and discourage diverse people from sustaining their historic hostilities. This may partially explain why the second half of the first millennium of the common era saw the reemergence of strong, vital empires in West Asia and China: Gupta India, Byzantium, and Tang and Song China.

Does an Empire Want More Land or More People?

Political scientists define a state, no matter how large it is, as an area ruled by a central government that has sovereignty over its land and subjects or citizens. An empire is a state that encompasses a very large area of diverse people and is usually created by force. Rulers of empires maintain a strong military in order to get more land and to hold onto the land they have, and they usually station troops along the borders to avert attack by outside groups, particularly nomads, or competing powers.

In some small states and even some empires, leaders want to attract people rather than claim more land. In areas where few people live, empire builders need to attract those who can supply the labor necessary to maintain the court and produce the needed goods. Force alone won't work, because in sparsely populated areas, people can flee. Instead, the government may provide a dazzling display of its wealth and power, including elaborate rituals, to attract people to the court. It helps if leaders can claim to have supernatural powers as well. Governments that use these strategies are often identified as "theater states" because of the methods they use to attract subjects.

In a large land-based empire, most subjects probably do not know or care very much who is ruling as long as they feel safe from neighbors or outsiders who might harm them or from unethical officials who abuse their power. They also want low taxes and reasonable corvée demands. In a people-based empire, those close to the capital are most directly affected by the government. Subjects on the outskirts may only think about the central government when they need protection or when some great festival is about to take place. Most subjects may think: "What care I who rules the land as long as I am left in peace?"

We might liken a land-based empire to a body of water that has been dammed. Leaders work hard to ensure that the dam holds and the boundaries are secure. Theater states can be compared to a lake into which someone has thrown a large rock . Ripples of water radiate from the place the rock hits. Nearest the rock's impact, a small whirlpool might form and pull in other objects. Farther away ripples become fainter and fainter and finally disappear. At the outer edges there may be hardly any movement in the water at all.

Subjects of a theater state who live close to the capital are probably very conscious of the government and are required to pay taxes, serve in the army, and perform corvée labor. Those far away are hardly aware of the government unless government officials or troops enter their areas or a special need arises.

All three of the empires in this act have characteristics of both land-based empires and theater states, and influences from all three will spread beyond their own borders. Like rocks thrown into a lake, their cultures and values will be strongest and clearest near the center, and like the ripples created by the rock's impact, their influences will radiate far afield.

The Importance of Cross-Cultural Interaction and Trade

Whether land-based or theater states, kingdoms and empires cannot ignore the importance of long-distance trade. Revenue from trade brings in resources that lighten the tax burden on local peasants. Even when income from trade makes up a relatively small percentage of the state's total wealth, merchants provide luxuries that rulers and affluent members of society want. These goods demonstrate their status and make their court more impressive. Moreover a favorable balance of trade, when the state exports more than it imports, is often an indication of a state's power and wealth.

States that want to buy more than they can sell are forced to pay the difference in something the sellers think is valuable. Throughout much of history the most desired payment has usually been either gold or silver. Both metals are attractive and quite rare and can easily be molded and smelted into ingots or coins and carried long distances. Consequently a state with a favorable balance of trade usually ends up with lots of silver and gold. At any given time, if we know which states are shipping out large amounts of gold and silver and which are accumulating these precious metals, we have a good idea which states are the most powerful and prosperous.

As we turn to consider the Guptas, Byzantium, and Tang and Song China, we shall be looking for characteristics of both land-based empires and theater states. We shall examine how influences radiate far from their centers as well as the ways these states are influenced by the many types of cross-cultural encounters taking place. We will try to assess their economic and political strengths and the stability of their governments. We shall examine the role played by the universal religions in each area. And because these societies could afford to support artisans, artists, religious leaders, philosophers, and other creative thinkers, we shall take special note of their cultural expressions.

SCENE ONE

THE GLORY OF THE GUPTAS

Setting the Stage

The Indian subcontinent has three distinct areas: the Indo-Gangetic plain in the north, the sparsely populated Deccan plateau in the center, and the area south of the Deccan. Two major groups populated the subcontinent: Aryans, who migrated into the Indus valley from the north around 1500 B.C.E. and settled in the Indo-Gangetic plain and Dravidians, who probably came by monsoon-driven boats from the Pacific Islands or Africa and settled in peninsular South India. Dravidian and Indo-European languages are very different, and some modern Dravidian-speakers argue that South India was initially an island that was later joined to the subcontinent. Some scholars also suggest that the Dravidians were refugees from the decaying Indus civilization. Whatever their origin, the Dravidian people developed a distinct civilization.

In addition to Indo-Europeans and Dravidians, India was also home to numerous tribal peoples who lived in small groups mostly in the country's dense forests and hilly regions. These people, some of whom still live by gathering and hunting and practicing a migratory form of slash-and-burn farming, may have come to India before any Indus, Indo-European, or Dravidian settlers arrived.

Far from being isolated from the rest of the Asian mainland, the Indian subcontinent was an integral part of Afro-Eurasian cross-cultural trade and contact. Merchants from the Indus Valley civilization (ca. 3000–1700 B.C.E.) traded with Sumerian city-states and Egypt. Later, Greek diplomats frequented the Mauryan court, and Emperor Ashoka's rock edicts (third century B.C.E.) mention Alexander's Hellenistic successor-states. Greek and Roman sculpture influenced Indian depictions of the Buddha, and there are intriguing similarities between Christianity and Mahayana Buddhism.

The Kushan kingdom in the first century C.E., stretching from north India into Afghanistan, thrust India into the midst of the currents of Eurasian exchange. Various groups traveled through the passes in the Hindu Kush Mountains, bringing new ideas and taking Indian concepts to other parts of Eurasia.

Taxila was a major trading city and a center of these exchanges. From there, lively trade flourished across the Indo-Gangetic plain. Standard coins and strong craft guilds of skilled artisans helped Indian merchants prosper. Many Indian businessmen became wealthy by supporting these guilds and financing merchant adventures. Some supported religious institutions and the arts. Chinese Buddhists had a keen interest in obtaining sacred Buddhist scriptures from India, and monks made pilgrimages to sites associated with the Buddha's life, including his birthplace. The growing wealth spawned by trade created an active group of merchants and businessmen that, together with wealthy kings, helped to create a very cosmopolitan civilization that both built on earlier traditions of Indian civilization and adapted new ideas.

An Eyewitness Account of the Gupta Empire

In 320 C.E., after the Kushan Empire disintegrated, the armies of Chandragupta I unified north India and established the Gupta Empire

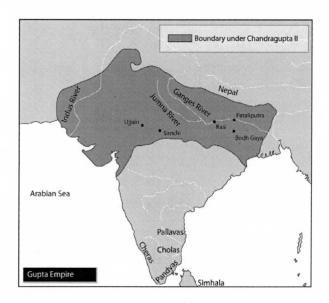

(320–550). Historians know very little about the dynasty's founder. By taking the name of the first ruler of the Mauryan dynasty, who had ruled 500 years earlier, he probably hoped to enhance his own legitimacy; there is no evidence that the two were related. Chandragupta also married the daughter of the leader of a powerful neighboring clan so that he could claim its military forces.

No official court histories remain to tell about the Gupta court, but several plays were written about Chandragupta II, and historians also have the report of a Chinese Buddhist pilgrim who traveled in South Asia during his reign. The monk, Fa Xian, recorded his travels in India from 405 to 441. Since he wanted to document Buddhist practices and beliefs and was not trying to impress or flatter anyone, historians believe his eyewitness account is fairly accurate. This is the way he described some of what he saw:

> [This country] has a temperate climate, without frost or snow; and the people are prosperous and happy, without registration or official restrictions. Only those who till the King's land have to pay so much on the profit they make. Those who want to go away, may go; those who want to stop, may stop. The king in his administration uses no corporal punishment; criminals are merely fined according to the gravity of their offenses. Even for a second attempt at rebellion the punishment is only the loss of the right hand. The men of the king's bodyguard have all fixed salaries. Throughout the country, no one kills any living thing, nor drinks wine, nor eats onions or garlic; but chandalas are segregated. Chandala is their name for foul men. These live away from other people; and when they approach a city or market, they beat a piece of wood, in order to distinguish themselves. Then people know who they are and avoid coming into contact with them.
>
> In this country they do not keep pigs or fowls, there are no dealings in cattle, no butchers' shops or distilleries in their market places. As a medium of

exchange they use cowries (shells). . . . The elders and gentry of these countries have instituted in their capitals free hospitals, and hither come all poor or helpless patients, orphans, widowers and cripples. They are well taken care of, a doctor attends them, food and medicine being supplied according to their needs. They are all made quite comfortable and when they are cured they go away. . . .

There is no lack of suitable things for household use. Although they have saucepans and stewpans, yet they do not know the steamer used for cooking rice. They have many vessels made of dried clay; they seldom use red copper vessels; they eat from one vessel, mixing all sorts of condiments together, which they take up with their fingers. They have no spoons or cups, and in short no sort of chopsticks. When sick, however, they use copper drinking cups. . . .

The taxes on the people are light, and the personal service required of them is moderate. . . . With respect to the ordinary people, although they are naturally light-minded, yet they are upright and honorable. In money matters they are without craft, and in administering justice they are considerate. They dread the retribution of another state of existence, and they make light of the things in the present world. They are not deceitful or treacherous in their conduct, and are faithful to their oaths and promises.

Fa Xian was impressed that a Buddhist monk could travel for nine years in complete safety, without any kind of passport. He never reported encountering hostility, persecution, or anyone trying to stop him from making extensive investigations into Buddhism. Buddhist monks traveled with merchants, spreading their beliefs. Monasteries built along important trade routes developed into commercial centers, ensuring that monks would have access to supplies and donors.

The Social Structure: Caste

Although Gupta rulers were tolerant of the many religious groups in their empire, they patronized Hinduism, which was emerging as the dominant faith in the subcontinent. By the time Fa Xian traveled there, most of the rulers were Hindu. However, Hinduism was not the Brahminic-dominated religious system of earlier times. Under Gupta patronage, Brahmin scholars brought earlier beliefs and practices into a common system called the Hindu synthesis. It included many Buddhist ideas, such as the principle that karma is shaped by one's intention, not just one's actions. It also incorporated the Jain ideals of non-violence, vegetarianism, and the sanctity of life. Several of Fa Xian's observations suggest how other faiths were being absorbed into Hinduism. For example, the absence of butcher shops was probably a Jain influence. It is interesting to note what he said India lacked.

Hinduism during the Gupta Age emerged as a total system that included not only the spiritual aspect of existence but also rules for organizing society and everyday life. The Hindu synthesis was built on the foundation of *dharma* (one's function, duty, job, or appropriate action), karma, and rebirth. Hinduism also advocated four lifetime goals—dharma, *artha* (survival, wealth and power), *kama* (pleasure), and moksha (release from rebirth)—and four stages of life: student, householder, going to the forest, and wandering holy man.

Dharma held the whole structure together, and everything in the universe had its specific dharma. The concept was so important in regulating Indian life that scholars compiled texts (*Dharma Sastras*) to codify behavior. Dharma is not a static idea and accepts the fact that people change during their lives. It describes the place of women in the social order and how each social group should behave. For example, directives in the *Dharma Sastras* seemingly were meant to establish male control over women's lives:

> In childhood a female must be subject to her father,
> in youth to her husband, when her lord is dead to her
> sons; a woman must never be independent.

We should remember that brahmins wrote these texts, and the rules they proposed are statements of their ideal society. Many statements

probably reflect efforts to limit women's former freedom and authority. In actual practice, although women's lives became more restricted
during Gupta times, some women owned businesses, served in positions of political leadership, wrote poetry, and were well educated.
Chandragupta II's daughter married a neighboring prince and ruled
his kingdom as regent for twenty years. Moreover, women in the
south were far freer than in the north.

The *Dharma Sastras* strongly uphold the concept of *varna* (the
four main castes), caste hierarchy and *jati* (the numerous subcastes),
and it appears that caste was strengthened in Gupta society despite
Buddhism's advocacy of greater social equality. The four varna were
brahmins, warrior-administrators, farmer-businessmen, and workers.
Jatis formed the core of what we call the caste system, and there were
thousands of castes all over India. Below the multiple castes was a
large group of outcastes.

RITUAL PURITY AND POLLUTION

Ritual purity and pollution constituted the basis for ranking castes.
Brahmins were the most ritually pure; outcastes were so impure that
they were considered "untouchable." (That explains Fa Xian's obser-
vation that chandalas had to indicate when they were coming so that
others could avoid contact with them.) Each village had a sense of
the ranking of the various castes within its community. In many villages, castes vied for position within the basic structure of brahmins,
craftsmen, farmers, workers, and outcastes.

Caste ranking usually influenced three aspects of life: what food
one could receive and from whom, whom one married, and one's
occupation. Higher castes had to eat ritually pure food, such as grains
cooked in a special way, and could accept certain foods only from
their own group or a higher caste. Fruits such as bananas or oranges
that are peeled were usually exchanged freely. The lowest castes
could eat polluted food, such as beef or pork, and accept food from
anyone. People were expected to marry members of their own caste,
but women might marry men from higher castes. A person was supposed to perform the job (dharma) that was appropriate to his or her
caste and hope to be born into a higher caste in succeeding births.
There was some social mobility in the society, but instead of individu-

als moving to higher castes, a whole caste would move up in the hierarchy by imitating a higher caste's behavior.

The caste system served as an important means of assimilating newcomers into Hindu culture. Incoming groups could find a place by adopting caste names and forming caste groups. For example, invading Huns gradually became Jats, and Rajputs took on Kshatriya status as warriors. Zoroastrians, Christians, and Jews were seen as castes. Caste hierarchy was so powerful that even the Muslims, who stressed the equality of all people, adopted caste hierarchy in India as part of their social organization.

Is Hinduism a Universal Religion?

Hinduism—a mix of Indus Valley practices: Brahmanism, the Vedic faith, Jain influences, and Buddhist reforms—developed some of the characteristics of a universal religion during Gupta times as a result of three important changes in Indian religious life. One was the adoption of Jain and Buddhist values, such as vegetarianism and non-violence (*ahimsa*). A second was reverence for images of deities and considering temples their homes. The third was the growing popularity of *bhakti,* personal devotion to a particular deity that loves and cares for the devotee, which was replacing the ritual sacrifices that brahmins performed.

VISHNU, SHIVA, AND THE GODDESS

The Upanishads, important new spiritual insights compiled between 700 and 200 B.C.E., described two strands of belief: monism and theism. Monists believe in a single ultimate reality identified as Brahman, which encompasses all that is and all that is not and they prefer to think of the Diving without form and beyond all pairs of opposites. Theists seek salvation by worshiping one of the major gods or goddesses. Given our dualistic outlook, we may conclude that one would have to be either a monist or a theist, but many Hindus mix these concepts together and can worship the gods and goddesses and also think of them as pointing beyond themselves to the greater cosmic mystery they are striving to understand.

Over time three major divinities emerged that had absorbed the attributes of lesser gods and goddesses: Vishnu, Lord of Preservation,

Durga slaying the buffalo demon

Shiva, a complex deity concerned with both creation and destruction that may have been worshiped as early as the Indus civilization, and Devi, the supreme goddess, who was worshiped in many different forms. Initially the goddesses had been powerful independent deities, but in the Hindu synthesis many of them became the dutiful wives or consorts (companions) of male gods. Lakshmi is Vishnu's consort. Parvati and Uma are the benign consorts of Lord Shiva. Durga and Kali are his aggressive and independent consorts, suggesting their earlier power. Each of these divinities encompasses all qualities, which helps explain why Shiva, the Lord of Destruction, is worshiped as the lingam, a symbol of creative potency, or why Kali, who has blood dripping from her tongue and holds severed heads in her hands, is adored as the Great Mother.

Lord Vishnu promised that he would appear periodically to ensure a balance in the world (sort of like putting a good player on a weak team to make the sides even). However, unlike the incarnation of Christ, which was a single event, Hindus believe Vishnu appears in ten different incarnations, which include a fish, tortoise, boar, man-lion, dwarf, Rama, Krishna, the Buddha, and Kalki, and that this cycle of incarnations keeps repeating The first six incarnations of Vishnu follow the process that modern scientists have identified with evolution. Kalki, the last, is a riderless horse that brings about the end of the world. (Could Kalki represent a distant memory of violent nomadic invaders who had once entered the subcontinent?) Many Hindus wonder whether the Age of Kalki is approaching.

Krishna swallowing Agni

Lord Vishnu's most popular incarnations are Rama, the hero of the *Ramayana*, and Krishna, the cowherd prince who loved the girls who took care of the cows. Rama was probably originally a tribal prince, but he became the seventh incarnation of Vishnu and the model ruler for how a good leader performs his dharma. Rama is an example of how local leaders or deities were absorbed into the larger faith.

Krishna means the "Dark One," suggesting that he may originally have been a South Indian (Dravidian) deity who gradually became an all-Indian favorite. Instead of destroying other deities, however, he absorbed their power or overshadowed them. For example, when frightened shepherds appealed to Krishna to save them from a fire, which symbolized Agni, a very important Vedic deity, Krishna swallowed the fire, thereby absorbing Agni's power. When devotees appealed to Krishna to protect them from a giant naga that was poisoning the waters, Krishna acknowledged that being venomous was the naga's dharma so he only banished it. Rather than denouncing the Buddha's teachings or persecuting Buddhists, Hindus took the Buddha into their system by making him the ninth incarnation of Vishnu.

THE DEVELOPMENT OF BHAKTI

The major divinities were not associated with any one area but rather were found throughout the subcontinent and Southeast Asia. In addition, their devotees believed they could absorb bad karma, much as Buddhist bodhisattvas were able to do, and help believers gain salvation. With these changes, Hinduism was moving away from the unbending laws of karma, toward bhakti, a more personal and loving relationship with a god or goddess. Bhakti used images of gods and goddesses as a focus of devotion.

Bhakti probably originated in South India, where it may have been a reaction against the growing influence of brahmins, who, as advisors to local leaders, were receiving large grants of land and exerting a great deal of political power. Brahmins championed a rigid caste system and elaborate rituals. Bhakti allowed worshipers to bypass brahmin rituals and establish a personal relationship with a god or goddess to whom they offered devotion, much as a lover would bring gifts to his or her beloved. Bhakti may have been influenced by contact with Christians who shared their belief in Jesus Christ as well as by the concept of the bodhisattva in Mahayana Buddhism.

Bhakti was an emotional form of worship, and many early South Indian bhakti poets wrote in local languages rather than in Sanskrit, the language of the court and scholars. Bhakti poets used various manifestations of human affection to mirror human/divine devotion, including the love a mother feels for her child and the love of husband and wife for each other. Married women longing for Krishna became an important metaphor for both ecstasy and the risk involved in one's complete surrender to god. For example:

> Holy and mighty will be his form,
> Rising to heaven, but his sterner face,
> Will be hidden, and he will show you
> The form of a young man, fragrant and beautiful;
> and his words will be loving and gracious—
> "Don't be afraid—I knew you were coming!"

In the Bhagavad Gita, written down sometime between 200 B.C.E. and 200 C.E., Lord Krishna, who serves as the charioteer of the reluctant warrior Arjuna, promises Arjuna he can realize moksha in several ways. The Gita adds Karma Yoga and Bhakti to meditation and profound knowledge, two earlier paths to moksha. Karma Yoga involves acting without concern for the consequences of one's actions. Krishna advised, "Be intent on action, not on the fruits of action." (2:47) This active approach owed much to Buddhism, and it offered warrior-rulers and merchants ways they could perform their dharma and still be seeking moksha. Bhakti, the other path, meant all, no matter their caste, wealth, or region, could seek moksha. Worship of a major god or goddess offered a more accessible and personal path for a large majority of Hindus With the increasing popularity of bhakti, Hinduism had become a far more open religion.

Intellectual and Artistic Achievements

Although Chandragupta sometimes used force to ensure that his subjects paid their taxes, the Gupta Empire is not noted for its military might but rather for its cultural accomplishments, including the Hindu synthesis, advances in math and science, and the splendor and beauty of its court. The dynasty brought peace, and taxes were generally fair. Gupta intellectual and artistic achievements suggest that the empire had many of the characteristics of a theater state. Visitors, awed by its rituals and ceremonies, wanted to be identified with such grandeur. Several Gupta kings attempted to redistribute land to those who did not have any, and the government sponsored several types of welfare programs for the poor. In addition, the Guptas care-

Sarnath Buddha

Buddhist cave temple at Ajanta

fully regulated trade and deployed armies when necessary.

As Hinduism matured, Buddhism was also enjoying a last great moment in the land of its birth. Indian artists created beautiful images of Hindu gods and the Buddha, built Buddhist stupas and monasteries, and created as many as five thousand extraordinary Buddhist, Hindu, and Jain cave temples. They illustrate the religious tolerance that existed throughout the land. Perhaps the most impressive temples are at Ajanta and Ellora in western India. Some were made by cutting away the surrounding rock, leaving freestanding structures. Most are excavations into the hillside. Besides impressive sculpture, several caves at Ajanta have beautiful paintings that suggest the luxurious life at the Gupta court.

SAKUNTALA *REVEALS MANY KINDS OF LOVE*
Sanskrit drama and poetry were among the Gupta court's major artis-

tic achievements. Rulers held poetic competitions and took great pride in the court poets known as the Nine Gems. One of the greatest of these "gems" was the dramatist Kalidasa, who lived around 400. He wrote many lyric poems that celebrate nature and the seasons and suggest that the splendor of the court rivaled the wonders of nature. Kalidasa is best known for his plays, particularly *Sakuntala*. The drama follows the heroine through her awakening love, her passion for her beloved, her sadness at leaving home, her rejection by her husband, her joy over the birth of a son, and her reunion with her husband.

Information about Gupta life can be gleaned from this play. For example, Sakuntala's foster father offers her advice on how to be a good wife:

> When you enter your husband's family:
> Obey your elders, be friends to the other wives!
> If your husband seems harsh, don't be impatient!
> Be fair to your servants, humble in your happiness!
> Women who act this way become noble wives;
> Sullen girls only bring their families disgrace. . . . . .

THE ZERO TRANSCENDS OPPOSITES

Gupta scientists and mathematicians also excelled. Astronomers knew the earth was round and rotated on its axis. They developed skill in geometry in order to lay out sites for sacrifices and temples, but they seem to have had little interest in geography. Indian mathematicians used positive and negative numbers, determined square and cube roots, and solved quadratic equations. They devised a decimal system and were the first to use place numbers with a system of one to nine. Arabs carried these notations to their centers of learning; European scholars, learning of them, called them "Arabic" numerals.

Most mathematicians believe the Indians were the first in the Eastern Hemisphere to invent the concept of zero—a major mathematical breakthrough. Zero seems to come logically from the Indian monistic view of reality that transcends opposites. They found the square root of 2, and in the eighth century solved indeterminate equations of the second degree that were unknown to Europe until a thousand years later. Indian scientists and mathematicians sometimes expressed their mathematical problems in poetic form. For example, one problem tells what happened when a young man hugged his beloved:

> . . . the lady's pearl necklace was broken. One third of the pearls fell on the ground, one-fifth went under the bed. The lady collected one-sixth and her lover collected one-tenth. Six pearls remained on the original thread. Find the total number of pearls on the necklace.

In Nalanda in North India, Buddhist monks founded what was probably the world's first university. It offered instruction not only in Buddhism but also in Hinduism, mathematics, medicine, and astronomy. Its excellent teaching and scholarly knowledge attracted students from throughout Eurasia, including many Buddhist monks from China and Central and Southeast Asia. At its height Nalanda housed and educated several thousand students. Only two or three out of every ten applicants could pass the difficult admission test.

Gupta scholars made many scientific achievements. Their skill in metallurgy is evident in the iron pillar that was cast by Gupta artisans and later erected near Delhi. This twenty-three-foot-high column has never rusted. Gupta manufacturers traded cotton, calico, and cashmere, all of which came originally from India, as well as manufactured items such as metalwork, pottery, and jewelry.

But Gupta unity lasted only two hundred years. By the fifth century nomadic peoples again began to move into India through the mountain passes in northwestern India. Although Gupta leaders recognized the threat, sending troops to that faraway frontier was costly. By 550 the dynasty could no longer raise the taxes necessary to pay armies to protect its boundaries. With the treasury exhausted, the dynasty crumbled.

Scholars have called the Gupta era India's golden age. Besides its vigorous cross-cultural trade, artists and writers created enduring masterpieces, and scientists and mathematicians made path breaking discoveries. Theravada and Mahayana Buddhism and Hinduism all thrived during the Gupta Empire. Philosophers absorbed much of Buddhism and combined seemingly contradictory ideas into mature Hinduism, which focused on bhakti, while retaining the concept of Brahman as ultimate reality. Gupta India also produced unsurpassed literature and art and fostered many scientific and mathematical achievements. One of the foremost scholars of Indian history concludes that under the Gupta Empire "India reached a perfection which it was never again to attain. At this time India was perhaps the happiest and most civilized region of the world." As this empire was waning, the Byzantine Empire, to which we now turn, was flourishing.

SCENE TWO

THE SPLENDOR OF THE BYZANTINE EMPIRE

Setting the Stage

The Byzantine Empire followed a path different from the usual West Asian pattern of invasions and empire-building. Byzantium was not created by invaders as had happened so often before; instead, it was a continuation of the Roman Empire. Nomadic groups that had successfully invaded and plundered Rome and its western territories were unsuccessful against the eastern provinces that became known as the Byzantine Empire or Byzantium, a powerful empire in its own right. Christianity was vital to its success and Constantinople, its impressive capital, was known as the second Rome and the people living there called themselves "Romans."

Constantinople was built on the Bosporus, a strait connecting the Black Sea and the Sea of Marmara, which separates Asia and Europe. Emperor Constantine had chosen this site because it was on high ground and surrounded on three sides by water, so it was relatively easy to defend. The Bosporus gave the city access to trade routes north to Kiev, on the Dnieper River, and to the richness of northern wheat fields and forests. The Sea of Marmara led to the Hellespont and the Aegean and Mediterranean seas. The city could easily collect tolls from ships as well as from merchants traveling overland. In addition, its hills made people think of the seven hills of Rome.

Emperor Justinian

Justinian, the first great Byzantine emperor, ruled from 527 until 565. Having little claim to the throne, Justinian adopted much of the pomp and ceremony Persian rulers had used to enhance their legitimacy, including wearing purple to designate his authority. Then, following a long-established pattern, he tried to enhance his authority by extending the area he ruled. He dreamed of conquering all the former Roman territory that invading nomads had taken over. Under his leadership

Byzantium briefly regained control of much land in North Africa, Italy, and parts of Spain. However, these military campaigns were very costly and put a great deal of strain on his subjects and the state's resources.

Law had been a cornerstone of Roman rule, and one of Justinian's major accomplishments was to establish a legal code. Under his leadership, scholars collected various Roman laws and compiled them into the Body of Civil Law, also called the Justinian Code. These laws included the Twelve Tables, which were the original laws of the Roman Republic, the summary of the opinions about disputed rulings, a textbook for students of the law, and 160 new laws that Justinian issued, mainly relating to economic matters and personal conduct. The Justinian Code was to become the basis for many subsequent legal codes.

Empress Theodora

Theodora, Justinian's queen, was a major force during her husband's reign. She had been an actress before their marriage, and many Byzantine aristocrats opposed the emperor's marriage to a commoner. Within five years, however, Theodora's strength and intelligence proved her worth, not only to her husband but also to the empire, and her insights and judgment influenced many of Justinian's decisions.

Resentment against Justinian escalated because he spent huge amounts of money on his military campaigns. In 532, as a way of expressing this resentment, subjects in Constantinople demanded that he release some prisoners and remove two unpopular government ministers. Justinian refused, and the crowds started rioting, in what became known as the Nika revolt. When Justinian ordered the rioters to stop, the mob turned on him. He wanted to flee, but Empress Theodora refused to go, challenging her husband and his advisors with these words:

> May I never be without the purple I wear, nor live to see the day when men do not call me "Your Majesty." If you wish safety, my Lord, that is an easy matter. We are rich, and there is the sea, and yonder our ships. But consider whether if you reach safety

you may not desire to exchange that safety for death. As for me, I like the old saying, that purple is the noblest shroud.

Justinian stayed. Later that day his troops put down the riot by slaughtering thousands of the protesters. His authority was never significantly challenged again.

What Made the Byzantine Empire Strong?

Most empire builders use military might and law to control their diverse subjects. While the Athenians experimented with direct democracy and Roman leaders attempted to institute a republican form of government, the overriding model that emerged in West Asia was the centralized authority of an absolute monarch. Large territories ruled by emperors, not independent city-states, became the model of leadership that Persian and other West Asian leaders followed, and Persian influences remained strong in Byzantium.

Constantinople's strategic position, along with the rich trade and manufacturing controlled by the city, were important reasons for the empire's strength and success. Other factors included the strength of the central government, its efficient use of the military, an effective system of land distribution that helped limit the development of large

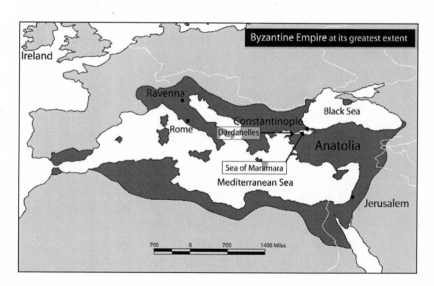

landed estates, and the government's relationship with the Church.

THE EMPEROR: THE ULTIMATE SOURCE OF AUTHORITY

The prestige of the emperor was a major reason for Byzantium's strength. Unlike the Roman Empire, Byzantium had a hereditary monarchy, though factions sometime fought over succession. Utilizing the pomp and ceremony associated with Persian rulers, Byzantine emperors made all who came into their presence bow and kiss the hems of their purple robes. Their elaborate dress and demeanor added to their enormous prestige.

The emperor controlled many aspects of Byzantine life. He made the laws, judged the people, and led the army. The bureaucracy was responsible directly to him, as was the army. He controlled an efficient core of administrators, including ministers of internal and foreign affairs, public revenues, military funds, and imperial estates. The top bureaucrats were recruited from the leading families. They answered directly to the emperor, and he could fire them at will.

Perhaps the most important source of the emperor's authority came from his relationship to the Church. Besides wielding all the royal powers of earlier Roman emperors, the emperor served as a "friend" and "imitator" of Christ. He was the head of both the Church and the state. Considered by many to be chosen by God, he made religion a department of the government and appointed the patriarch of Constantinople and other important Church officials. The emperor and his advisors often made decisions on religious doctrine as well. The clergy gave frequent sermons in support of the political policies of the emperor, who was said to be carrying out the will of God. Anyone who opposed him was guilty of blasphemy, normally a religious offense. The only legitimate way to overthrow the emperor was to allege that he had strayed from the godly path.

ECONOMIC STRENGTH

After the collapse of the Roman Empire, there was virtually no trade to the west. The Sassanids, by insisting on high tolls, were strangulating trade with India and China. Justinian tried to bypass the Sassanids via the Crimea and southern routes that used the Red Sea instead of the Persian Gulf, but the Sassanid navy controlled the sea lanes.

To circumvent the Sassanids, the Byzantines wanted to produce silk themselves. The Chinese government had maintained a monopoly on silk production for a thousand years and put anyone to death who attempted to give away the secret of how silk was made. Historians claim that during Justinian's reign, two Nestorian Christian monks smuggled silkworms out of China in their hollow bamboo canes, which helped Byzantine merchants figure out how the precious cloth was made. With newfound wealth from silk production and other industries, Byzantium gradually became a major trading center in the hemispheric system.

Constantinople was ideally situated for commerce, and this entrepôt became a great warehouse and market. The city controlled the trade routes that ran both north-south and east-west, from Europe and West Asia to India and China. Products arrived in Constantinople and were then sent out again to buyers in other areas. All goods were taxed a straight ten percent import duty. Resources to support the bureaucracy and pay the soldiers came in large part through trade.

Most merchants in Constantinople were middlemen, and they used other peoples, including Jewish merchants, to carry the goods beyond their borders. Many residents of Constantinople were employed in manufacturing goods from the raw materials brought to the city. Byzantine artisans produced numerous goods, especially glassware, linen and wool cloth, jewelry, icons, inlaid boxes and badges for ceremonies; many of them were expert in gold and silversmithing.

MILITARY STRENGTH

Besides its strong central control and economic strength, the Byzantine Empire maintained a well-trained professional army of about 120,000 men, half of whom were cavalry. Legally every man in the empire had to serve in the military, but many rulers distrusted their subjects and preferred to accept money rather than service from them. They used that money to hire an army of well-paid mercenaries (soldiers who fight for pay). Because soldiers received good salaries, it was relatively easy to recruit them.

From the outset Byzantium faced almost constant pressure from nomadic groups on its borders. To this was added the vigorous expansion of Muslim Arab forces. Because the borders were vast and the army was expensive, Byzantine rulers attempted to resist nomadic threats with diplomatic strategy as well as tactics such as flattery and bribery. Byzantine diplomats assumed every man had a price, and they appealed to the greed or vanity of local rulers, often bribing them with riches or impressive titles. They also pitted feuding tribes against one another. Often diplomacy proved more effective and less expensive than fighting.

To ensure that there were enough soldiers, in the seventh century the government organized the provinces into *themes* (military districts) and appointed military generals to rule them. Generals had jurisdiction over both defense and civil administration and acted as provincial officials as well as generals. Free peasants were given land in return for military service, underscoring the importance of military preparedness and ensuring a large supply of willing soldiers.

The Byzantine navy was also a formidable force. By the middle of the seventh century, ships were armed with firebombs that sailors hurled at enemy vessels, usually causing panic among the opposing forces. The incendiary weapon known as "Greek fire" even burned on water, so it was an effective weapon against the enemy's wooden ships. The Byzantine navy controlled the Mediterranean until the ninth century.

DEALING WITH DIVERSITY

Byzantine leaders worked hard to unify the many different peoples in the empire. Many subjects were Greek speakers who felt loyal to their Hellenic culture. The imperial administration encouraged everyone to speak Greek and practice common customs but they never forced people to do so, nor did they mistreat those they conquered. Instead, little by little, they tried to win people over by welcoming their leaders into the bureaucracy if they had learned Greek, letting the upper classes intermarry with the Byzantine elite, and permitting them to serve in responsible positions in the military.

Commerce was another reason for Byzantium's attitude of tolerance. Because trade was essential to the state's prosperity, outsiders were welcomed. Influences from many areas came to the capital, and the Byzantines wanted to make the foreigners feel at home.

Everyday Life in Byzantium

Few records tell how the average person in the Byzantine Empire lived. Merchants must have prospered. Peasants had a harder time because there was a high tax on land. Collecting taxes was the bureaucrat's most important job, and there were taxes on individuals, called a head tax, and on land, buildings, and services. One method for collecting taxes was to group people together and make each person responsible for the taxes of everyone in the group.

In theory there was social mobility, and the bureaucracy, the army, commerce, and service to the Church all offered people ways to raise their standing in the community. As long as at least one son maintained the family occupation, the others were allowed to seek different jobs. In practice, however, probably little mobility actually occurred. Byzantium was most prosperous when the empire had a large free peasantry farming small plots of land. Some were able to build a surplus and move up the social scale, but most remained at the subsistence level and were often threatened by local landlords who coveted their land.

Agriculture-based empires must try to control the buildup of large private estates. When powerful individuals buy or seize large plots of land, there is less available for free peasants, who, as a result, often become tenant farmers and vanish from the tax rolls. Conscious of the threat that large landowners posed, the central government periodically broke up large estates. Until the twelfth century the government made an effort to limit the amount of land an individual could own. The theme system also helped ensure a free peasantry because generals gave part of the land from their themes to peasants who served in the military.

Constantinople

An impressive capital enhances a ruler's power and legitimacy and serves as an important symbol of the empire. In an effort to make Constantinople imposing, Justinian supervised the construction of the Church of the Holy Wisdom, known as Hagia Sophia. Completed in 537, Hagia Sophia was characteristic of Byzantium's synthesis. Its balanced proportions reflected Greek influences; its engineering required the skills of Roman artisans; and its dramatic domed roof, a

Virgin Mary between Constantine and Justinian

sphere set on a rectangular base, was based on Persian examples. A row of windows along the base of the dome made the dome appear to be floating on air. Worshipers entering Hagia Sophia felt as if they had entered sacred space where time was suspended. When Justinian approached the altar to dedicate the church, he declared, "Glory be to God, who has thought me worthy to finish this work. Solomon, I have outdone thee!"

The city was a political, commercial, and intellectual center. Scholars from many areas came to study in the vast libraries filled with Greek, Latin, Persian, and Hebrew documents. The language of the empire was Greek rather than Latin. Tutors instructed those who hoped to enter the bureaucracy, as well as wealthy merchants and aristocrats. Byzantine monks and scholars engaged in the subtlest of religious arguments and sought to merge Jewish and Christian teachings with the teachings of Plato, Aristotle, and other Greek philosophers.

Many Greek and Roman traditions spread from Byzantium to the Muslim world, while Muslim, Indian, and Chinese ideas reached Byzantium. In 863, two monks — Cyril and Methodius — left Constantinople to take the Christian message to Slavic people who had settled in the western Balkans. They translated the Bible into an alphabet Cyril created consisting of modified Greek characters adapted to the Slavic languages. (The Cyrillic alphabet is still used in parts of Eastern Europe and Russia.)

Byzantium had elements of a theater state. Constantinople dazzled visitors from all walks of life. The pomp and prestige of the capital impressed foreigners when they visited it and dulled their desire to oppose Byzantine influence. An ambassador from Kiev once exclaimed, "For on earth there is not such splendor or such beauty, and we are at a loss how to describe it." During the first crusade, when Western Europeans saw the great city for the first time, one military leader explained:

> . . . Those who have never seen Constantinople mar-
> veled greatly at it, for they could not conceive that the
> world held so mighty a city, when they saw the height
> of the walls, the great towers enclosing it all around,
> the splendid palaces, the lofty churches (the number
> of which was so great that none could believe it who
> had not seen it with his own eyes), and the length and
> breadth of the city that lorded it over all others. And
> know ye that there was no man so bold that his flesh
> did not creep thereat, and this was no wonder.

Why Fight Over Icons?

Over the years Byzantine Christianity and the Roman Church grew apart. One difference was the attitude toward icons—venerated images of Jesus, the Virgin Mary, and various saints. Gazing at and kissing them were important parts of worship in Byzantium, and many icons adorned the walls and ceilings of church buildings. Believers told how they had been miraculously cured by merely touching an icon. Merchants hung icons in their shops to protect their goods, and soldiers carried them into battle. The importance of divine images came in part because of Greek and Persian influences in Byzantium.

Perhaps fearing that icons might replace the Eucharist (Holy Communion) as the focus of worship, some Roman church leaders began to disapprove of the use of religious images. Some may have been sensitive to the fact that Judaism and particularly Islam, the most rigorous monotheistic faith, were totally opposed to images. Pope Leo III (r. 714–41) decided that icons were a form of idol worship and that they violated the commandment prohibiting making "graven images." In 726 he and his supporters in Rome launched the iconoclastic movement, which led to the fierce iconoclastic controversy in Byzantium. (Iconoclasm means destroying icons; it now refers to anyone who tries to undermine familiar ideas and symbols).

The Virgin and Christ Child

Some Eastern church leaders maintained that veneration of religious objects was a legitimate form of worship. The gaze from an icon caused "deep thoughts" and allowed the worshiper to communicate directly with the saint. Bishops argued that "simple folk" needed them. Icons helped remind believers of the full humanity of Christ. What might seem like worship of an icon was really paying reverence to the person it pictured. Moreover, they claimed it would be hard for Byzantine Christians to give up their beloved icons. Other Byzantine church leaders opposed the use of icons. Those who believed that Christ had only one nature argued against portraying him as a human being and stressed that it was impossible to portray his divine nature. The debate raged until 843, when the iconoclasts finally gave up the cause. Slowly icons were restored to a prominent place in worship.

Emerging from the iconoclastic struggle, Byzantium experienced a period of enormous cultural vitality. One symbol of that revival was the vibrant intellectual life at the University of Constantinople, first chartered in 425. The university was not just a school for training clergy but the major institution for educating civil servants. It also offered courses in law and medicine, philosophy, mathematics, astronomy, and rhetoric, and attracted numerous Muslim and European students. Many of the major intellectual leaders of the time, including Cyril, who developed an alphabet for much of eastern Europe, graduated from this distinguished university.

The iconoclastic controversy was only one of the issues that separated the eastern and western halves of the Christian Church. Language was another: the Roman Church used Latin, and the Eastern Church used Greek. Minor differences included the wearing of beards, whether to use unleavened or yeast bread in Holy Communion, and differences in the liturgy.

The biggest issue was the relationship between the pope of Rome and the patriarch of Constantinople. In the first centuries of the papacy the patriarch of Constantinople played an important role in the pope's selection. Even Gregory, one of the most important early popes, wanted the blessing of the patriarch of Constantinople but did not want him to have more influence than the other three patriarchs. After the Muslims captured Jerusalem, Antioch, and Alexandria, three of the patriarchal cities, the patriarch of Constantinople thought of himself as co-equal with the pope in Rome, but the pope did not agree. Unable to settle the various issues that separated them, they formally separated in 1054 into the Eastern Orthodox Church and the Roman Catholic Church.

Byzantium had many of the characteristics that make an empire powerful: strong centralized control, prosperous trade, a well-trained and motivated army, a good tax base, and toleration coupled with a sense of unity. For more than a thousand years, Christian Constantinople was the richest, most beautiful, and most cultivated city in Europe. Byzantium, along with the Islamic states, not only carried on Greek and Roman learning but made important new contributions. Exciting innovations were also taking place in other parts of the world. We now move farther east to see what was happening in East Asia at the same time.

SCENE THREE

THE GOLDEN AGE OF THE TANG AND SONG

Setting the Stage

Humans have lived in East Asia for at least 600,000 years. East Asians probably joined in the Agricultural Revolution about 10,000 years ago, sometime after settlers in West Asia had done so. Southeast Asian farmers were probably the first to domesticate rice, and the new grain soon became a staple throughout South and East Asia.

Farmers in North China prospered by farming the rich *loess* (soil) in the valley of the Yellow River. The loess erodes easily, and the silt that collected in the riverbed resulted in frequent floods causing people to call the river "China's Sorrow." Communities had to cooperate to build flood control and irrigation works. By the start of the common era, during the Han Empire (206 B.C.E.–220 C.E.), Chinese civilization had spread to the Yangzi River valley, where the farm land

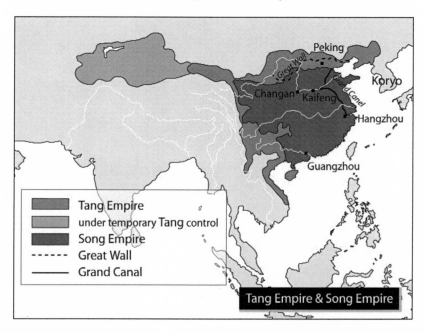

Tang Empire & Song Empire

was even better than in the north.

After Han rule ended, China splintered into many separate, small kingdoms, and for nearly four hundred years new states came and went. None lasted very long nor was able to reestablish the Han Empire. During this period of disunity, the most successful smaller state was the Northern Wei, a nomadic group that conquered and ruled part of northern China from 386 to 584. They adapted many Chinese ways, including using Chinese as the official language of their court, dressing like the Chinese, and using Chinese surnames. Because the Wei had no written language, they employed Chinese scholars, so the bureaucracy remained Chinese. At the same time, independent families, particularly in the southern part of China, continued to amass a great deal of wealth and power.

The Northern Wei was one of the nomadic groups that tried to gain acceptance in China. Wei rulers supported Buddhism so they would be considered "more civilized" and gain legitimacy. They invited Indian architects and sculptors to help build impressive Buddhist cave sanctuaries modeled on the Indian cave temples of Ajanta. The Yungang and Longmen caves are among the world's great art treasures. Wei rulers also commissioned the building of fine Buddhist temples and the translation of Buddhist texts from India.

The Sui Dynasty

The first dynasty to reunite the various small kingdoms in China, initially by force, was the Sui. Wendi, who founded the Sui dynasty in 581, decided to use religion to help unite the empire. He supported Buddhism and also relied heavily on Confucianism to establish his dynasty's legitimacy. He tried to bring back the examination system based on the earlier Han model, requiring officials to take written examinations on Confucian classics to prove they were fit to rule. To support the examination system, Wendi opened several government schools and held periodic examinations. Although he hoped to recruit bureaucrats on the basis of their intellectual and scholarly merit rather than their family ties, this system failed significantly to weaken the power of large landholders.

The two Sui emperors commissioned grand building projects that required massive numbers of workers. Their major project was a canal that linked the Yangzi with the Yellow River. The government ordered hundreds of thousands of men to build this 100-foot-wide "Grand Canal" that was to run from Hangzhou to Changan. The population had increased significantly, especially in the Yangzi Valley, and the canal enabled the government to tax southern rice-growing farmers. One section, featuring forty rest houses along the way for the emperor, connected Hangzhou to Peking so goods could be shipped easily to troops protecting the border.

These canals were a great engineering feat, but their construction brought immense suffering to the countless people who were involved in building them. Resentment grew as a result of the massive hardships.

The suffering did not stop there. Wendi and his son Yangdi (r. 604–18) launched military campaigns to extend the kingdom's borders. Chinese troops conquered the Red River Valley in northern Vietnam, re-established colonies along the western trade routes, and made Turfan, a major trading center on the Silk Road, a tributary state. But when three campaigns against Korea were unsuccessful, and many men were drafted to fight two separate groups of Turks from Central Asia who were threatening China, discontent increased.

Peasants who were forced to fight were not the only people who were upset. The two Sui emperors made numerous enemies among the aristocracy by trying to break up the large estates. Rebellions broke out all over the empire, and in 618 the Sui dynasty collapsed. However, like the Qin dynasty in the third century B.C.E., the Sui had weakened the landed aristocracy and unified much of the country. Even though the dynasty was short-lived, its public works and governmental reforms laid the basis for the Tang dynasty that followed.

The Tang Take Control

The shift from Sui to Tang did not cause any fundamental change in Chinese life, even though the intense fighting in 618 had destroyed the estates of a number of the most prosperous families. Many early Tang officials had served the Sui; the first Tang emperor, Emperor Guozu, had been a general in the Sui army and was related to the Sui rulers. During his eight-year reign, Tang forces averted several rebellions and pushed back the nomads on the northern border.

The Tang benefited from the bad reputation of its brutal Sui predecessors. Although Taizong, Guozu's second son, eliminated his elder brother and forced his father to resign so he could become emperor, he clearly understood that a successful Chinese leader must not rely on the sword to rule. In order to establish a successful dynasty, he would have to honor the scholar rather than the soldier.

During the majority of Taizong's reign (627–49), China was prosperous, and in general its subjects felt far more secure than they had for centuries. Chinese engineers and workers completed the Grand Canal, which doubled the area from which the government could collect taxes. Transportation on the canal was cheap because humans as well as animals could haul barges filled with as much as several tons of merchandise. The imperial government received all the grain it needed and encouraged local craftsmen to produce other goods that they could sell, which stimulated commerce.

Taizong supported Buddhism, Daoism, and Confucianism and tried to use all three faiths to legitimize his rule. He performed public rites for the general good rather than concentrating on his own ancestors. He was generous to Buddhists and made a great public display over Xuanzang, the Buddhist pilgrim who had traveled to India during his reign even though he had initially forbidden him to go. Taizong also patronized Daoism and included elements from the writings of Chuang Zi (a famous Daoist author) in the government examinations.

How Can the Government Bring Stability?

During the first century and a half of Tang rule, revenues more than covered the government's expenses, and the country prospered. Using military force and diplomacy, the Tang defeated the Eastern Turks and took control of areas in Inner Mongolia. All able-bodied peasants were given military training and organized into regular forces. In addition, special self-supporting military colonies of soldier-farmers were placed at strategic places along the northern frontier, and there were Chinese garrisons all the way to Kashgar, a city in Central Asia where the northern and southern silk roads meet. However, because the frontier was extremely dry, northwest farmers were not productive.

In an attempt to guard against the gradual rise of large tax-free landed estates, the Tang reintroduced the "equal field" system, the Northern Wei's method of taxation. Peasants were to be awarded land, and at a peasant's death most of the land was to be returned to the government. The peasants who held these parcels of land had to pay tax in grain and give the government a certain number of days of corvée labor. To collect taxes, the Tang divided communities into groups that were mutually responsible for one another's taxes.

Despite good intentions, these reforms did not break the power of the large landholding families, mainly because only new land was brought into the equal field system. Before long the drift toward large self-sufficient estates began anew. In addition, much land was not redistributed after peasants died, so there was little available land for the growing population.

Empress Wu Zetian

When Taizong died, the court followed the usual procedure and put his concubines, including Wu Zetian, in a Buddhist convent. Their heads were shaved, and they were expected to spend the rest of their lives mourning in seclusion. However, Wu-Zetian had other plans. When the new emperor, Gaozong, a weak young prince, visited the convent, she caught his eye and, against all custom, enticed him to bring her to the palace as his concubine. She soon became his full consort and because this emperor was not a very ambitious person, he willingly left most of the business of government to her. "Promotion and demotion, life or death, were settled by her word. The emperor sat with folded hands."

Wu Zetian was as ruthless as any male ruler. Because she was only the preferred concubine of Emperor Gaozong, she feared competition from his wife and another beautiful concubine, so she ordered her guards to kill them. Her own secret police kept her informed about possible enemies, and in 697 she had thousands of them killed or exiled and their sons banned from holding office.

In 690 she was proclaimed "Heavenly Empress." Although other women had ruled in China, this was the first and only time a woman was given the title empress. She tried hard to extend China's power, strengthen the central government, and satisfy her subjects' needs. In an effort to break the power of the Confucian bureaucrats who opposed her, she started a school dedicated to Buddhist and Confucian scholarship and appointed officials from areas far from the imperial court who had passed the required examinations. Recognizing the enormous popularity of Buddhism, Empress Wu used it to help give legitimacy to her rule, and she even proclaimed that she was an incarnation of Maitreya, the Buddha-yet-to-be. She supported work on the Buddhist Longmen caves and commissioned an enormous sculpture of Maitreya Buddha that is reported to have resembled her. As a result in no small part to her strong support, Buddhism became very influential in China during her reign.

Changan, Xuanzong's Capital

Following Empress Wu, Xuanzong, the greatest Tang Emperor, ruled from 712 to 756. During his reign Tang China was perhaps the richest and most cultured area of the world. The emperor loved horses and is reported to have kept forty thousand in the royal stables. He also kept thirty thousand musicians and dancers in the imperial palace. Tang artists excelled in creating landscape paintings, porcelain figures, and poetry.

At the center of Tang splendor was Changan, the capital. It was a cosmic city, the symbolic center of the world, "the place where earth and sky meet, where the four seasons merge, where wind and rain are gathered in, and where yin and yang are in harmony." By choosing a site near the capital of the earlier Han and Sui dynasties and carefully

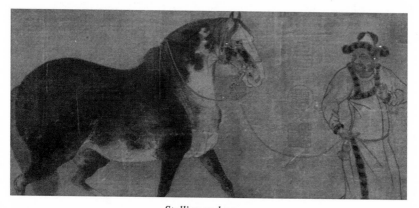

Stallion and groom

following the prescribed pattern for a city, Tang rulers created sacred space from which the power of T'ian (Heaven) and the emperor radiated over the land.

> The capital . . . was a city of cosmic order,
> The pivot of the four quarters.
> Glorious was its renown,
> Purifying its divine power,
> Manifested in longevity and tranquility
> And the protection of us who come after.

The city was the major political center, where the emperor lived and from which political power emanated. The energies of the earth passed through the city in an auspicious manner and were diffused outward from the center through its gates. The 500-foot-wide north-

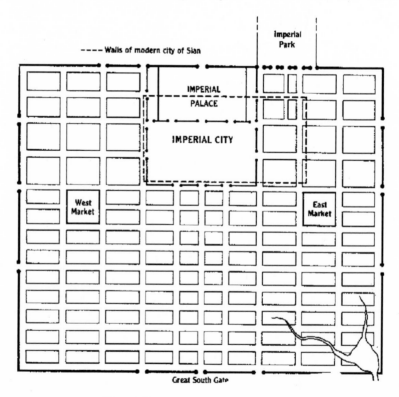

Plan of Changan during the Tang Dynasty

south axis was the most important and impressive avenue. (By way of comparison, Fifth Avenue, in New York is only 100 feet wide.) Changan in many ways was a good example of how the opulence, excitement, and power of the capital can impress visitors .

The fame of the Tang court spread far and wide and drew curious foreigners anxious to learn about China. Four groups of diplomats from Byzantium came between 643 and 719, presumably to ask for support against the Muslims who threatened their empire. The Chinese had heard about Islam by 638 and had even allowed an Arab delegation in 713 to come before the emperor without kowtowing (bowing down) because, the Chinese record noted, "Court etiquette is not the same in all countries."

Changan was also a major trading center. The city had a West Market for traders from places such as India, Iran, Syria, Arabia, and even farther west. Tang records show that the city was the temporary home for four thousand families from these areas. Tang authorities allowed foreigners living in the city to practice their own religions and build their own temples and churches. The Nestorians, whom the Chinese called Iranian Christians, were the largest Christian community. There were also many Manicheans, whose religion, shaped by Zoroastrian dualism, attempted to combine elements of Christianity, Buddhism, and Zoroastrianism. Additionally, there were substantial Jewish and Zoroastrian communities. In 640, when Changan's population reached two million, it was the largest and perhaps most cosmopolitan city in the world.

The Tang tried to keep all commerce within the tribute system. This system was based on the assumption that Chinese culture was the most exalted in the world and that foreigners would be honored to come and pay their respects to its leader and bring tribute. In return, the visitors would gain the blessing of the emperor, who might confer titles on them, and they would receive gifts that were often far more valuable than the tribute they had presented to the court. Even with this attempted restriction, the late Tang experienced a spectacular rise in overseas trade beginning with large-scale business with Southeast Asia. A lively trading system developed in the East and Yellow seas, carried largely by Korean ships, and Korean merchant communities emerged in many of the port cities along China's coast.

Guanyin bestowing a son

Xuanzong Champions Buddhism

Xuanzong's reign was the high point for Buddhism in China, even though it was not the only religion in China. Four different Buddhist schools developed, but Pure Land Buddhism was the most popular. It focused on Amida, the Buddha of Infinite Light, who presided over the Paradise in the West, and on Guanyin (Kuanyin), the Bodhisattva of Mercy, "the one who hears the cries of the world." Married and pregnant women sought her special blessing.

Chan Buddhism (which became Zen Buddhism in Japan) taught that meditation rather than good deeds or study was the means to pierce through illusion. Scholarly writings and words in general were of little use. Incorporating Daoist meditation and intuition together with earlier Hindu traditions of Yoga, Chan Buddhists taught that the Buddha nature is immanent in all beings. Experiencing the Buddha nature, which can come through meditation, brings release from illusion. Northern Chan Buddhism taught that insight comes gradually, while the southern school taught that it can come suddenly, in a single moment of insight.

What Was Life in Tang China Like for Women?

Empress Wu demonstrated how much official power women could achieve, but because of the way Confucian values influenced Chinese historians, there are few official records of the role average women played in Tang society. Society was divided into three classes — the elite aristocratic families that lived near the capital, the scholar-officials, and the commoners. Marriages were arranged with members of one's class. Upper-class women owned property and could move about in public and remarry without being criticized. Women, including unmarried daughters, could inherit property if all other male heirs had died, and they remained close to their own families after marriage.

Much of the information about women that has survived reflects Confucian attitudes toward how they should act, as this selection from *The Family Instruction of the Grandfather* illustrates:

> A wife serves her husband
> Just as she serves her father.
> Her voice should not be heard
> Nor her body or shadow seen.
> With her husband's father or brothers
> She has no conversation.

A popular ballad called "A Woman's Hundred Years," well known during the Tang era, gives some insights into an upper-class woman's private life.

> At ten, like a flowering branch in the rain,
> She is slender, delicate, and full of grace.
> Her parents are themselves as young as the rising moon
> And do not allow her past the red curtain without a reason.
>
> At twenty, receiving the hairpin, she is a spring bud.
> Her parents arrange her betrothal; the matter's well done.
> A fragrant carriage comes at evening to carry her to her
>   lord.. . .
>
> At forty, she is mistress of a prosperous house and she
>   makes plans.
> Three sons and five daughters give her some trouble.
> With her *ch'in* [musical instrument] not far away, she toils
>   away at her loom,
> Her only fear that the sun will set too soon.

At fifty, afraid of her husband's dislike,
She strains to please him with every charm,
Trying to remember the many tricks she had learned since the
    age of sixteen.
No longer is she afraid of her mothers- and sisters-in-law.

At sixty, face wrinkled and hair like silk thread,
She walks unsteadily and speaks little.
Distressed that her sons can find no brides,
Grieved that her daughters have departed for their husbands'
    homes. . . .

Tang Poets Express Social Concerns

Poetry reached impressive heights during the Tang era. Li Bai (Li Bo/
Po), Bai Juyi (Bo Juyi), and Du Fu (Tu Fu) are generally considered
to be among the twenty-five greatest poets of all time. Li Bai (701–
62) often wrote about longing for home.

Before my bed there is bright moonlight,
So that it seems like frost on the ground.
Lifting my head I watch the bright moon,
Lowering my head I dream that I'm home.

Another poem by Li Bai reads:

A girl picking lotuses beside the stream—
At the sound of my oars she turns;
She vanishes giggling among the flowers,
And, all pretense, declines to come out.

Li Bai is said to have drowned during a boating party when he leaned
over the side of his boat trying to scoop up the moonbeams reflected
in the water.

Many Tang poets wrote about parting from a friend. Because educated gentlemen often became officials, and officials were stationed
all over the country, friends might never see each other again. Bai
Juyi wrote:

We did not go up together for Examination;
We were not serving in the same Department of State.
The bond that joined us lay deeper than outward things;
The rivers of our souls spring from the same well.

In the following poem, Bai Juyi wrote about his responsibilities as
a scholar-official:

From my high castle I look at the town below
Where the natives of Pa cluster like a swarm of flies.
How can I govern these people and lead them aright?
I cannot even understand what they say.

But at least I am glad, now that the taxes are in,
To learn that in my province there is no discontent.

Underneath the splendor of the Tang court, peasants were suffering, and poems often reflected the gap between the rich and poor:
"Inside the red gates wine and meat go bad; / On the roads are bones
of men who died of cold." Du Fu (712–70), the greatest poet of
China's mid-eighth-century hardships, was perhaps best loved for his
poems of compassion, as well as social criticism. Knowing how
important it was to have sons, he ends a poem about ceaseless and
senseless wars by writing:

Now we peasants have learned one thing:
To have a son is not so good as having
A daughter who can marry a neighbor
And still be near us, while a son
Will be taken away to die in some
Wild place . . .

In a poem entitled "On Asking Mr. Wu for the Second Time," he
pleads:

Do please let your neighbor
Who lives to the west of you

Pick up the dates in front of
Your home; for she is a woman
Without food or children; . . .
It would be good of you to try
And help her, and save her
Feelings; so do not fence off
Your fruit. . . . heavy taxation is
The cause of her misery; the
Effect of war on the helpless
Brings us unending sorrow.

What Did An Lushan Want?

In spite of the wealth and brilliance of his reign, two major setbacks
marred Xuanzong's rule. The first involved conflicts with border
areas and Muslims armies. In 751 a small state in Yunnan defeated the
Chinese forces, leaving the Chinese on the defensive in the southwest,
and Arab Muslim soldiers defeated the Chinese at the Talas River
near Samarkand. In the wake of these defeats, the Chinese government began to withdraw from its central Asian frontiers, even though
the Muslims did not take full advantage of their victory. (The
Umayyad dynasty had just fallen, and many Muslims returned to West
Asia to await the new caliphate.) Huge expenditures were needed to
control hostile subjects and to maintain the empire that had expanded
into areas that were not suitable for farming and brought in little revenue.

The second major setback was a serious rebellion in which a
woman played a major role. The emperor, now middle aged, fell in
love with Yang Guifei, one of his son's consorts, and made her one of
his own concubines. As the years went by, he allowed her to handle
more and more of the affairs of state. At this time An Lushan, an officer of mixed Turkic ancestry, started to visit the court, making everyone laugh at his crude, uncultured ways. The young consort, with
more than a friendly interest, adopted him as a "son" and encouraged
the emperor to allow An Lushan to visit frequently.

Eager to please his young mistress, the emperor often invited the
officer to private dinners and state affairs. He was deaf to his advisors
who warned that the officer was not the fool he appeared to be but

was really plotting a rebellion, and he was blind to the growing intimacy between the general and his pretty concubine. He also ignored the resentment people in the south were feeling at having to send vast quantities of grain upriver to support the ever-increasing population in the north and what they considered to be the wasteful court.

An Lushan made his move in 755. By then he controlled 200,000 troops, including many of the best soldiers of the empire, and had built up a power base on the northeastern frontier. From there he quickly and ruthlessly subdued the north, taking Loyang, the Eastern Capital, and causing the emperor and his court to flee from Changan, which An Lushan's forces destroyed. Blaming the trouble on Yang Guifei, the emperor's troops demanded that unless he had her killed, they would not continue to support him. Reluctantly, he allowed them to strangle her. He then abdicated, a broken man.

The rebellion was finally suppressed, but its effects were long-lasting. Not only did it become a favorite subject for poets and writers (both Li Bo and Du Fu lived through it), it was a humiliation for the emperor and his officials. The raging civil war impoverished the countryside and greatly weakened the central government. Although the Tang stayed in power for another century, it never again reached its earlier level of grandeur.

Why Did Buddhism Decline?

One indirect legacy of An Lushan's rebellion was the persecution of the Buddhists Although the faith had become very important, many Chinese still considered it a foreign religion. Cremation and celibacy troubled many who were brought up with Confucian ethics and wanted to have sons who would continue their lineage. In addition, renewed emphasis on the examination system revived interest in the Confucian classics, weakening the practice of Buddhism among the educated. When Buddhists made a great commotion in 819 over what was reported to be the Buddha's finger, a scholar urged the emperor to outlaw such foolishness and argued:

> Now the Buddha was of barbarian origin. His language differed from Chinese speech; his clothes were of a different cut; he did not pronounce the pre-

> scribed words of the former kings [the sage emper-
> ors] . . . He did not recognize the relationship be-
> tween prince and subject, nor the sentiments of father
> and son. . . . How . . . is it fitting that his decayed and
> rotten bone, his ill-omened and filthy remains, should
> be allowed to enter the forbidden precincts of the
> Palace?

Much of the anti-Buddhist sentiment was due to its increasing economic and political power. The rapid growth of Buddhist schools,
monasteries, and temples had transformed Buddhism into a major secular power in China. Temples and monasteries had extensive land
holdings and ran mills, pressed oil, conducted banking services, and
provided the best medical care available. Monasteries also ran schools
for children in remote areas, and popular stories, such as Mulan's trip
to the underworld to try to save her mother, helped spread the faith.
Buddhist institutions had grown very wealthy, and their holdings were
tax exempt. Monks did not pay taxes or serve in the military. Many
wealthy patrons avoided taxation by registering their land with
Buddhists. During the hard times following An Lushan's rebellion,
people became especially resentful of prosperous Buddhists and considered their temples, images, and rituals a wasteful use of scarce
resources.

Between 841 and 845 the Tang launched a massive anti-Buddhist
campaign, and the emperor issued an edict calling for the destruction
of 4,600 monasteries and 40,000 private shrines, and ordering
260,500 monks and nuns to return to secular life and begin paying
taxes. His charges against the Buddhists included:

> Wasting human labor in building, plundering the peo-
> ple's purses by golden decorations, neglecting both
> husband and wife by vigil-keeping, no teaching is
> more harmful than this Buddhism. . . . The public
> monasteries and temples are . . . so gigantic and
> imposing that they vie with the Imperial Palace in
> splendor!

Despite the harsh persecutions, Buddhism continued to flourish in China and enjoyed revivals during the Song and later dynasties. Although many of their formal institutions had been destroyed, Buddhism would continue to be a significant force in Chinese culture. Large numbers of Chinese continued to follow the teachings of several schools of Buddhism. At the same time an increasing number of the scholarly elite began to explore ways that Buddhist values could be incorporated into traditional Confucianism.

The Rise of Neo-Confucianism

Neo-Confucianism was one important way that Buddhist values continued to influence the Chinese elite. Although scholars strove to create a new form of Confucianism that would be free of foreign influences and ensure China's uniqueness, they incorporated many Buddhist concepts into this new philosophy. In fact, Neo-Confucianism was a synthesis of Confucianism, Buddhism and Daoism, and it gained popularity during the Song Dynasty.

The Neo-Confucianists grafted the Buddhist concern with transcendent values onto the more humanistic Confucian focus on human relations, and they stressed the importance of individual self-improvement. They retained the Confucian belief that human beings are basically good or can become good by working hard to overcome weaknesses and suppressing impure thoughts. Striving to perfect oneself through self-cultivation became an important aspect of Neo-Confucianism.

The continuous process of self-cultivation that the Neo-Confucianists advocated could be achieved in two ways: by acquiring greater knowledge and by engaging in deep meditation that would result in "illumination." The philosophy stressed the role of education, a very important aspect of Confucianism. It advocated controlling one's desires and thoughts and developing inner concentration through meditation, which was an important aspect of Buddhism. Neo-Confucianists believed both techniques would lead to a better society, a long-standing goal of Chinese civilization.

Neo-Confucianism gradually moved to the forefront of Chinese philosophy and would soon have a great influence in Korea and Japan as well.

Transition to the Song

As the central government weakened, local leaders once again began to exert their power and built up local power bases. The central government could no longer collect enough taxes to run the government effectively or feed the people in times of famine. Nomadic groups on the borders again started to raid and invade, and peasants felt the burden of taxation and corruption so heavily that they often revolted. In 906 opposing armies overthrew the Tang dynasty. For about fifty years five successive dynasties in the north and ten states in the south competed for control; many were ruled by nomadic groups that had invaded from the north.

In 960 a Chinese army achieved a series of military victories and established the Song dynasty. During the Song, which lasted until 1279, the population of China approached 100 million. Rice production more than doubled because of newly opened lands in the south, improved tools, use of more fertilizers, and new varieties of rice, particularly an early ripening variety from central Vietnam. Farmers also planted strains that grew well on drier land, which greatly increased the yield. The government encouraged rice farming by giving tax relief, extending credit, and setting up model farms. Wheat cultivation also spread in the south, and in the southwest farmers grew two harvests a year: either two of rice or one of rice and one of wheat.

How Did the Song Treat Its Neighbors?

In its traditional dealings with neighboring peoples and to control trade and contact with foreigners, the Chinese followed the tribute system. Song leaders had to decide not only how to reestablish that system but also whether to try to conquer additional territory in the north or west. Although some advisors wanted China to expand, they realized that the Battle of Talas and An Lushan's rebellion had dramatically weakened China's military and the government was in no position to require outsiders to acknowledge its superiority.

The new government did not want to risk unsuccessful military efforts that might result in the loss of even more territory. In addition, it seemed counterproductive to waste resources trying to control hostile territories, especially ones that were not productive. Rather than admit they were too weak to challenge their neighbors, however, officials argued it was stupid to waste men and resources fighting the barbarians who were little more than animals. It seemed wiser to be flexible in dealings with them and to "fight with other means," such as humble words and generous gifts.

The Khitans, who threatened the northern border, were especially worrisome. In 1005 the Song negotiated the Treaty of Shanyuan, that required the Chinese to pay the Khitans 200,000 bolts of silk and 100,000 taels of silver to maintain peace on the border. This amounted to about three percent of the Chinese government's total revenue. This treaty placed an enormous financial burden on the Song and all but established the Khitans as equals. Even so, the language of the treaty tried to maintain China's superiority. It read in part:

> If indeed Heaven above regrets calamity and [causes] the rogues to appreciate our humanness [*ren*] and they thus accept our wish for friendly alliances and extinguish the beacons on the frontiers, that would indeed be a great fortune to our ancestral altars.

Examination Hall

Ensuring Talented Bureaucrats

The late Tang and early Song emperors were the most successful in appointing bureaucrats on the basis of merit rather than choosing rich landholders or members of the imperial household. Tang emperors, building on the Han example, had tried to use examinations as the basis for selecting their bureaucrats. Empress Wu-Zetian, in part to break the power of the old military elite who opposed her, had strengthened this trend. However, most candidates were still judged by family connections and their appearance and speech, and many tried hard to influence the officials who graded the exams.

In an effort to provide a common education for those who took the examinations, the Tang had opened new schools and an imperial academy. By the late Tang the vast majority of those in government jobs had passed the examinations. By relying on the examinations, the Song succeeded in ensuring that most government officials were selected on the basis of their ability.

Three levels of exams existed. The local level exam only lasted several hours; the middle exam, given at the capital, took longer and was more difficult. The most prestigious exam was held at the palace under the emperor's strict supervision. Candidates put numbers, not their names, on their exam papers in order to prevent graders from giving preference to friends or family members. In theory, a man could "sit" for the exam as many times as he wished. If he passed, he became a member of the gentry, "an advanced scholar worthy of government appointment." The emperor was expected to select administrators from the gentry.

The Song used several means to ensure that officials performed their work honestly and remained loyal to the emperor. Regional quotas ensured that officials came from all areas of the country. Each official served three-year terms and was not to stay in one area for more than six years. To prevent family loyalty from conflicting with loyalty to the throne, no official could serve in his native province. When an official's father died, he had to observe a three-year mourning period during which he performed no official duties. This "sabbatical" cut him off from his potential power base and gave him time for reflection on life's true values. In addition, censors (the eyes and ears of the emperor) traveled around to observe how the officials were acting.

The examination system helped to check the growth of a landed aristocracy and aided in the creation of a powerful intellectual and moral elite with common cultural values based on Confucian ethics. Even those who did not pass the difficult examinations still modeled the same values. The examination system also provided the possibility (even if largely unrealized) of upward mobility, promising that a man's promotion resulted from his talent and diligence rather than who his relatives were or how much land and wealth they controlled. However, the system had weaknesses. It divided China into two strata, the educated elite and everyone else. In addition, the content that the scholars studied in order to pass the exams created a conservative outlook that often made it difficult for them to support reforms.

Why Was There So Much Internal Trade?

Cities, kingdoms, and empires have a vibrant class of merchants, traders, and professionals, as well as artisans who manufacture both necessities and luxury items for local markets and for export. These groups, sometimes referred to as the "middle class," are interested in exchanging goods.

Confucius had been wary of merchants, calling them parasites who lived off the honest labor of farmers and artisans. In his view merchants added nothing to the value of the goods they sold. Despite this Confucian bias, merchants grew in importance under the Song, in part because as the population grew, more goods were produced and there were more people to buy them.

To carry on commerce, artisans and businessmen need some form of money and a banking system. They also need to devise ways to track the flow of money and merchandise, ways to extend credit and protect individual merchants from catastrophic loss. The Song minted copper coins called "cash," and as early as 1024 they introduced paper currency. Different regions, connected by the canal system, began to specialize in making different goods. Even poor peasants began to sell a little of their surplus food and use the money to buy other things, which contributed to the increasing demand. Officials also began collecting taxes in cash, not in kind (goods).

Artisans and merchants often used their wealth to educate their sons, hoping that at least one would pass the exam and bring gentry status to the whole family. Although few actually became gentry, the possibility of upward mobility gave legitimacy to the whole social system.

Internal trade traveled on the waterways, especially the Yellow and Yangzi rivers and the Grand Canal. The geographic center of Song power shifted from the north, where previous dynasties had built their capitals, to the richer Yangzi Valley and farther south. The Song moved their capital to Kaifeng, the world's second largest city in 1000. This change symbolized the importance of trade and commerce and brought in a new source of leadership.

The Song Excel in Manufacturing

Chinese Daoists' interest in alchemy resulted in the invention of gunpowder, made by mixing sulfur, saltpeter, and charcoal. The Chinese first used the mixture to treat skin diseases and to kill insects. In the tenth century the military started producing explosives. In 969 the Song emperor gave a prize to the inventors of a new "fire arrow" that probably carried a charge of gunpowder. A 1044 military handbook described the many uses of gunpowder weapons, including a bomb that released poisonous gas. Twenty years later the government banned the sale of sulfur and saltpeter to foreigners and made gunpowder production a state monopoly. They ran large workshops that employed more than 400,000 workers who produced gunpowder weapons. They also developed iron coats of mail and bombs that fragmented on impact and could pierce leather armor and the bodies of men and horses.

With the rise of trade, Kaifeng became one of the half-dozen major manufacturing and commercial centers of the world, producing guns, cannons, moveable type for printing, and water-powered mills and looms. One scholar suggests that by the eleventh century China was producing as much as 125,000 tons of iron and steel a year, more than all of Europe produced in any single year until 1750. The Chinese also produced more coal in the twelfth century than England did in the eighteenth century. For about two hundred years the Chinese had been using coke, a form of soft coal, for cooking. Now they began to use coke as well as harder coal to fire their blast furnaces. There was a large demand for both iron and steel: one order alone called for

19,000 tons of iron for coins, and two arsenals produced 32,000 suits of armor. Song China had more per capita production than any other country in the world.

Artistic Expression During the Song

Art, especially landscape paintings, is among the greatest accomplishments of the Song. Landscape paintings from the Song period celebrate nature, especially awe-inspiring mountains and waterfalls. Paintings showed scholars silently contemplating such things as the moon, a vast lake, or a gnarled tree. Although artists made little use of color, the landscapes created a vast sense of three-dimensional space. Humans, dwarfed by the environment, were pictured in harmony with nature.

Song scholars also produced many historical works and were great calligraphers. Li Qingzhao was a renowned poet whose life "is one of the great literary romances and tragedies of Chinese history." In her poem "Remorse" she writes:

I loved the Spring,
But the Spring is gone
As rain hastens the falling petals.
I lean on the balustrade,
Moving from one end to the other.
My emotions are all disordered.
Where is he?
Withered grass stretches to the horizon
And hides from sight
Any road by which he might return.

Social Structure

Although China under the Tang and Song continued to look to Confucian values as the basis of its social order, many changes had taken place since Han times. According to the Confucian tradition, society was divided into several hierarchical groups with the emperor, the moral example for the state, at the top of the pyramid. Next came the gentry—the landholding, literate, and highly cultured families—who carried on Confucian values. Peasant farmers, because they fed

A King of Hell as a bureaucrat

the people, ranked next. Artisans were slotted beneath the farmers. Next came merchants. Citing the philosopher Mencius, who had stated, "Good iron is not used for nails nor do good men become soldiers," the Chinese put the military at the very bottom.

Despite this official attitude, all through Chinese history soldiers had fought in countless wars. China under the Tang relied on disciplined soldiers and extensive cavalry to build a great empire to the west. Similarly, the Song needed large armies to defend its northern borders and keep peace at home. The Song, especially after the fall of the northern provinces, relied heavily on merchants and traders for the prosperity of the empire, and by lending money, paying taxes, and promoting prosperity, merchants wielded great influence on both the leaders and the gentry. Cash, paper money, insurance, banking, systems of credit, and civil law were just a few examples of the sophistication of Chinese businessmen.

At the same time the gentry clearly enjoyed the highest social status and the most privileges. As bearers of the age-old Confucian tradition, the gentry alone had real access to the civil service and exercised the greatest political and moral authority. More often than not they also controlled the choicest land.

Were Women Unproductive?

Song historical records include some information about how women lived. In both the law and the economy, women's status during the Song was relatively high. Palace ladies had their own "bureaucracy" within the court, and ladies from gentry families took charge of household budgets and even managed estates. Some served as cloth-makers and religious devotees. A woman kept her dowry throughout her marriage, even if she married a second time. For that reason "the status of women as widows . . . was relatively high." With increases in population, manufacturing, and commerce, women had more opportunities to work in jobs such as running restaurants or selling fish and vegetables. Wealthy families hired cooks, maids, dressmak-ers, and entertainers. One Song source claims that in Hangzhou,

> the middle class and poor families do not care about getting sons. When a girl is born, she is deeply loved and given good care. Once she grew up to be a wo-man, she was taught, according to her beauty and ability, arts, skills so that she would be ready to be picked up by the scholar-official [families that need-ed her for] entertainment or service.

Fearful that outside job opportunities might make women less attentive to their husbands and homes, some men emphasized wifely fidelity and discouraged widow remarriage. One influential writer stressed that a wife should consider her husband heaven. No matter how destitute she was, a widow should never remarry: "to starve to death is a minor matter; to lose one's virtue is a matter of utmost importance."

The practice of binding a girl's feet began to spread in court circles during the Song. This custom may have origi-nated with aristocratic ladies who wanted to have small feet like one of the Tang emperor's concubines or those of Turkish dancers enter-taining the court. Among prosperous families where women performed little or no

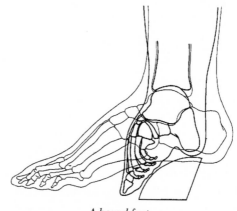

A bound foot

physical labor, bound feet became a sign of a family's wealth and status. Mothers bound the feet of their six- or seven-year-old daughters so that they would have a better chance for a good marriage. Although this extremely painful custom seriously limited a woman's ability to walk, many men found the "golden lilies" appealing and were excited by the way a woman with bound feet walked. Few peasants could afford to bind their daughters' feet because women with bound feet had to work in the fields on their knees.

The Song are Forced South

After the Song had relied on scholarly bureaucrats for a century, military and economic problems began to weaken the dynasty. Giving scholars control over the professional army undermined its effectiveness, even though the military still consumed a large portion of the total budget. New threats appeared on the northern borders, and in an effort to meet the rising costs of defense, the Song printed too much paper money. By 1107 its value dropped to one percent of its face value, prices soared, and famine was widespread.

The government rejected attempts at reform that would have reduced the interest rates moneylenders charged or replaced large monopolies with a state trading company. They made no effort to establish new tax rolls that included large landholders or to cut military expenses by asking each district to supply a number of men for the army. As a result, again peasant uprisings shook the empire. With so much internal unrest, the country was unable to withstand the nomadic threat. In 1126, even with catapults, flamethrowers, and bombs, the Song could not hold back the invading nomads who captured Kaifeng and took over the northern half of their kingdom.

The Southern Song Excels in Overseas Commerce

Forced south, the Song established the Southern Song kingdom and made Hangzhou, situated where the Yangzi River and Grand Canal meet, their capital. The Southern Song ruled a much smaller area and had less taxable land. As a result, it turned to commerce to raise the revenue it needed. Hoping to increase commerce, merchants began to employ new techniques for trade and travel. They used cotton sails in place of bamboo slats, and constructed boats with sturdier hulls and a centerboard keel that could be raised in shallow water. They also created the world's first paddleboat. By 1100 Chinese sailors were using the "south-pointing needle," a magnetic compass (300 years before the Europeans learned of it), and they could sail ships across the open sea even in cloudy weather without losing their course. The Song navy became one of the most powerful in the world.

By the middle of the twelfth century the revenue from trade made up over half of the government's income, and the official prejudice against merchants softened. The government began giving official ranks to merchants, even Muslim merchants, particularly those who were doing a large volume of business carrying porcelain, tea, and silk. Large Muslim diaspora communities grew in the port cities. The numerous pieces of broken Chinese porcelain found near Cairo and along the east coast of Africa suggest how extensive trade during the Song dynasty was.

Increased trade and the rapid rise in the importance of merchants, manufacturers, and overseas trade resulted in the Southern Song becoming a leader in Afro-Eurasian commerce. It developed the most sophisticated financial institutions of the time and anchored the eastern end of the vibrant Indian Ocean trading network.

The Southern Song dynasty lasted until 1279. This golden age of good government, prosperity, and artistic expression has rarely been surpassed. The Southern Song's political stability, resulting in large part from its talented bureaucracy, and the country's impressive economic growth, seemed to promise further development.

But in spite of the tightly knit bureaucratic system and the vibrant economy, increasing pressure from nomads to the north, China's age-old nemesis, continued to threaten the dynasty. Even though the Southern Song built up its naval strength in an effort to protect its northern border and tried to make alliances with the various nomadic groups, the nomads continued to build up their power. And now a new nomadic group, the Mongols, are about to pose the greatest threat of all.

The Gupta, Byzantine, and Tang and Song empires and the increasingly powerful Muslim states were preeminent in Eurasia in the period from 300 to 1279. Each area was guided by its distinctive

worldview. Under the Gupta both Buddhism and Hinduism flourished, although Hinduism gradually absorbed many Buddhist ideas
and moved to the forefront of Indian life. Byzantium developed its
own Eastern Orthodox style of Christianity, ultimately leading to a
widening split between the Roman and Eastern Orthodox churches. In
China the Sui and Tang dynasties supported Buddhism until its wealth
and power seemed to pose a threat. Under the Song, elements of
Buddhism were absorbed into Neo-Confucianism, much as Buddhism
in India had been integrated into Hinduism.

In each of these empires, wealth acquired from taxation and the
support of manufacturing, trade, and conquest was used to support
vast building projects, to patronize the arts and sciences, and to stage
impressive rituals. Byzantium instituted the theme system in an effort
to control the growth of landed estates, and China's examination system tried to ensure that bureaucrats were selected on the basis of
merit.

Beyond these three centers of power, the energetic drive of Islam
that had inspired the formation of the first Muslim caliphate under the
Umayyads continued as a major political force across Eurasia. The
second caliphate, launched by the Abbasids in 751, clearly meets the
criteria for an empire, and it had many of the same strengths that char-
acterize the areas we have discussed in this act. However, after a hundred years of Abbasid control, the huge and expanding territory of
Islam began to fragment into a number of new states. We have therefore decided to examine the impressive Abbasid Caliphate and the
other Muslim areas that became part of Dar al-Islam in the next act.

Outside these major centers of power, new states were forming
across the hemisphere even as existing ones were changing and ever-
increasing cross-cultural exchanges were knitting together peoples
from the Pacific to the Atlantic oceans. It is to the new states and the
expanding network of exchanges that we now turn.

ACT THREE – THE FLOWERING OF EMPIRES

Setting the Stage

1. What is the difference between a land-based empire and a theater state?
2. How do leaders in a theater state try to attract and impress potential subjects?
3. What is a favorable balance of trade? Why do states hope to maintain a favorable balance of trade?

SCENE ONE
The Glory of the Guptas

1. What are the sources for information about the Gupta Empire? Why do historians consider Fa Xian's account fairly accurate? Cite an example of how his own values influence what he notices and reports.
2. Review the major ideas of the Hindu synthesis. Why is dharma so important?
3. What is the basis for ranking castes? Discuss whether the caste system is a way to provide a place for everyone and/or a way to keep everyone in his or her place?
4. What does the quote from the Dharma Sastras suggest about the position of women? Suppose you substituted "mother" for "father, "mother-in-law" for "husband," and "daughter" for "son." Why might that have actually been the reality?
5. Make a case for Hinduism being considered a universal religion. What ideas or practices might prevent it from being considered a universal religion? The Bhagavad Gita offers four ways to reach moksha (salvation): knowledge; meditation; acting with complete indifference to the results of your actions (karma yoga); and bhakti. Who might try to follow these paths? Do karma yoga and bhakti make Hinduism a universal religion? What about caste?
6. Search the Web for illustrations of Indian cave temples; <www.WHEN.org>. What do the caves at Ajanta suggest about religious tolerance in Gupta India? What do the various sites at Ellora suggest about artistic expression in Gupta India?

7. Identify some Gupta intellectual achievements. Imagine doing math problems without a base-ten system and zero.
8. Would you like to have lived in Gupta India? Why or why not?

The Splendor of the Byzantine Empire

1. What was Byzantium's relationship to the Roman Empire? What did Justinian hope to accomplish by his military exploits? How did Justinian strengthen the rule of law?
2. Identify the reasons for Byzantium's strength. What was the basis of the ruler's authority? What contributed to the empire's military strength?
3. What role did trade play in Byzantium? How did its position strengthen its commercial role?
4. In what ways was Byzantium a theater state? What role did Constantinople play in the empire's strength? How did merchants get by? How did peasants manage? Which groups fared the best?
5. What was the basis of the Iconoclastic controversy? What role might Jewish and Muslim attitudes have played in that debate? What did Church leaders fear?
6. Identify several reasons for the split between the Roman Catholic and Eastern Orthodox churches.
7. Would you like to have lived in the Byzantine empire? Why or why not?

The Golden Age of the Tang and Song

1. What policies did the two Sui rulers—Wendi and Yangdi—use to unite and strengthen their empire? Why did they commission the building of the Grand Canal? What were its effects?
2. How did Emperor Taizong bring stability to the Tang Empire? How did he try to check the power of the large landlords?
3. Why did Empress Wu Zetian and Emperor Xuanzang support Buddhism? How did political support contribute to the increasing strength of the Buddhist communities in China? Why did the government eventually turn against the Buddhists?
4. Identify aspects of the Tang court that fit a theater state. What was the role of the capital? Of merchants and commerce?
5. What insights do Tang poems give about the lives of women? What were some of the social concerns Tang poets expressed? Identify some of the roles women played in Song China. What were some reasons for binding a girl's feet?
6. Who was An Lushan? What were the immediate and long-term results of his rebellion?

7. In what ways did Neo-Confucianism incorporate both Buddhist and Confucian principles?

8. Describe the tributary system. What was its relationship to cross-cultural trade?

9. Evaluate the role and importance of the examination system.

10. What economic advances did the Southern Song achieve? Why did the Southern Song participate actively in overseas commerce?

11. Would you like to have lived under either the Tang or Song? Why or why not?

Summing Up

1. Identify the significant factors that make an empire strong. Compare the strength of the Gupta, Byzantine, and Tang and Song empires, focusing on one of these factors.

2. How did rulers of these empires promote their power and legitimacy? What factors—either internal or external—weakened the government's authority?

3. What role did religion play in these three empires? In what ways and why did the governments support religious activities? In what ways and why did they try to limit the influences of various religious groups? Compare with the role of religion in other areas you have studied, particularly the Umayyad Caliphate.

4. Assess the importance of both internal and cross-cultural trade in these three empires and in the Umayyad Caliphate. What was the official government view of commerce in each area? How did they either support or try to limit it? How does the commercial strength of these areas compare with that of other empires you have studied such as the Han and Roman?

5. If you had a chance to come back and live in one of these areas, which would you choose? What job would you want to have? Would you want to return as a man or a woman? Explain the reasons for your answers.

ACT FOUR

New States Emerge in Afro-Eurasia (500 to 1450)

The Gupta, Byzantine, Tang and Song empires and the Muslim caliphates thrived during the first millennium of the common era. Because of their relative stability and wealth, each made important innovations in manufacturing, artistic expression, and trade. These empires were also open to innovative ideas as travelers and traders carried information from one end of Afro-Eurasia to another.

We have defined a state as an area ruled by a central government that has sovereignty over its land and people. A state can be as small as a city or as large as an empire, with many options in between. Because many of us have been taught that the nation-state is the highest form of political development, we often mistakenly believe that other political organizations are less "developed" than our modern idea of a nation-state. However, between 500 and 1450, leaders created a variety of political organizations, and each in its own way functioned quite well.

Many Stones, Many Ripples

We have likened the central government of an empire to a large rock thrown in a pool of water, suggesting the government is strongest at

163

the center or capital, the point of impact, and its power and authority diminish as people move away from the capital. But suppose you threw a handful of stones into the water. Many small ripples would result, and the outer rings might bump into one another and even overlap.

We can compare these smaller stones and radiating ripples to more decentralized political organizations such as city-states and feudal states. A very weak king might rule over a large area or there might not be any central control. What happens at the borders of these territories or when areas overlap? Can small centers of authority provide protection for its subjects? What prevents different groups from fighting? To which center will people pledge their allegiance? Is it possible to give one's allegiance to several layers of government?

Suppose No Central Authority Exists?

Scholars sometimes use the term "stateless society" to designate areas that are not governed by a single central authority or where there is no clear line of authority. But this term may suggest that these societies lack something essential. Rather than calling these areas "stateless", some scholars suggest that we should think of them as *heterarchies*: areas where political control is shared instead of concentrated in any particular person or elite group. In this type of state, authority is shared among different groups, based on such factors as lineage, craft, age-set, or secret society; each group's authority is limited to discrete aspects of community life, and checks and balances prevent any group from becoming dominant.

A heterarchy can be just as effective in creating a stable and prosperous society as a hierarchical state with a single sources of authority. Further, a centralized state has certain drawbacks. It tends to require a great deal of wealth to support its elite members. It may also be slow to respond to dramatic changes in such things as the environment or the population, in part because those at the top do not want to lose their exalted position and tend to ignore the concerns that the people are expressing. Where no single elite exists and many groups share the power, members of the community must cooperate rather than compete, and they may be better able to respond quickly to needed changes.

Who Will Do the Work?

Whatever type of leadership exists, communities, cities, kingdoms, and empires all need men and women who will do the work. Land-owners, businessmen, military and political leaders, among others, could not survive without farmers and laborers working for them. Getting workers and finding ways to pay them can be difficult. The solution has often been to use forced labor.

Throughout history the most common source of free labor has been the family. Parents expect their children to work on the family farm or business, and children learn important skills while they are growing up. Although we do not usually think of this work as forced, more often than not children have no choice in the matter.

We usually think of forced laborers are either serfs or slaves. Slavery has existed since very early times. Slaves were usually men and women captured in battle or bought from other groups, although an individual might also become a slave if he could not pay his debts.

There was a wide spectrum of how slaves were treated. A slave's life was often harsh. Those who were forced to work in mines, row ships, and perform dangerous and degrading work were at the very bottom of society and lived without dignity or much hope for the future. Slaves who served at court or in the military were often not only armed but given a great deal of responsibility. Some lived quite well, and a few Muslim slaves (Mamluks) even governed kingdoms. Female slaves most often became servants, entertainers, and prosti-tutes.

After 500 C.E., most slaves in West Asia were Turks and Slavs (the origin of the word "slave") who were purchased or captured in Eastern Europe. Race and ethnicity were not major criteria. Muslim communities made widespread use of slaves but were not allowed to enslave other Muslims. Many African communities depended on slave labor, and wars were often fought to obtain slaves, not territory.

Slaves could sometimes achieve their freedom by paying the owner or completing a specified number of years of service. Children of a slave woman and a freeman were often considered free. In sparsely settled areas, such as Southeast Asia, slaves might earn their freedom by agreeing to settle near the court and pledging their loyalty to the ruler. Slaves in Africa often became members of the family that owned them.

Serfs were tenant farmers, but unlike tenants, serfs were bound to the land they farmed and they had to give part of what they produced to the landlord. While serfs were not allowed to leave the land, landlords were not supposed to evict them.

Monsoons Enhance Ocean Travel

Besides laborers to do the work and produce goods, states need commerce to survive and thrive. While local farmers and artisans produce much of what the population needs, necessities not available locally must be acquired by cross-cultural trade. For these encounters to occur, merchants and travelers must be able to move from one place to another.

The monsoon wind system made extensive interaction across the Indian Ocean possible. The monsoon, which actually means "winds," is caused by the difference in temperature between land and water. Land heats and cools faster than water, and air over land moves from cooler areas toward warmer ones. In the spring the landmass between South China and India becomes very hot, while the Indian Ocean remains cooler. The hot landmass draws the air from over the cooler Indian Ocean, creating the southwest summer monsoon that blows south to north between April and August. Because those winds carry

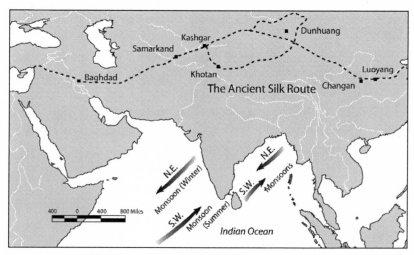

Monsoons and Silk Routes

lots of moisture, they also bring heavy rain.

In the summer months the southwesterly monsoon pushes sailing ships from West Asia, Arabia, the Persian Gulf, and East Africa toward India, Southeast Asia, and China. Half a year later, from December to March, because the landmass cools faster than the ocean, the Indian Ocean attracts winds from the lands to the northeast. These northeasterly winds permit ships to sail westward.

Merchants from the Roman Empire and traders from Meroë and Axum used the monsoons to get to East Africa as well as to Gujarat and the Malabar coast on the western shores of India. Because they had to wait several months for the reverse monsoon that would propel their ships home, they created diaspora communities composed of people from their own homeland. Merchants waited in these communities until they could return to the African coast or West Asia on the reverse monsoon. The monsoon also moved ships to and from the eastern coast of India to ports in Southeast Asia, so diaspora communities grew up there as well.

Over Land by Camel

Travelers and traders also journeyed over land, and overland traders created diaspora communities, in part because few merchants ever made the entire trip. Instead, "stayers" lived in their own communities processing goods, and "movers" traveled back and forth from one area along the trade routes to another. Stayers and movers felt at home in their diaspora communities.

While we often associate overland travel with wheeled vehicles or horseback riding, camel caravans virtually replaced wheeled vehicles during the millennium from 300 to 1300 C.E. The camel became known as the "ship of the desert," and gradually most overland transportation along the Silk Roads and the vigorous trade across the Sahara went by camel.

Merchants strung their camels in a line called a caravan. They traveled in groups for mutual protection and to avoid becoming lost. Strings of ten to twelve camels were common, but very large caravans might include as many as 10,000 animals. Camel caravans could transport goods more cheaply, more quickly, and with fewer interruptions than any other form of overland transport.

A camel caravan crossing Gobi Desert

Camels are relatively cheap to maintain because they eat the sparse grasses of the steppes. They can find food even in semi-arid lands and can go up to nine days without water. They can endure the rigors of desert travel: a covering protects their eyes from sand, and their fur insulates them from the desert's extreme temperatures of daytime sun and nighttime cold. Further, their hooves do not sink into the sand. Good camel grooms can forecast when a sandstorm will occur by studying the behavior of their camels. Finally, camels provide insurance against the loss of food or water. They are a vital source of milk and can be forced to gorge themselves on water and food and then be made to regurgitate what they have swallowed.

Traders used the single-humped dromedary in hot dry desert environments from North Africa to Arabia to Northwest India. The two-humped camel evolved in the colder areas of the Iranian Plateau and central Asia. Over time, breeders along the Silk Roads crossed both types to develop a hybrid camel suited to all types of climate and topography. The hybrid camel was especially suited for the difficult trip from China to Western Asia and for trade across the Sahara.

Caring for camels became an important industry along the Silk Roads. Cities that grew up along these routes were centers of entertainment and trade, and they all had caravansaries—buildings where the men and animals ate, rested, and, when necessary, were nursed back to health. Many people who lived along the trade routes were drawn to the caravan cities and made their living training and caring for camels in the caravansaries.

In this act we examine the expansion of Byzantium's influence northward into what is now Russia, North Indian civilization's expanding role beyond the Deccan in the Indian subcontinent and into Southeast Asia, and China's influence in Vietnam, Korea, and Japan. We will also investigate developments in West and East Africa, Europe, and the many areas under Islamic control and influence that became part of Dar al-Islam. We shall be especially interested in examining the development of new states, including those that have more than one source of authority.

As cultural and political contacts increase, arteries and arenas of overland and maritime trade and interactions continue to expand. We will look for examples of voluntary conversion—enhanced by individuals, merchants, and political leaders—and forced conversion, resulting from military expansion and political pressure. We will pay special attention to the many kinds of changes that take place as a result of increased encounters and interactions.

EXTENSION OF INDIAN, BYZANTINE, AND CHINESE INFLUENCES

Setting the Stage

The Guptas in India, Byzantium in the Mediterranean, the Tang and Song in China, as well as the Umayyad Caliphate that expanded from West Asia, developed into prosperous and powerful states. Each created a distinct civilization and developed advanced science and technologies, fine art and literature, and superior administrative systems.

It is not surprising that these areas sought to extend their influence and authority beyond their borders, attracting the attention of their neighbors who came looking for new knowledge and goods. Merchants and traders carried cultural values that strangers often found appealing. Sometimes major civilizations invaded and tried to force their way of life on their less powerful neighbors.

To the north and west of Byzantium, Swedish Norsemen (Vikings) were arriving in great numbers and beginning to settle into an agricultural way of life. South and east of China, Koreans, Japanese, and Vietnamese were building new states. And chiefs in Southeast Asia were looking for ways to attract trade to their ports and enhance their power. Newly emerging states were developing ways to bring diverse peoples together and provide legitimacy for those who sought to rule.

As ideas spread between older established civilizations and new states, people took what they wanted and rejected what they did not find useful. Sometimes they attempted to borrow institutions, only to find they did not work well in the new setting. New states readily accepted cultural elements that seemed similar to their own practices and beliefs and supported their institutions. They also adapted the older forms to their own purposes, making some more symbolic than functional. Additionally, each new state combined the imported forms into a unique synthesis.

Byzantium's Influence Spreads North

In spite of the disintegration of the western Roman Empire, Greco-Roman traditions and Christianity were exerting a significant influence on most of Western Europe by 500 C.E., and Byzantium, seen by many as the second Rome, was carrying on the imperial tradition.

In the ninth century the Vikings, whom the Slavs called *Rus* (seafarers), began to travel from the eastern Baltic to the Black and Caspian seas, conquering a number of Slavic settlements. At the beginning of the tenth century, Oleg, a Viking leader, settled in Kiev, a city on the Dnieper River. His successors gradually became the recognized leaders of a loose confederation of city-states known as Kievan Rus, whose inhabitants intermarried and merged with other Slavic people.

In 987 Prince Vladimir convened his vassals and explained that he wished to select a new religion for himself and his state. His speech reveals the extraordinary range of Kiev's contacts with the outside world. He said: "Behold the Bulgarians came to me urging me to accept . . . [Islam]. Then came the Germans and praised their own faith, . . . [Roman Catholicism]. After, came the Jews. Finally, the Greeks appeared . . . and their words were artful and it was wondrous to listen and pleasant to hear them." He then dispatched ambassadors to each religious center to report on these faiths. The emissaries who reached Constantinople were "led to the edifices where the Greeks worship their God, and did not know whether they were in heaven or on earth." They returned to Kiev praising the magnificence of Constantinople.

A year later Vladimir assumed the Christian name Basil. He was baptized and proclaimed Greek Orthodox Christianity the state religion. In an effort to eliminate existing religious practices, he directed that existing idols should be destroyed, and some were smashed into pieces and burned. He appointed twelve men to beat Perun, the Slavic thunder god, with sticks so as to "affront the demon. . . ."

As happened with the spread of universal religions in other areas, the form of Russian Christianity that slowly evolved incorporated many Slavic beliefs, customs, and sacred objects, not unlike how the Celtic goddess Brigid became identified with the Christian saint Bridget. Saint Parasceva, the patroness of women, and the Virgin

St. Sophia, Kiev

Mary both resembled the Slavic mother goddesses, and the Russian devotion to Nature was symbolically transformed into the Christian festivals of Easter. This synthesis produced a "double faith" in which Christianity and earlier beliefs existed side by side.

However, Vladimir's expectation that religious unity would lead to political unity did not work out as it had in Byzantium. At its height in the eleventh century, Kievan Rus remained a loose confederation of city-states. Merchants, artisans, freemen, slaves, and peasants lived under the control of their princes to whom they paid tribute, generally in goods. Yet Kiev's international flavor, particularly as a result of its conversion to Christianity, should not be discounted. The Cathedral of Holy Wisdom, St. Sophia, which was located in the center of the city, was as important to Kiev as was its namesake in Constantinople. In both churches worshipers enjoyed the great beauty of the holy icons as well as the divine light emanating from the mosaics. Slowly Kiev was building a new state, and, as it developed its own version of Christianity, was becoming a part of the expanding world of Christendom.

South Indian States

While diplomats from Kiev made a conscious effort to seek out information about Christianity, in other areas traders and migrants spread new insights. North Indian brahmins carried their religion across the Deccan into South India, and southern bhakti saints took their mystical form of Hinduism north. In the popular form of Hinduism practiced widely in the south, brahmins dominated village politics as well as larger provincial assemblies. They were at the top of social hierarchy, non-brahmin castes were grouped in the middle, and untouchables were on the bottom. There was virtually no social mobility, and untouchability became a major feature of South Indian life.

By the end of the sixth century two kingdoms were dominant in South India: the Pandyas in the center and the Pallavas in the east. The Pandyas ruled from their capital at Madurai and the Pallavas ruled from Kanchipuram and their port at Mahabalipuram, one of modern India's archaeological treasures. From 846 to 1279 the Chola dynasty dominated south India. They controlled the southern coast and participated actively in long-distance trade. Their navy was one of the largest in the Indian Ocean, and Chola merchants were second only to the Muslims. At their height the Cholas won victories as far north as the Ganges River, and their navy undertook a number of expeditions against important trading centers in Southeast Asia. The South Indian kingdoms exported textiles, gems, and spices and imported many thousands of horses, mostly from western Asia. Since wars were increasingly fought on horseback, the most successful Indian warriors used horses to compete. Armed soldiers on horseback were able to run circles around the cumbersome elephants that had been the "tanks" of many Indian armies.

The southern states adapted characteristics of theater states rather than those of highly centralized kingdoms. Although they had strong armies, they tried to attract subjects with dazzling displays of wealth and elaborate rituals. Southern rulers sought legitimacy by granting large tracts of land to their brahmin advisors and financing temple building. They collected sufficient taxes from surrounding villages to maintain their courts and engage in expensive temple building. The Cholas built some of the finest Hindu temples in the world.

Nataraja

Much of the economic, social, and political life of these South Indian kingdoms focused on the elaborate temple complexes, especially in the Chola era. Lively trade took place in temple corridors and courtyards, and the temples supported bankers, merchants, and craft guilds. Temple administrators supervised farming and irrigation projects and stored surplus food for less prosperous times. Brahmins conducted temple schools and provided higher education for selected young men. Besides the impressive outpouring of bhakti poetry in Tamil, the Chola courts and temple complexes also supported Sanskrit scholarship and kept classical Hindu learning alive.

Lord Shiva as Lord of the Dance (Nataraja) was a major artistic expression in South India. This sculpture symbolized the essence of Hinduism. In his upper right hand Lord Shiva holds the drum of creation. In his left hand he holds fire, symbolizing destruction. Creation and destruction continue in a seemingly never-ending cycle. But his other right hand says, "Be not afraid," because there is a way out. His other left hand points to the upraised foot that symbolizes release from rebirth (moksha-nirvana). Shiva dances on the dwarf of ignorance: if one can dispel ignorance, moksha is realized.

Indian Influences in Southeast Asia

Geography has influenced life on the mainland and islands that comprise Southeast Asia as much as anywhere else in the world. The seas invited communication and trade throughout the region, and the Strait of Malacca, between the Malay peninsula and Sumatra, has played a major role in cross-cultural trade. Southeast Asia's location between India and China, two major early civilizations, also placed the area in the middle of one of the world's most active trading zones.

Water is especially important in the lives of people in Southeast Asia The monsoons, periodic flooding and the warm climate were ideal for growing wet rice. Farmers grew enough surplus to support large populations, and wet-rice cultivation spread throughout Asia to become the major staple of that part of the world. Homes built on stilts and water puppet shows performed in flooded fields suggest how pervasive water is in people's lives. Puppeteers stand waist-deep in flooded fields, using the water to activate the puppets and conceal how they are manipulated. Water almost becomes a character in the show. Flooding makes recessional agriculture possible, and the rice plant grows as the water recedes.

It is uncertain where the numerous early inhabitants of mainland Southeast Asia came from. Many probably migrated south from Mongolia or China. Others, who probably came by sea from as far away as Africa, settled initially on Polynesian islands and then migrated from there to Southeast Asia. However, large-scale settlements in Southeast Asia occurred long after India and China were populated, and it was not until the start of the second millennium C.E. that people began to move into the Mekong River valley and settle the Mekong delta region.

Indian merchants played a prominent role in the early contact Southeast Asia had with the outside world. At first they sailed to the Malay Peninsula and went overland at the Isthmus of Isa. That route was partly responsible for the development of the Kingdom of Funan in the first century C.E. A Chinese document written in the third century C.E. reported that in Funan "Merchants come and go in great numbers to transact business. . . . More than a thousand Buddhists from India resided there."

After traders began to sail through the Strait of Malacca in the sixth century C.E., the kingdom of Srivijaya (670–1025) grew in importance. It included Sumatra, the eastern tip of Java, and the

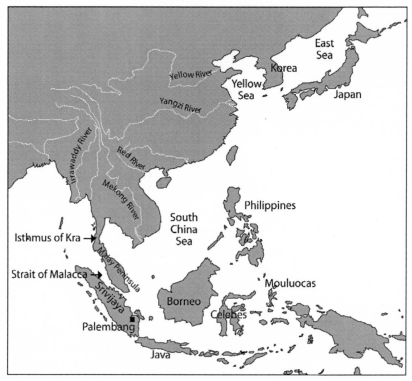

Southeast and East Asia

northern parts of the Malay peninsula. Palembang, Srivijaya's major city, became the region's dominant trading center. Chola merchants from India carried on lively business ventures and even a naval expedition against Srivijaya. Other smaller states flourished on Java, including the Salendras who commissioned Borobudur, a monument that combines both veneration for local ancestors, a sacred mountain, and the Buddhist goal of nirvana.

The Rise of the Khmer Kingdom

At the same time that Srivijaya was flourishing, newcomers were migrating into the Mekong valley in Southeast Asia. The Mekong is the third-largest river in Asia, after the Yangzi and the Ganges. The Chams, a dark-skinned people who came from the east by sea, settled along the mainland's eastern coast. The Khmers migrated overland into the area that is now Cambodia.

At the end of the eighth century a prince from the Salendra court brought Hinduism and Buddhism to the Mekong delta. After a successful military campaign, he established the Khmer kingdom (802–1431) near the Great Lake, the Tonle Sap. When the snow on neighboring mountains melts and the monsoon rains come, the Mekong River floods. Water flows into its tributaries, causing the Siem Reap River to reverse its course and flow upstream. As a result water pours into the Great Lake, which triples in volume and fills with fish, an important food source. Farmers plant rice in the water and fertile silt that is left as the water level subsides.

In 802 Brahmin priests installed Jayavarman II as a Khmer *devaraj* or god-king. Recalling that Salendra leaders had called themselves "mountain kings," he named his capital "Mountain of the Great King of the Gods." To symbolize his connection to the gods, he had his palace built on a hilltop. He hoped it would remind people of the Hindu idea of the cosmos: Mount Meru, the home of Indra and the other gods that was surrounded by vast oceans and other mountains. Platforms and *barays* (large reservoirs of water) around the temple complexes represented the land and oceans surrounding the sacred mountain/temple.

The Hindu cosmos fit what the Khmer people already believed about sacred mountains, so syncretism helped Hindu influences spread. Subsequent kings wanted to make their own cosmic cities, and they supervised the construction of even larger palace/temple complexes that resembled Mount Meru. Leaders hoped worship of both Lord Vishnu and Shiva would enhanced their legitimacy.

In many ways the Khmer kingdom was a theater state. Impressive rituals helped the god-kings "control" the sun and rain, so important for growing the rice that supported the kingdom.

ANGKOR WAT AND ANGKOR THOM:
MODELS OF THE COSMOS

Suryavarman II, who ruled from 1113 to at least 1145, was one of the greatest Khmer kings. He is responsible for the construction of Angkor Wat, his temple-mountain. The walls of Angkor Wat are covered with exquisite reliefs, including lovely nature spirits, worshiping ascetics and illustrations from Hindu mythology. Nagas (sacred serpents), line the entrance ways. The Churning of the Ocean, Lord Vishnu's incarnation as a tortoise, when the devas (gods) and asuras (anti-gods) used the naga king as the churning rope, is illustrated numerous times throughout the complex. This myth equates the crowing of Indra as king of the gods with the crowing of Suryavarman as the Khmer king. In addition, this remarkable monument marks where the sun rises on the solstices and equinoxes.

In 2001 Ploy Pritsangkul, a young tenth-grade Cambodian student, wrote about her first visit to Angkor Wat:

> At first sight, the stone temples strike you with immense force. You would be dazzled and amazed by the monstrous size. As you walk in towards the entrance, a sense of serenity would rise in you despite all the tourists, souvenir sellers and beggars that are surrounding on all sides. That feeling would linger on and grow until you would feel like you are a part of this wonder. As your eyes lay on the bas-reliefs, the carvings on the stone walls, you could just close your eyes and see the lovely scenes of life from the past millennium. You see the women graciously talking

Angkor Wat

and giggling as they sit upon a floating barge while picking up sweetly scented lotuses. Soldiers in armor suit . . . march right across your eyes. You see kings, queens, princes and princesses wearing their royal garments with jewels glittering and playing in the sunlight. . . . These scenes, too lovely to be true, become a reality in Angkor and Angkor alone.

Scholars assumed that the large *barays* that surround Angkor Wat were constructed primarily for irrigation, which the government supervised. However, recent research has questioned whether channels connected these reservoirs to land farther away. If they did not, the water from them could not have irrigated the fields. Most scholars now suggest the brays were used for both ritual purposes and for irrigation. Most Khmer farmers probably relied mainly on recessional agriculture and various forms of relatively small scale irrigation.

Jayavarman VII (r. 1181–1218) was another great Khmer ruler and the country's greatest builder. He introduced Mahayana Buddhism as the state religion, but the people continued to worship their local gods and spirits. Angkor Thom, his two-mile-square city, contains the Bayon, his temple-mountain. Two hundred giant smiling faces look out from its towers in the four cardinal directions. They may symbolize the bodhisattva Avalokatesvara, the Bodhisattva of Compassion, or the way the ruler's power radiates over the land, or both.

Unfortunately, Jayavarman VII's many expensive projects depleted the country's resources and led to the Khmer's gradual decline. The people gradually adopted Theravada Buddhism. The Thais, who lived to the north and west, sacked the severely weakened Angkor in 1369 and 1389. The area was finally abandoned in 1431 and memory of the once great kingdom was all but lost.

The Development of Nam Viet

East of Cambodia, the Viets had settled in the valley of the Red River well before the start of the common era. "Viet," which refers to an ethnic group, means "beyond" in Chinese, suggesting that the Chinese were describing people who lived outside their kingdom. Nam means "south," so the area became known as Nam Viet and later as Vietnam. Local hereditary chiefs ruled over Viet communities.

For much of its early history, China controlled the Viets. Emperor Han Wudi's armies incorporated Nam Viet into the Han Empire in the early second century B.C.E. The Han divided the country into nine military districts and attempted to turn their subjects into proper Chinese. They instituted Chinese rituals, emphasized Daoist and Confucian teachings, and taught the Chinese language. The Nam Viets were even required to wear Chinese clothing and hairstyles. The Chinese never used the term Nam Viet; they called the area Annam, which means "pacified south."

DAI VIET (GREAT VIET)

Many Chinese influences were beneficial, but the people in the Red River delta wanted to preserve their own culture and build their own style of civilization. For centuries the Viets resisted Chinese occupation and developed a strong sense of their own uniqueness. Even educated Viets who knew Chinese and wrote only in Chinese continued to speak their own language.

In 39 C.E. the Viets revolted against the Han. When the Chinese executed a Vietnamese aristocrat whom they accused of treason, his widow and her sister, Trung Trac and Trung Nhi, managed to raise an army and drive the Chinese out. The two sisters, who are revered as national heroines, were proclaimed queens of an independent Vietnamese kingdom. When the Chinese retook Vietnam, they drowned themselves.

Three years later Nam Viet was placed directly under a centralized Chinese administration that intensified efforts to assimilate the Vietnamese into Chinese culture. Although challenged several times, Chinese rule remained relatively secure until the Song dynasty. In the early eleventh century, the Viets finally founded the independent state of Dai Viet, in the heart of the Red River delta, made Hanoi their capital, and gradually began to move into the Mekong Delta.

In spite of centuries of struggle against the Chinese, the legacy of Chinese civilization in Dai Viet was profound, and Confucian values had seeped into everyday life. The Viets, following the Chinese example, practiced a form of Mahayana Buddhism, the only people in Southeast Asia to do so. The new government replaced local lords with officials trained in a civil service institute that was similar to the Chinese Confucian academies. But the Viets also retained a great many of their own values and practices. Vietnamese Buddhism included many local practices, especially the belief in spirits that needed to be propitiated and local figures that became bodhisattvas.

One major difference between China and Dai Viet was the role of women. Even in early times, women throughout Southeast Asia could inherit property, keep their own names after marriage, and pass their names on to their children. Men often paid a bride price (payment given to the bride's family), and it was relatively easy for a woman to get a divorce. Women also took an active role in courtship and enjoyed greater equality in sexual and financial matters than did women in either China or India. Throughout Vietnamese history women served as diplomats and military and political leaders and had more access to education than elsewhere in Asia.

The Korean Peninsula

The position of the Korean peninsula, located in the northeastern part of Asia near China, Russia, and Japan, has influenced much of Korea's history over the past two thousand years. To the north is China; to the southeast lies the Japanese archipelago. "Like a shrimp caught between two whales," the peninsula has been affected by geopolitical rivalries among its neighbors. Numerous invaders have entered Korea from Manchuria, Mongolia, and Japan. China regarded the peninsula as a buffer zone on its northeast frontier, shielding it from outsiders, and it served as a bridge connecting Japan to the Asian mainland. Korea's precarious position as a small country has prompted the people to acknowledge that, "When whales fight, the shrimps' backs are broken."

Around 4000 B.C.E., people began migrating into the Korean peninsula from Inner Asia and Southern Manchuria. These newcomers lived by gathering and hunting. Later they learned to farm and to domesticate goats, sheep, and pigs. After the fall of the Shang dynasty (ca. 1100), a wave of refugees from China migrated to the peninsula, bringing with them knowledge of wet-rice farming and bronze smelting. By about 400 B.C.E. the Koreans had learned iron smelting and were also producing beautiful pottery.

Life in the Three Kingdoms

During early Korean history, small clan-based communities with agriculture as the core of their economy emerged. Farmers cultivated rice and raised livestock for consumption and trade. Gradually three main kingdoms emerged: Koguryo in the Yalu River region, Paekche in the lower region of the Han River, and Silla in the southeast.

Korean society was highly stratified. Silla rulers developed a strict hierarchy called the Bone Rank system. (Bone Rank refers to "closeness to the bones" that one inherits from his or her parents.) In this hereditary system, people were born into a certain rank and stayed there; there was no social mobility. One's position in the hierarchy determined how one should act as well as one's family's occupation. It dictated such things as the size of one's house, the color of the clothes one could wear, the kind of vehicle one could have, and even the kinds of utensils used in the house.

In all three kingdoms, religious beliefs and practices focused on nature spirits. Men and women worshiped the sun and moon and looked with awe at spirits of the mountains, rivers, trees, and stones. People believed the spirits could bring good luck and health, peace, and prosperity. These beliefs are identified as Shamanism. Like their Chinese neighbors, they revered their ancestors and believed their spirits traveled freely, bringing either good or bad fortune to their living descendants. Originally both priests and priestesses officiated at Shaman rituals, but gradually women who could receive divine inspiration became dominant. Young girls who showed signs of possession learned to contact ancestors' spirits and exorcise evil spirits.

Chinese Influences Reach Korea

In 618 the Silla defeated the other two kingdoms and united the peninsula, and the United Silla ruled until 935. The Silla elite worked hard to strengthen ties with China. Korean students studied in Tang universities, and pilgrims journeyed to China to learn firsthand about Chinese Buddhism. Buddhism became very important in United Silla and leaders, following the Sui example in China, used the faith to gain legitimacy and strengthen their state. They argued that since all good Buddhists follow the way of the Buddha, everyone should unite and follow the Korean monarch. In turn, Buddhist monks prayed for the state, and Buddhist temples were dedicated to its protection. Monks also encouraged troops to fight bravely to protect the state, its ruler, and the Buddha.

Confucian values also influenced the Silla government. Confucian ethics increased the status of the aristocracy and strengthened families. A national Confucian college was established, and Confucian classics became important Korean texts. The kingdom was then divided into provinces, prefectures, and districts, similar to Tang China. The capital at Kyongju, the seat of government, developed into a

Stone Pagoda at Pulguksa

large city of around a million people and was modeled on the Chinese capital at Changan.

Koreans had a talent for bringing together seemingly contradictory ideas, and they succeeded in making a synthesis of both Buddhist and Confucian influences and Korean ideas. That synthesis is illustrated in the life of Wonhyo (617–86), a scholarly Buddhist monk who attempted to merge the various Buddhist schools of thought. He was married for three days to a Silla princess, long enough to father their son, who became a renowned Confucian scholar and was later honored in the Confucian academy.

The two queens who ruled during the United Silla period also demonstrate the importance of Chinese influences. Queen Sondok sent students to China for higher education, and supported the building of Buddhist temples and pagodas as well as the first observatory in Asia. Queen Chindok strengthened royal power, adapted Chinese court styles and the Chinese calendar, and encouraged the use of the Chinese writing system.

By the Koryo dynasty (918 to 1392), Buddhism had permeated the country. It became the state religion and profoundly influenced

Korean life. The government commissioned the building of many temples and monasteries, and monks and temples acquired a great deal of land as Buddhist economic and political power grew.

But the Koreans, like the Viets, were selective about what they took from China. Although Confucian/Buddhist thought seemed to have removed Shamanism from both private and public life, in reality it remained important, particularly for women and the farmers in the countryside. Buddhist rituals, ancestor rites, and Shaman practices existed side by side and complemented each other in a uniquely Korean synthesis. While men were responsible for public rituals outside the home, Shaman rituals, conducted by women, actively supported the spiritual well-being of individual households and were believed to help ward off misfortune. During ceremonies Shaman priestesses gave women practical advice on health, childbirth, and how to keep harmony in the family.

The important role women played in Shamanism and the existence of Korean queens attest to the authority women had in United Silla society. During the Koryo era women had nearly equal status with men. Both sons and daughters could inherit property, and husbands moved in with their wives' families for the first year of marriage. But an epitaph that a grieving husband wrote in 1146 about his dead wife could also have been written by a Confucian gentleman. He praises her by saying that she was pure, modest, literate, and "diligent in her wifely duties. She was the first to perceive and carry out the wishes of elders and with filial piety she nourished my now dead mother . . . and faithfully offered sacrifices for my dead father."

Despite attempts to institute Chinese-style examinations, Koreans continued to use the Bone Rank system to determine in which of the seventeen levels of the government bureaucrats might serve. Recruitment in the top ranks was limited to those in the highest ranks. While the Chinese system offered the possibility of social mobility, this was virtually impossible during the United Silla era.

"The Flower Dedication Song," one of only twenty-five Silla poems that have survived, suggests the social hierarchy and the wide gap between the rich and poor. Picture an official and his pretty young wife traveling along a narrow stretch of road. Looking up at the rocky cliffs, the lady takes a fancy to a lonely flower. Just then a decrepit

Tripitaka Koreana

old man leading a cow passes by. Although he is acutely aware of his inferior status, he says:

> If you would let me leave
> The cattle tethered to the brown rocks,
> And feel no shame for me,
> I would pluck and dedicate the flower.

The Koryo dynasty maintained the strict Bone Rank hierarchy and there was almost no social mobility. Powerful aristocratic landowners threatened both the central government and the freedom of the peasants who were bound to the estates. The government set up granaries to supply food for those in need, but most peasants were very poor and survived by bartering a portion of their produce for other essentials.

During the Koryo dynasty, Korea built up an impressive printing industry that produced copies of Korean histories and Buddhist classics. Koreans also developed the beautiful celadon ceramics, featuring a distinctive blue-green glaze, that remain among the most prized pottery in the world.

When Mongol forces threatened the country in 1232, Buddhist monks prayed to the Buddha to help ward off the invaders. They carved 81,258 wood blocks with which they printed the Tripitaka, a complete Buddhist canon. Each time they carved a character, they bowed three times. The Tripitaka strengthened the people's resolve to resist the Mongols, and it has become a national treasure. We will examine what effect this impressive act of dedication had on the Mongols when we consider the sweep of Mongol power in the next act.

Japan

Japan, the "Source of the Sun," is an archipelago southeast of Korea. It has four main islands—Hokkaido, Honshu, Shikoku, and Kyushu—that stretch north and south for about one thousand miles, comparable in latitude to the eastern coastline of the United States from Maine to Florida. Kyushu is separated from Korea—its nearest neighbor—by 120 miles (whereas England is a mere twenty miles off the coast of Europe).

Water and the sea have influenced Japanese life and culture from its earliest history. Even though farmland was scarce, abundant moisture supported the growth of rich vegetation, and the people supplemented their diets with fish and edible seaweed. The seas offered protection from invaders and sheltered the islands from outside influences. Rugged mountains isolated inland areas, the sea separated one area from another, and it was difficult to travel over land. Only one-fifth of the land in the archipelago was arable. On the other hand, the Inland Sea connected the southern three Japanese islands in a common trading and communication network.

Mountain streams provided abundant waterpower, but there were few mineral or coal resources. It is not unusual for three or four minor earthquakes to occur each day somewhere on the islands. Severe ones occur every seven years or so. Volcanoes often erupt violently. Mount Fuji is the most famous volcanic mountain in Japan, although it is no longer active.

One of the earliest peoples to settle in Japan was a group of Caucasians known as Ainu, but most of the early settlers came originally from Mongolia. Over time the more powerful Japanese pushed the Ainu into small enclaves and dominated their culture. Early

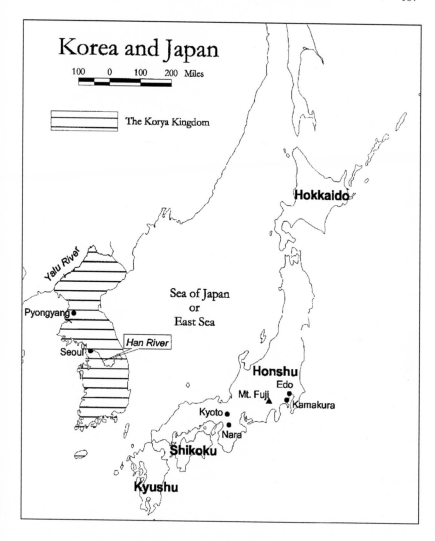

Japanese settlers were also in contact with Polynesian people in the thousands of islands that dot the western Pacific.

Geography encouraged the development of small, isolated, and more or less independent communities where men and women developed loyalty to neighbors in their particular area. Each community was self-sufficient and claimed a common ancestor. Clan members cooperated and depended on one another like a large, extended family, even though they were not always related by blood. Children learned to honor and respect their parents and ancestors.

From earliest times most Japanese followed Shintoism, the way of the spirits. Like Korean shamanism, Shintoism focused primarily on natural forces. The Japanese looked at their surroundings with a sense of wonder coupled with an acute aesthetic appreciation. Nature was awe-inspiring, and they believed everything possessed a spirit called *kami*. These spirits could be found in such things as special stones, streams, old trees, a mountain, or a sunset. Shinto shrines were built to honor the kami and reflect the Japanese aesthetic admiration of nature. The first Japanese ruler, a member of the Yamato clan, claimed descent from the supreme Shinto deity, the Sun Goddess.

Korea and China. had a profound influence on Japanese culture as it developed in the third century B.C.E., around present-day Kyoto and Osaka. Early Japanese tombs and jewelry closely resemble Korean styles. Farmers learned wet-rice farming, how to use the potter's wheel, and how to work with bronze and iron from Korea and China. Koreans brought Chinese technology, language, and Buddhist teachings to Japan.

Will the Japanese Clans Unite?

By the seventh century, the Yamato clan was exercising religious and cultural influence on other clans but it had little political power. When the Yamato learned about the reunification of China under the Sui dynasty (581–618), it wanted to copy the Chinese model of empire and create a strong unified Japanese state. Prince Shotoku, who ruled during the first part of the seventh century, established diplomatic relations with the Sui dynasty and sent scholars to learn about its culture.

Drawing heavily from the Chinese example, Prince Shotoku made a major effort to unify his kingdom. He composed a seventeen-article constitution that instructed the people to obey the ruler and carry out all his commands. It established appropriate rewards and punishments and recommended creating a bureaucracy based on merit. The constitution praised Confucian values, especially the parent-child relationship and filial piety, and it also urged people to respect Buddhist ideals. Buddhist influences are clearly reflected in Article 10 which reads in part:

Let us cease from wrath, and refrain from angry looks.

Nor let us be resentful when others differ from us. For all men have hearts, and each heart has its own leanings. Their right is our wrong, and our right is their wrong. . . . How can anyone lay down a rule by which to distinguish right from wrong? For we are all, one with another, wise and foolish. . . . Therefore, although others give way to anger, let us on the contrary dread our own faults. . . .

THE NARA PERIOD

Despite these lofty goals, strong clan leaders resented Prince Shotoku's attempt to strengthen the central government, and they largely ignored his document. Other efforts at unity failed as well, and Japan remained divided among clans. The Fujiwaras were the dominant clan from 710 to 785. They continued to send emissaries to learn more about China and they modeled Nara, their first large city and their capital, after Changan.

The Nara government was the strongest Japan had known. Even so, in a society dominated by powerful landowning clans, introducing a Chinese-style bureaucracy based on merit proved impossible. As in Korea, the government still appointed the heads of important families to be bureaucrats and saw no point in using a written examination to select officials. A strict hierarchy developed. An individual was expected to act in ways appropriate to his or her hereditary position, age, and gender. Individuals were very sensitive to the hierarchical relationships in each situation, and they treated one another accordingly.

Maitreya

Although adopting a Chinese style of government and meritocracy proved elusive, the Japanese enthusiastically embraced Buddhism. Japanese monks returning from China brought firsthand information about the faith. During the early seventh century the Koreans sent a beautiful image of Maitreya—the Buddha of the Future—to Japan. Soon the Japanese were making similar images.

As Buddhism spread throughout the country, Japanese Buddhists created their own version of the religion, as Chinese, Koreans, and Southeast Asians had done before them. They added a strong aesthetic dimension to the faith, transforming Chan Buddhism into Zen Buddhism. This uniquely Japanese form inspired countless beautiful gardens and temples. The government supported monasteries and temples and their number and wealth increased dramatically.

ARTISTIC EXPRESSION IN THE HEIAN PERIOD

Fearing Buddhist institutions were becoming too powerful, the aristocrats decided to build a new capital at Heian (Kyoto) and ushered in the Heian Period (794–1185). Soon after the court moved to Heian, the Japanese cut off contact with China and concentrated on expressing Japanese cultural values. Court life in Kyoto resembled the Chinese model in many ways, but it had a uniquely Japanese aesthetic dimension. Members of the court pursued a lavish lifestyle, and nobles cultivated an elegant sensibility. Successful men and women learned beautiful calligraphy that was thought to reflect one's character. Architecture developed along uniquely Japanese lines with sliding door panels, the simple but elegant use of wood, and some of the loveliest gardens in the world.

Women at the court dominated Japanese literature. While male scholars labored to write histories in Chinese, women wrote in *kana*, a phonetic Japanese written language. Their works celebrate beauty, refinement, and romantic love. One of the most famous compositions composed during this period was *The Tale of Genji*, the world's first novel (and one of the most remarkable works of world literature). Lady Murasaki, a lady-in-waiting to the empress, composed this romantic story about a "shining prince." Her novel recounts his many romantic encounters as well as glimpses of the refinements of the Heian court. Romance was enhanced by the fact that men might see only a woman's sleeve nestled on the window of her carriage and had to rely on their imaginations to picture the rest.

Both men and women wrote poems in which they expressed their awe and appreciation of nature. Less was more: with a few words, a key detail or by juxtaposing two contrasting images they tried to evoke an emotional response from the reader. For example:

> Rather than that I should pine for you
> Would I had been transmuted
> Into a tree or stone,
> Nevermore to feel the pangs of love.

Japanese women in the early days had wielded significant power. Female chieftains could rule clans. During the Heian period marriages were easy to arrange and equally easy to dissolve, and husbands and wives often lived apart or with the wife's family. Wives regularly inherited from their husbands and frequently owned land, Priestesses dominated religious life.

Gradually Japanese women lost much of the power that they had formally had. By the tenth century men were being appointed to fill most of the government jobs. Women could no longer exert direct authority. Instead, they had to exert their influence behind the scenes by trying to influence their husbands, brother or sons to do as they wished. Wives and grandmothers arranged marriage partners for their daughters, often with an eye to gaining status for them and for the family by marrying them into strong clans.

Chinese influences may have contributed to the reduction in women's position. Many aristocrats and rich merchants adopted the Confucian attitude toward women and began to practice polygamy and keep concubines. The Chinese values they adopted took the form of *tatemae* (outer official behavior), while the indigenous Japanese traditions made up *honne* (inner, or what people really want). *Honne* remained the soul of the culture. Men controlled the public roles of authority and power (*tatamae*), while women retained their authority in the private (*honne*) dimension of life and exerted a powerful role in socializing children and controlling domestic finances.

Both Emperor and Shogun

The Heian court, despite its many artistic and cultural achievements, grew wasteful and corrupt. The leadership became detached from the people and was unable to provide security for the country. Many viewed the court as a small group of effete snobs who had lost all sense of the masculine ideal. As a result, regional chiefs led family-centered warrior bands that tried to maintain order.

With the rise of strong military leaders and the growing isolation of the Heian court, two different but simultaneous systems of government emerged. One was the emperor and his court that presided in Kyoto. The other was a military dictatorship, centered in Kamakura (near present-day Tokyo). It was based on the powerful landholding clans that exercised the real power throughout the country. A shogun (supreme general) controlled the centralized military government (the *bakufu*, or "tent government"). Different military lords were bound to the shogun through personal and political ties based on the amount of land they controlled.

Those who had sought to build a centralized Japanese state by importing the Chinese concept of emperor had been unable to do so. Instead, a feudal society developed, and Japan was divided into regional units based on military power. After 1333 these regional military leaders with large landholdings became known as daimyo. The daimyo established binding relationships with men called samurai (warriors) who fought for them. The samurai, a military class similar to European knights, served as vassals to powerful lords and lived on their estates. They promised service and protection to their lords in return for the lords' patronage and other assistance. The emperor served merely as the symbolic head of the country and provided legitimacy for the military rulers.

The Samurai's Code

The samurai, who fought both on horseback and on foot, became the new heroes of Japanese society. Besides fighting, they also managed farmlands, taught martial arts, and led hunting parties. A successful samurai might acquire land and become a daimyo.

Samurai followed a system of conduct that was later officially codified into Bushido (The Way of the Warrior). A samurai was expected to be absolutely loyal to his lord. For example, a popular story related how the son of a lord was kidnapped. When one of the lord's samurai discovered where the child was being hidden, he secretly substituted his own child for the lord's son. The kidnapper, unable to tell the difference between the two infants, killed the samurai's son and the lord's son was saved. The Japanese greatly admired this samurai's devotion to his lord.

Samurai were to be fearless in the face of death. A warrior should welcome death before allowing dishonor to befall his lord or himself. Self-control was also important. The warrior must endure all kinds of physical hardship without complaining. "When the stomach is empty, it is a disgrace to feel hungry," samurai were taught.

Finally, the warrior should be skilled in the arts of war. His sword was his honor and should never be out of his sight. He carried two swords, one for killing his enemies and a shorter one to use—in case of cowardice or disgrace—to take his own life. Much of the best Japanese literature of this period elevated the warrior's selfless devotion to duty, even in the face of death, and combined that theme with the beautiful but transitory nature of experience.

Stories also reflected how Buddhist values were combined with the warrior's code. Once a rebel army attacked a Buddhist monastery. The general who burst into the abbot's room felt insulted when the abbot did not greet him with any particular respect. "Don't you know you are looking at someone who could run a sword through you without batting an eye?" the general screamed.

"And you," replied the abbot, "are looking at one who can be run through with a sword without batting an eye." The general smiled, bowed, and left. Brave samurai were expected to conduct themselves like the abbot.

People all over the world have been selective in what they adapt from other societies, and they find extraordinary ways to use new ideas to support and refine their own values. It should not be surprising, therefore, that the Japanese significantly transformed Chinese influences to fit Japanese values and sensitivities. For example, China created a strong central government and placed the warrior at the bottom of society, maintaining that good men should not become soldiers. They also had established a bureaucracy based on merit. In

contrast, by the twelfth century the Japanese emperor was purely symbolic, and a government of military force based on large landholding
clans ruled the country. Turning the Chinese hierarchy upside down,
the Japanese made the warrior the most honored figure in literature
and society.

In addition, the Japanese adapted Confucian, Buddhist, and Shinto
ideals that are inherently non-violent to reinforce the warrior's code.
The Confucian emphasis on mutual respect between a father and son
was used to strengthen the relationship between a daimyo and his
samurai. Not fearing death mirrored the Buddhist belief in life's
impermanence and strengthened the warrior's willingness to face
death and reinforced the Japanese sense of the transitory nature of
life. Moreover, Shinto values were reflected in the emphasis on sim-
plicity and reverence for nature.

Kiev, Khmer, Korea, Nam Viet, and Japan were all selective and innovative in what they adapted from other areas. Although the Viets were
under Chinese authority for about a thousand years, they clung to
their sense of uniqueness and eventually established their own independent kingdom. Koreans welcomed both Confucian and Buddhist
influences but kept their faith in shamans and retained the Bone Rank
system that ensured hereditary privileges. Southeast Asian leaders
merged Hindu-Buddhist ideas with existing beliefs in sacred mountains, nagas and the influence of ancestors and used Indian models of
kingship and the Hindu-Buddhist concept of the cosmos to enhance
their legitimacy and power. And the Japanese incorporated Confucian,
Buddhist, and Shinto ideals into a code for warriors. The men and
women in each of these areas forged a new synthesis that mixed their
own ways with new ideas. As they did, they entered the mainstream
of hemispheric civilization as original and creative actors with their
own styles of civilization. We now turn to see what has been happening in Africa.

SCENE TWO

CITY-STATES AND EMPIRES IN AFRICA

Setting the Stage

Africa, the second largest continent, contains twenty-three percent of the earth's land surface, three times as much as the continental United States. The continent has numerous distinct ecological zones, especially over the 3,500-mile area running north to south. The northern coastline borders the Mediterranean Sea. South of this coastal zone is the Sahara Desert, which now almost divides the continent in two. The sahel (a dry grassy steppe) runs along the southern edge of the Sahara. If we think of the Sahara as a sea of sand, then the sahel is the coastline bordering that sea, and the towns and cities in the sahel are similar to seaports.

South of the Sahara and sahel is the savanna, the grassland where both herders and farmers live, and farther south is the tropical rain forest that covers about twenty percent of the continent. The Sudan refers to the savanna south of the desert and north of the forest. As one moves south of the rain forest, there is another band of savanna, then areas of desert, and finally the southern coastline.

Geography has had a profound influence on life in Africa. Poor soils and heavy rainfall make it difficult for farmers to produce large surpluses. The tsetse fly, which thrives in the rain forest, causes a sleeping sickness that infects people and kills large animals such as horses and donkeys, and riverbanks host malaria-carrying mosquitoes. All these factors have kept the population relatively low. The Sahara is a formidable barrier to north-south travel, and rapids in the river near the coasts make navigation inland difficult, contributing to the continent's isolation. Even so, from the early centuries of the first millennium C.E., traders went back and forth across the sahel, savanna, and rain forest, exchanging goods among West Africa's very different ecological regions.

Beyond the desert and rapids, several major rivers enhance internal contacts. The Congo River drains a basin larger than the area of India. The Niger River runs through both the savanna and the rain forest and is West Africa's major east-west trade route. It flows northeast until it reaches an inland delta area called the Great Bend and then flows southeast for about a thousand miles to the Atlantic Ocean.

Urban settlements existed along the Upper Niger perhaps as early as the third century B.C.E., long before trans-Saharan trade made the area even richer. Rapids at both ends protect people from attack, very much as the cataracts do in the Nile Valley. At the Great Bend the river floods periodically, spreading rich silt along its shores and making recessional agriculture possible. The silt makes the land fertile enough for farmers to produce a surplus and for cattle to graze on grasses that grow along its banks. Communication and trade were relatively easy along the Niger as well, and traders carried surplus food downriver by canoe.

Bantu Migrations and the Spread of Iron

During the first millennium C.E., large numbers of people living in the interior of Africa began to migrate to new areas. This movement is called the Bantu migrations because most of the people spoke Bantu-related languages. Bantu-speaking migrants, who probably came originally from what is now northeastern Nigeria, spread south, east, and west. Some of them went as far as the East African coast and southward to present-day South Africa.

Historians speculate on the reasons for these migrations. Some Bantu-speaking people were probably forced to move as the Sahara spread south. Increases in population caused others to start new settlements in less populated areas. Although iron smelting was known in what is now Rwanda as early as 800 B.C.E., and had reached West Africa, probably from Carthage, around 600 B.C.E., early Bantu-speaking migrants often brought knowledge of both improved farming techniques and ironworking to the sparsely populated areas in which they settled. Iron technology enabled them to make better farming tools so they could grow more crops, which led to more people and additional movement. High-yield crops, such as bananas and "water yams," introduced by Indian Ocean traders who had originally come all the way from Indonesia, resulted in even more population growth. Iron

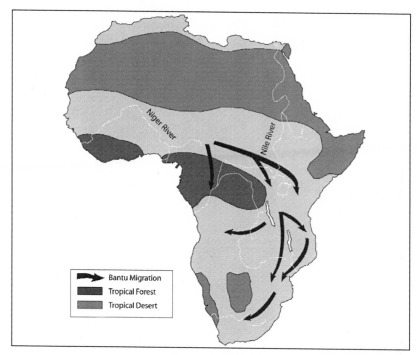

Bantu migrations

weapons enabled the migrants to defeat hunters or herders they encountered, and in areas where people were already farming, improved iron tools and weapons probably gave the newcomers an advantage.

Using Oral Sources

When historians consider Africa's early history, they are hampered by a lack of written sources. Archaeological remains provide much important information, but few written records exist that are more than a thousand years old. Reports from travelers and traders from as early as the eighth century C.E. give clues about Africa's past, but many of the outsiders who wrote were not always sympathetic or did not fully understand what they were seeing.

Africans preserved their history orally. Because personal memory seldom goes back beyond three or four generations, professional record-keepers called *jeli*s (often identified by the French term *griot*s) commemorated individuals, family genealogies, and important events and passed their reports on to succeeding generations. Jelis possessed impressive powers of memory and eloquence. To strengthen their memory, they sometimes used short, dramatic narratives enhanced by proverbs, songs, and chants. Jelis often interspersed recollections from their own experiences to enliven significant historic episodes.

It is perhaps not surprising that for a long time European and American historians questioned how useful the African oral tradition was in revealing what had happened. After all, they called the period before there were written records "prehistory" and pointed out that memory is not always reliable. African oral tradition, they maintained, might be especially unreliable because jelis were supposed to praise the leaders they served. They might give a current ruler credit for achievements of the past or change the sequence of events by moving important earlier events forward or more recent events back. In addition, they often did not notice or mention gradual changes. Even with all these possible distortions, however, historians now realize that the oral tradition provides much valuable information about Africa's past and is not necessarily less accurate than many written sources.

But the scarcity of sources was not the only reason scholars ignored much of Africa's history. Many historians focus on political history, equating civilization with states and empires. Some dismissed Africa because they had trouble identifying rulers or governments or they could not identify any fixed hierarchies. With so many states to study, it seemed pointless to report on so-called stateless societies.

Heterarchies and States

Many African communities were heterarchies in which authority and decision-making were shared among different groups. Instead of a single ruler and his officials, communities were often composed of numerous lineage or kinship groups, each of which had its own chief. Lineage usually determined who participated in the decision-making, and a council consisting of the clan elders made decisions about issues affecting the whole community. Individual leaders might have only temporary power, or their authority might be limited to certain areas or a small number of people.

Size was not the criterion for distinguishing areas with shared authority from other types of political organization: areas that had multiple centers of political authority were often quite large, and the area some centralized states controlled might be very small. The difference lay in the way authority was exercised.

Of course centralized states also existed in Africa, and a central authority offered certain advantages. Defense was one. Decentralized groups have trouble mobilizing enough military force to withstand an attack or invasion. States can more effectively organize and control long-distance trade. Governments can control production and prices and collect taxes on what enters and leaves their territory. And a central government can mobilize resources for public works, such as irrigation systems or monumental building projects.

If empires develop from smaller heterarchies, the type of central control that results may be different from the kind that develops from a centralized kingdom. If that is the case, what appears to be an empire may be closer to a loosely organized confederation of self-ruling, economically autonomous political groups in which the central government's authority is more limited.

Early History in West Africa

Besides North Africa and the Nile Valley, urban life also developed in western Africa, particularly along the upper and middle Niger River. Iron tools helped farmers produce surplus food, and surpluses, as we have seen, make specialization, trade, and complex societies possible. Urban centers developed along the Niger for many of the same reasons that cities that grew up along other river valleys. Following the periodic flooding, farmers in the inland Niger delta and the southern edge of Lake Chad planted in the areas from which the water receded, much as farmers would do in the Khmer kingdom and had been doing in the Nile valley for millennia. Intensive recessional agriculture proved very effective.

Trade was critical in western Africa. Salt, which is essential to survival, was scarce, so merchants must have been trading agricultural products for salt from the mines in the Sahara Desert for almost three thousand years. Exchanges developed among the diverse environmental zones in the savanna as well, and trading centers developed along interior overland trade routes.

Jenne-Jeno

Jenne-Jeno, "Old Jenne," located near the inland delta of the Niger River, is one of the oldest known cities in western Africa. Herders forced south by the expanding Sahara Desert probably founded the city in about 250 B.C.E. The site was relatively easy to defend: rapids protected it from invaders and so did swamps and twisting canals.

Jenne-Jeno probably developed into a trading center where merchants carrying salt from the Taghaza mines in the Sahara met traders with gold from mines in the western Sudan near the Gambia River. In addition, the river provided fish, and farmers cultivated crops in the receding waters on the floodplain. Iron implements found at Jenne-Jeno that were made during the early centuries of the common era confirm the existence of trade, because the closest iron is fifty kilometers away. Craftsmen cured animal hides for clothing, made pottery, and supervised the mining of gold and copper. By 1000 C.E., Jenne-Jeno's population exceeded fifty thousand.

Archaeological evidence suggests Jenne-Jeno was a city but had no central government. Instead it had a heterarchy, a collection of perhaps sixty-nine urban clusters that existed side by side. These communities specialized in different occupations, and no one group dominated the whole area. The clusters were interdependent because they needed one another's specialized activities.

West African Kingdoms: Ghana

Whoever controlled the gold and salt mines or trade routes, or both, could become rich and powerful. The most important area was where the caravans emerged from the desert, especially near the western end of the Niger River. During the fifth or sixth century C.E., leaders became wealthy by dominating that trade route, and they were able to establish what became known as the kingdom of Ghana. (Do not confuse this state with the modern nation of Ghana, also in West Africa, that chose to identify itself with this ancient kingdom.)

The wealth and prestige of Ghana's leaders resulted from their control of the gold mines to the south and trade routes leading across the Sahara. Ghanian merchants traded gold, ivory, and slaves for glassware, horses, cloth, and salt, which was often worth its weight in gold. Leaders taxed goods coming into the cities and goods going out as well. In addition, they kept tight control over how much gold was in circulation to ensure that its value remained high.

The following description of the capital of Ghana, probably Koumbi-Saleh, was written in the middle of the eleventh century:

> The city of Ghana consists of two towns situated on a plain. One of these towns, which is inhabited by Muslims, is large and possesses twelve mosques . . . In the environs are wells with sweet water, from which they drink and with which they grow vegetables. The [non-Islamic] king's town is six miles distant from this. . . . Between these two towns there are continuous habitations. . . . The king has a palace and a number of domed dwellings all surrounded with an enclosure like a city wall. In the king's town, not far from his court of justice, is a mosque where the Muslims who arrive at his court pray.

These two centers, one for Ghanians and the other for Muslim traders and other foreigners, as well as the mosques, indicate active trans-Saharan trade and the growing importance of Islam. Wealth from trade and taxes on trade gave the leaders enough resources to finance the construction of imposing buildings that may have impressed other groups and made them willing to ally themselves with Ghana. But Ghana was probably more like a collection of several small, somewhat independent areas than a kingdom with one powerful ruler. Most of the farmers, fishermen, and herdsmen over whom the government claimed to have authority probably continued to obey the directions of their local chiefs. However, when the kingdom was threatened, men from the local communities would fight with the Ghanian leader. It is estimated that in the mid-eleventh century Ghana could put together an army of 200,000 warriors. Horses, which the Ghanians got by trading with Berbers in northern Africa, gave Ghana a military advantage over neighboring areas.

Cities such as Timbuktu were not situated on the best agricultural land but prospered because they participated in the trans-Saharan trade. Traders transferred goods at Timbuktu from camels to canoes

Mosque in Timbuktu

or donkeys. Trading centers also developed along the border of the rain forest, where, because of the tsetse fly, goods were transferred from donkeys to humans who transported the goods on their heads.

A reduction in trade and a prolonged drought contributed to Ghana's decline. As the soil in the sahel deteriorated, farmers could no longer support the large population. Muslim armies, hoping to spread a conservative form of Islam, made repeated raids, further weakening Ghana, as did neighboring groups, including the Soninke. In addition, once the leaders of Ghana accepted Islam, they may have had difficulty keeping non-Muslim territories loyal. By 1200 its authority had ended.

Sunjata Establishes the Kingdom of Mali

Mandinka people living in Kangaba near the headwaters of the Niger River were probably subjects of Ghana, sending tribute and serving as middlemen in the gold trade. As Ghana declined, several groups, including the Mandinka and the Soninke, fought for control over the lucrative trade. At first the Soninke, led by Sumanguru, prevailed. Sumanguru, head of the Sosso clan, was known for his cruelty and skill at witchcraft. He was so oppressive that the Kangaba prince fled and his brother Sunjata [Sundiata] was banished.

Sunjata was an unlikely candidate to challenge anyone. The national oral epic of Mali indicates that as a child he had been weak and unable to walk. He could not protect his mother, the Kangaba ruler's second wife, from the ridicule of the ruler's first wife. Finally, when she taunted Sunjata about being unable to bring his mother even a few leaves from the baobab tree, the young boy suddenly stood up and dragged the whole tree to his mother's compound. Fearing his newfound strength might make Sunjata a threat, Sumanguru banished him. The exiled Sunjata built alliances with leaders in neighboring areas, and in 1230 they helped him seize power. "After that," the jeli sang, "Sunjata ruled over an immense kingdom. His justice spared nobody. He followed the very word of God. He protected the weak against the strong. Under his sun the upright man was rewarded and the wicked one perished."

In the lavish festivities marking Sunjata's victory over Sumanguru, the "twelve kings of the bright savanna country" struck their spears in the ground before Sunjata, symbolizing their acceptance of his authority. Sunjata then gave each king back his spear and his kingdom, acknowledging his alliance with them all.

> One by one all the kings received their kingdoms from the very hands of Sunjata, and each bowed before him as one bows before a Mansa [king, sultan]. . . . To each he assigned its land, he established the rights of each people and ratified their friendships.

MANSA MUSA

During the next hundred years, Mali leaders extended their territory to include the central and western regions of the Sudan, making it one of the world's largest empires at that time, and he also promoted Islam. During his twenty-five-year reign, from 1312 to 1337, Mansa Musa (King Moses) controlled not only the trading routes Ghana had dominated but also Gao and Timbuktu, important trading cities, and his hegemony extended to the Taghaza salt mines.

Mansa Musa is best known for his 1324–25 pilgrimage to Mecca. His entourage was so grand and the gifts he distributed so lavish that, years later, scholars still thought of him as "the most powerful, the richest, the most fortunate, the most feared by his enemies, and the

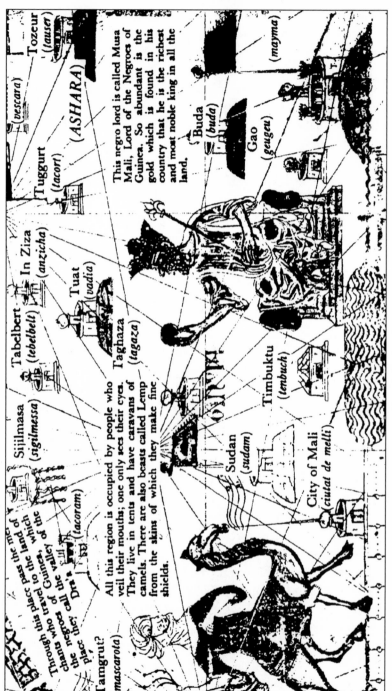

Key to the Catalan Map

most able to do good to those around him." Mali was recognized as a world power, and its ambassadors attended courts in Egypt and Morocco. Maps such as the Catalan map showed both Mansa Musa and Mali.

Trade linked Mali to other parts of the world. Traders used cowrie shells, which came almost exclusively from the Maldive Islands off the west coast of India, as currency. Gold that came from Ghana and Mali provided the basis for the currency in Europe during this era. In addition to gold, traders from Mali carried ivory, ostrich feathers, kola nuts, hides, and slaves that they traded for salt, textiles, copper, silver, books, paper, swords, perfume, and horses.

Islam's influence increased dramatically in Mali, especially after Mansa Musa's pilgrimage. Sunjata had converted to Islam, but judging from his jeli's accounts, he practiced traditional rituals as well. Mansa Musa was a devout Muslim. He brought Muslim scholars from Mecca to Timbuktu, supported the building of mosques in Gao and Timbuktu, and helped make Timbuktu a center of Islamic learning. Travelers reported that merchants in that city traded more books than any other item. Rulers tried hard to balance the interests of their Muslim subjects and the non-Muslim majority.

Ibn Battuta, a fourteenth-century Berber Muslim traveler who visited Mali in 1352, was impressed by the people's honesty. He reported that "neither traveler there nor dweller has anything to fear from thief or usurper." He noted that men claimed descent from their mother's brother, not their father, and that their sisters' sons, not their own, were their heirs. The women, he reported, dressed in fine Egyptian fabrics and "are of surpassing beauty." He was impressed that people diligently observed the hours of prayer, studied the books of the law, memorized the Qur'an, and showed profound respect for their ruler. However, this devout Muslim was shocked that women entertained male friends freely and that their husbands did not object.

Perhaps Mali's success contributed to its weakness in the years after Mansa Musa. The kingdom's vast area was difficult to control, and distant areas often did not pay tribute to the court. After 1400 many areas revolted and gradually the empire fell apart.

As Mali weakened, Songhai, one of Mali's tributary kingdoms, became more powerful. As in earlier western African kingdoms, trade was very important. Songhai conquered enough diverse groups and territory by 1450 to become an impressive empire that we will consider later in the human drama.

Christianity Becomes the State Religion in Ethiopia

Christianity was also important in Africa. Rulers in Axum had converted to Christianity at about the same time as Emperor Constantine, and a Christian community continued to thrive in what is now Ethiopia. In 1150 leaders began to unify the area. Expanding from their capital in the central highland, they installed Christian military commanders to supervise the land they conquered and to build monasteries.

King Lalibela, who ruled sometime between 1200 and 1250, supervised the construction of eleven churches cut from solid rock. These extraordinary structures were sculpted from the top down by cutting away the surrounding rock and were named after buildings in Jerusalem, as if they were trying to build a new Jerusalem. In 1320, settlements on the northern coast of present-day Somalia became part of the kingdom.

In 1270 the Solomonids established a new dynasty. They claimed to be descendants of the Axumite kings, who, in turn, believed they were related to King Solomon and Makeda, the Queen of Sheba. According to their national epic, Makeda had visited King Solomon's court in the tenth century B.C.E. She was impressed with his judgments and decided to adopt his religion instead of worshiping the sun. Before leaving, she agreed to dine with him as long as he did not try to make love to her. He gave his word, and in return she

Church at Lalibela

promised not to take any of his possessions. But the extremely spicy food he served her made her thirsty, and she took a drink of water without asking permission. Having tricked her into breaking her word, he was freed from his oath and made love to her. When she returned to Ethiopia, she gave birth to their son, Menilek.

Later, when Menilek went to Jerusalem, King Solomon recognized his son and crowned him king of Ethiopia. As a result, the Solomonid rulers claimed that the Ethiopians were a uniquely chosen people who shared the glory of Solomon's descendants who ruled Rome, and that the kings of Ethiopia and those of Rome were brethren. Their ability to unite the fifty tribes that lived in Greater Ethiopia came in part from their belief in that unique heritage.

East Africa: The Swahili Coast

The east coast of Africa played a critical role in the Indian Ocean trading network. The area was a vibrant mixture of peoples and products. By early in the first millennium C.E., Bantu-speaking Africans had settled along the coast and built independent market towns. At about the same time people from islands in Southeast Asia journeyed some 6,000 miles to the island of Madagascar, about 200 miles off the coast of East Africa. They introduced new products, such as bananas and yam, which African farmers adopted, and aspects of their culture were incorporated with African beliefs and practices. Some of their descendants reached the mainland in the tenth century, as did Arab merchants who were active in the Indian Ocean trade.

By the mid-twelfth century many Arabs from the Arabian Peninsula and the Persian Gulf area also began to settle along the coast. Merchants in these towns traded ivory, rhinoceros horn, wax, tortoise shells, and coconut oil from the interior for iron tools, weapons, cotton cloth, and some wheat and wine.

Traders, traveling in single-sail monsoon-driven ships called dhows, were carried south from Arabia and then brought home by the reverse monsoon. As merchants traveling up and down the coast, mingling and intermarrying with local inhabitants, the area stretching from Magadish in the north to Sofala in the south became known as the Swahili coast. "Swahili" means "coast-dwellers." Gradually their Bantu language incorporated some Arabic phrases and became

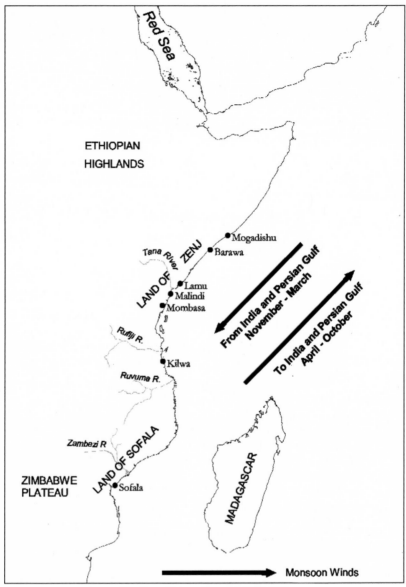

The East African Coast to 1000 C.E.

known as Swahili; it was written using the Arabic script.

Certain common characteristics developed along the Swahili coast. The most prominent feature was the development of a series of independent city-states, each ruled by an Islamic dynasty that regulated trade and officially chronicled its achievements. The upper class of each city-state was composed of government officials and wealthy merchants who spoke Arabic and Swahili. Nearly all of them were Muslims. Next came Swahili-speaking craftsmen, artisans, clerks, and minor court officials. Non-Muslim laborers and slaves from the interior of the mainland made up the lowest class.

Another common feature in the Swahili city-states was the importance of Islam: to be Swahili came to mean being Muslim. Believers supervised the construction of impressive domed mosques made of local coral blocks from the sea. Ibn Battuta, who traveled to the Swahili coast in the 1330s, described the mosques he saw at Mombasa as "very strongly constructed of wood. Beside the door of each mosque are one or two wells."

Each city-state endeavored to maintain its independence, and all depended on income from trade. Traders had already introduced new crops from South and Southeast Asia, such as sugarcane, coconuts, bananas, Asian rice, and certain root vegetables. African traders brought gold, ivory, copper, and slaves from the interior to the coast. Some were exchanged for cloth, beads, and glazed ceramics from as far away as China.

By and large, relations among the Swahili city-states and the interior of East Africa were peaceful. Sometimes, however, adventurers from the coastal city states raided the mainland for goods and slaves. Because labor was scarce, slaves were used on local plantations

Ruins of the Great Mosque of Kilwa

in coastal Africa. Others were imported from as far away as Oman and India.

Kilwa was the southernmost port to which traders could sail on the monsoon in one season. After 1250 Kilwa controlled the southern trade in gold and copper from Sofala. As a result Kilwa became one of the most important and probably wealthiest Swahili city-states as well as the key trans-shipment point for trade with Central and Southern Africa. Ibn Battuta identified Kilwa as the "principal town on the coast." He wrote that most of its inhabitants were

> Zanj of very black complexion. Their faces are scarred. . . . Kilwa is one of the most beautiful and well-constructed towns in the world. The whole of it is elegantly built. The roofs are made of mangrove poles. There is very much rain. . . . The chief qualities are devotion and piety. . . .

Great Zimbabwe

Great Zimbabwe was the center or capital of what was perhaps the first prosperous state in Central Africa. It developed during the early centuries of the second millennium on the Zimbabwe plateau near the Zambesi River. Zimbabwe means a "building of stone," and archaeologists have uncovered many stone buildings. Each had dry stonewalls with broad bases that encircled small buildings and cattle compounds.

Geography played an important role in Great Zimbabwe's development. The plateau, a thousand feet above sea level, was relatively cool, well watered, and lightly wooded. Because it had few tsetse flies, both cattle raising and farming were possible. The number of cattle rather than the amount of land one owned was the measure of a person's wealth. Whenever a drought occurred, which was about every five years, people could eat some of their cattle and also trade them for grain.

Great Zimbabwe probably started as a sacred center, not unlike Teotihuacan in Mesoamerica, and its sacred quality invested it with great importance. Smooth mud dwellings had existed on the plateau before the first millennium, when people began raising cattle. When nearby gold mines were discovered and Zimbabwe became wealthy and powerful, residents of the city built monumental structures that included altars, large pedestals supporting giant soapstone birds that may have represented ancestral spirits, and a large stone tower.

Great Zimbabwe's largest structures were built between 1250 and 1450. The city's elliptical walls, thirty-two feet high and sixteen feet wide, were all constructed with carefully cut granite, which splits evenly and leaves a smooth surface. They laid the stones in various patterns without mortar. The walls appear to have encircled the homes of between two hundred and three hundred of the community's elite families and were probably primarily intended to emphasize their status rather than to protect them. They also suggest the leaders controlled a great number of laborers. Five to eighteen thousand people probably lived near Great Zimbabwe.

The Great Enclosure, in the valley, was the political and commercial section of this remarkable city. It included the market and was surrounded by residential areas. Its outer wall was over eight hundred feet long, made of finely cut granite blocks. It was the largest single structure in sub-Saharan Africa for several centuries.

Gold merchants controlled trade between the gold fields and the

Walls at Great Zimbabwe

Swahili coast. Craftsmen worked copper and gold into jewelry. Copper was mined in distant areas and shipped through Great Zimbabwe's bustling markets to Sofala. People also worked as potters, stone carvers, cotton weavers, and farmers. Pieces of Chinese ceramics made in the thirteenth century, as well as Indian and Persian goods that archaeologists have unearthed, provide evidence of the prosperous trade. The elite grew rich taxing trade and from the tribute in iron, ivory, gold, and food that came from neighboring areas.

Great Zimbabwe was abandoned by 1500, probably because of a decline in the metal trade as well as ecological problems. Trying to raise so much food, cutting so much timber, and grazing and hunting so many animals seriously damaged the ecosystem, and eventually the area's resources could no longer support a large population.

The Importance of the Community

We have looked closely at only a few of the thousands of different groups that existed in Africa before 1450. Each formed its own community and often claimed a common ancestor. Significant language diversity existed as well. There are five main language families but literally thousands of subgroups. This diversity made political unity difficult. Despite the enormous diversity, however, there seem to be certain common cultural elements, some of which may also have existed in ancient Egypt and Nubia.

Perhaps the single most important aspect of African life was the importance of the community. Individual security and happiness came from everyone working together. The following statements reflect the value placed on community.

To be human is to belong to the whole community.

The individual does not and cannot exist alone....I am because we are, and since we are, therefore, I am.

The individual was practically nothing; the family almost everything. Family rights transcended all other rights.

> The perception of belonging to a group—whether family, age-grade, village, clan or nation—is almost always paramount over a sense of individuality.

Often the outward signs of belonging to the group were circumcision and scarification. Inward signs were reflected in people's names. Music, dance, and other rituals also helped build a sense of unity. Choruses or refrains in the jeli's message were often interrupted by responses from the audience, and the call and response tradition continues to the present.

Age groups played an important role in the life of the community. An age group usually included all the boys or girls who were born within a five- or six-year period. Rites of passage, particularly initiation rites, were an important source of solidarity among age group members. Many initiation ceremonies included days or even weeks of seclusion during which those being initiated learned the history and secrets of their community and age group, practiced skills, and assumed their responsibilities for helping to strengthen their age group and serve the larger community. As they grew older, members of an age group would become community leaders, then respected elders, and finally revered ancestors.

THE ROLE OF THE EXTENDED FAMILY

The family was the most important group and the basis for the whole society. The family provided the services that other institutions in the United States, particularly schools and the government, provide. It was the source of social security, of law and order, of education and rituals of remembrance, and of praise and punishment. One's status was determined by one's position in the family and lineage. Political power in many communities was organized around families and lineage groups, and family rights transcended all other obligations.

Even the physical layout of homes contributed to the sense of community. Family compounds in villages were usually grouped in a circle. Individual dwellings in the compound were like rooms in a house, and the central courtyard was an open area where women and children shared the work and the family gathered. Each wife within the family compound was expected to control her own children, and if she worked, she could keep what she made. The various compounds in the village, in turn, were also often laid out in a circle. Perhaps this setting suggested the cycle of life and emphasized the nonhierarchical nature of some communities; some other communities were highly stratified.

Young people imitated the example of family members and other community elders. Stories about the clan's history provided another source of education and helped children learn values. Some stories stressed cooperation while others suggested that survival depended on following the example of tricksters who continually had to improvise ways to get out of trouble. When heroes were given an impossible task, they might counter with impossible conditions. In this way, they got out of having to do something that was unfair without being disrespectful to the person who had ordered it.

REVERENCE FOR ANCESTORS AND FOR THE ELDERLY

Ancestors have been important in African society from very early times. Families included ancestors as well as living members. Men, women, and children all felt connected to their ancestors and bore a sense of responsibility to future generations. Terra-cotta statuettes of kneeling male and female figures discovered in a niche in a doorway of one very old home in Jenne-Jeno might have represented ancestral spirits that family members prayed to for protection.

Many believed that when someone died, that person gradually moved from the world of the living to the spirit world. As long as he or she was remembered, that person belonged to the "living-dead." Being remembered gave the ancestor a kind of personal immortality. The living-dead returned to family members via dreams and maintained an interest in the family. Often living persons received instructions from the living-dead and tried to obey what they said, just as children would dutifully try to obey their parents.

Community members participated in acts of remembrance by pouring libations (liquid offerings) to departed ancestors or leaving their favorite foods in shrine houses. Usually the oldest family member performed these ceremonies because he remembered the most. These acts were not ancestor worship but rather rituals of remembrance. Much of the artwork was connected with veneration of ancestors, and masks were used to receive ancestral "voices."

The land on which the community had been established was sacred because the ancestors, not the living, owned it. Their feet had sunk deep into its soil, and they were buried in it. Acts of remembrance gave the living a way to serve the dead and often eased grief. When the last person who knew and could remember an ancestor died, that ancestor's spirit merged with earlier spirits and ceased to have any direct contact with anyone in the community.

WHAT ABOUT SLAVES?

Slavery was a common feature of African society, in part because there was often a shortage of laborers. Most slaves were captives in war; in fact, many wars were fought to get slaves, not to conquer territory. Muslim travelers reported on the many slaves they saw in the markets. Some claimed female slaves were more valuable than male slaves because men were likely to be killed in raids. Female slaves did needed work and also bore children.

To be a slave in a society that focused on the extended family and revered ancestors was especially tragic. Slaves had no ancestors to venerate nor family or lineage to protect them, so even if they gained their freedom, they were marginalized. On the other hand, a child born to a female slave and a free man was often treated like a distant relative rather than a slave, and his or her children were usually considered full-fledged members of the family.

Beliefs about the Supreme Spirit

Although different communities told their own stories of creation, most Africans seem to have believed that the world was created by a single, all-powerful divinity. That Supreme Spirit is self-sufficient, self-contained, all-knowing, and unchanging. In fact, it is so awe-inspiring that there are almost no images of it nor even attempts to symbolize it. The Pygmy say:

> In the beginning was God
> Today is God
> Tomorrow will be God.
> Who can make an image of God?

He has no body.
He is as a word that comes out of your mouth.
That word! It is no more,
It is past and still it lives!
So is God.

In describing the Supreme Spirit, the Gikuyu of Kenya say:

No father nor mother, no wife nor children;
He is all alone.
He is neither a child nor an old man.
He is the same today as he was yesterday.

This Gikuyu hymn suggests that the most other-than-human quality is being alone, reinforcing the belief that "to be human, you have to be connected." At some point the all-powerful divinity separated itself from the world of men and women. Its existence in another realm led to the belief in two worlds: the visible world in which people live and the invisible world of spirits. Spirits of living-dead ancestors connect the two worlds, serving as intermediaries between the living and the spirit world. Some of those spirits are related to nature, and their presence encourage people to try and live in harmony with the environment.

Nature is a part of the Supreme Spirit's creation, and there is little distinction between the sacred and the secular. Spirits can influence life in this world for good or ill. Rituals help people get in touch with the spirit world, forces of nature, and their ancestors. Through sorcery, evil spirits may be called upon to punish or harm others. In order to appease the spirits, men and women use divination to find out which spirits to address and what rituals those spirits require.

African civilizations, among the oldest in the world, created their own distinctive styles of organization and values. In part because of the continent's geographic conditions, most urbanized centers in African could not expand their control over much territory, although some empires, such as Ghana and Mali, did cover large areas. The Niger River was an important avenue for trade, and impressive cities, such as Gao and Timbuktu, thrived because they participated in that trading network. The vital Swahili city-states were connected to Indian Ocean trade, which accounted for much of its wealth. African values stressed the importance of the family, community and ancestors, and a complex system of social interdependence and cooperation characterized many of the early states.

Islam was increasingly important in various areas of Africa. After Mansa Musa's pilgrimage to Mecca, Timbuktu became a center of Islamic learning. Islam dominated life along the Swahili coast, and Muslim traders brought their faith to many areas. We shall now focus on the Abbasid Caliphate and examine the increasing influence of Islam not only in Africa but throughout Afro-Eurasia.

FROM THE ABBASID CALIPHATE
TO DAR AL-ISLAM

Setting the Stage

By 750, less than 130 years after Muhammad's first revelations, Muslim political and military power had spread from the Arabian Peninsula, over North Africa, into the Iberian Peninsula, and across western Asia. Impressive Muslim communities existed in West Africa and Ethiopia, and in 711 Muslims established a Umayyad province in Sind in northwestern India. Muslims were active traders all along the Silk Roads and supported diaspora communities as far away as China.

Conversions to Islam, which increased significantly in the eighth century, created problems for Arab Muslims who tended to look on non-Arab converts as inferior. During the Umayyad Caliphate, Arabs had the highest status, half-Arabs next, and non-Arab Muslims of whatever racial background next. Non-Muslims were at the bottom of the social hierarchy.

Although one of Muhammad's strongest directives had been the brotherhood of all believers, Arabs did not want to share their superior position with non-Arab Muslims. Understandably, non-Arab and half-Arab Muslims began to demand equal status. Many Arab soldiers had taken conquered women as concubines, and their half-Arab children demanded to be treated equally. This debate caused growing resentment against the Umayyad Caliphate, which was essentially an Arab-dominated government, and in 750 there was a major uprising against Umayyad rule.

The leader of the revolt was a distant relative of Muhammad. He was joined by Shii and non-Arab forces. They defeated the Umayyads and established the Abbasid Caliphate. In an effort to distance themselves from the former Umayyad dynasty, they moved their center of government into what had been Persian territory and allowed some Persians to hold government jobs. Although Arabs remained important at all levels of leadership, Egyptians, Syrians, and especially

Persians rapidly rose to position of power in the Abbasid Caliphate.

The Importance of Baghdad

In 756 al-Mansur, the second Abbasid caliph, ordered the building of Baghdad, a new capital. Baghdad was built on the Tigris River near the former Sassanid capital. It was a planned city and served as a political and commercial center. It was laid out in three concentric circles. By placing the ruler's palace at the center and the Friday Mosque to its side, al-Mansur attempted to underscore the Abbasids' political authority. The surrounding large plaza was used for drilling and the troops. Fearing that it was dangerous to have markets so near the palace, the caliph relocated the markets outside the original central city, while still maintaining the importance of trade in the capital.

Baghdad was heir to the wealth and sophisticated culture of the Sassanid and earlier Persian empires, and the court adopted many features of those earlier groups. The Abbasids chose not to focus on expanding their territory, but instead worked to consolidate and strengthen their empire and support urbanization that not only facilitated commerce, the arts and architecture but also the process of Islamization. By 800, Baghdad had become the second-largest city in the world at that time. Only Changan was larger.

Descriptions of Baghdad in the *Thousand and One Nights* illustrate the city's wealth. The story of Sinbad the Sailor suggests the vibrant commerce that existed in the Indian Ocean, and Muslim shippers and merchants dominated that trade. From Baghdad al-Mansur boasted: "There is no obstacle between us and China; everything on

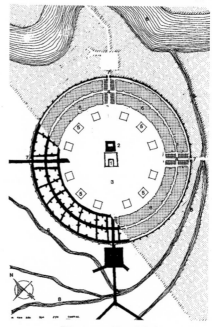

Diagram of Baghdad

the sea can come to us." One ninth-century Arab geographer described the area around the Persian Gulf as "the center of the world, the navel of the earth."

Achievements of the Abbasid Caliphate

The early ninth century Abbasid Caliphate has been described as the "world's richest and most powerful state, its capital the center of the planet's most advanced civilization"

> [Baghdad] had a thousand physicians, an enormous free hospital, a regular postal service, several banks (some of which had branches as far afield as China), an excellent water-supply system, a comprehensive sewage system, and a paper mill.

During the Abbasid Caliphate, Islamic civilization extended well beyond the area under the Caliphate's direct political control. Muslims merged aspects of Hellenic, Hellenistic, Roman, Byzantine, Persian, and Arab civilizations. Islamic civilization's impressive commercial strength and cultural achievements stretched from the Iberian Peninsula to the Indian subcontinent.

The wealth of the Muslim world resulted in part from many technological innovations. Improved irrigation projects increased agricultural yields, thus enlarging tax revenue. Islamic artisans created centers for manufacturing pottery, fabrics, rugs, metalwork, glass, and jewelry. They imported and distributed paper from China, and after the Battle of Talas in 751, when they captured Chinese soldiers who knew how to make paper, Muslims set up their own paper mills. Paper was better and cheaper to make than parchment, and cheaper books meant more people could own them, which stimulated literacy.

SCHOLARLY INNOVATIONS

Muslim scholars made significant scholarly advances in mathematics, science, and philosophy. In response to a request for books on mathematics, the Byzantine emperor sent al-Mansur Euclid's *Elements* and some works on physics. Borrowing the Indian concept of zero, place-numbers, and the base-ten system, in the ninth century al-Khwarizmi created algebra. Muslim mathematicians also worked out longitude and latitude.

The Persian scientist al-Razi (865–925) wrote about philosophy, logic, astronomy, math, physics, medicine and music and was also a renowned physician. He understood that a relationship exists between psychological and physical health: "The body is indeed changed by emotions. The emotions include: anger, joy, apprehension, sorrow, shame."

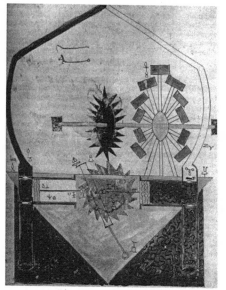

Two cylinder reciprocating pump

Al-Biruni (973–1048) used longitude to plot the coordinates of cities. His famous chessboard problem still intrigues scholars: a ruler was asked to give the amount of grain that would correspond to the number of grains on a chessboard with one grain on the first square, two on the second, four on the third, sixteen on the fourth and so on up to the 64th square. (Should the ruler agree to provide that much grain?)

Ibn Sina (Avicenna, 980–1037), a brilliant Persian scientist, wrote many books on topics as varied as astronomy, geometry, philosophy, theology, and art. He is most renowned for his medical discoveries, which were considered the best medical knowledge at that time anywhere in the world.

Ibn Rushd (1126–1198, known as Averroës in the west) was an authority on Aristotle and made extensive commentaries on the Greek scholar's work. He stressed that there was no conflict between scientific study and religious beliefs.

Poets played a very important role in Muslim culture as journalists, preachers, and entertainers. Like Homer in early Hellenic society, they were esteemed members of society. Baghdad was the home of

Omar Khayyam (d. 1120), a famous mathematician as well as poet, who wrote a collection of four-line verses called the *Rubaiyat* celebrating such things as nature, the transience of life, and the pleasures of love. Khayyam wrote during the decline of the Abbasid Caliphate, which may help explain the sense of sadness and impermanence that permeates his work. For example:

> But helpless Pieces of the Game He plays,
> Upon his Checker-board of Nights and Days;
> Hither and thither moves, and checks, and slays,
> And one by one back in the Closet lays.

> The Moving Finger writes: and, having writ,
> Moves on: nor all your Piety nor Wit
> Shall lure it back to cancel half a Line,
> Nor all your Tears wash out a Word of it.

SUPPORT FOR EDUCATION

Muslims made donations to foundations that supported worthy causes, such as establishing mosques, hospitals, schools, and orphanages. Because the Qur'an was central to Islam, Muslims considered literacy important and held each community responsible for producing scholars. Young people could attend schools affiliated with mosques free of charge, and elementary schooling was almost universal. Students gathered around learned men in the mosques to hear recitations from the Qur'an or scholarly texts. They memorized those texts and paid close attention to what the scholars had to say. The scholars gave successful students letters indicating which texts they had learned and were now allowed to teach.

The House of Wisdom in Baghdad, founded in 830, had an enormous library, observatory, museum, and training academy. Scholars from many different areas gathered there to study and exchange insights. Muslim scholars actively sought out Greek, Persian, and Syrian texts and had them translated into Arabic.

As Islamic knowledge advanced, educators needed a more systematic form of higher education, and in the early tenth century they created colleges called *madrasas* (places for giving lessons) near mosques. Soon madrasas were established in most of the large cities such as Baghdad, Damascus, and Aleppo as well as in Egypt and Jerusalem. They offered instruction in religion and law, and advanced study in science, mathematics, astronomy, physics, philosophy, literature, and history.

Because an increasing number of graduates of madrasas wanted more education, wealthy Muslim patrons supported the creation of universities. The most prominent university was built in Baghdad in the thirteenth century. Others were located in Cordoba, Toledo, Granada, and other cities. Al-Azhar, the University of Cairo, has been enrolling students continuously for more than a thousand years.

ARTISTIC EXPRESSION

Islamic artists and architects excelled in architecture, especially the construction of mosques and tombs. Nothing in the Qur'an prohibits representing living forms, but it was said that on the Day of Judgment, Allah would demand that everyone who had created an image of a living thing must bring it to life or be thrown into hell. Muslim artists may not have wanted to risk that fate. Islamic art uses the arabesque, geometric shapes, and calligraphy Many mosques and other public buildings are decorated with these patterns and with numerous quotations from the Qur'an.

Most Muslim paintings are book illustrations known as miniatures. Instead of using a vanishing point to create the illusion of distance, objects were placed higher up in the miniature. Some artists even tried to suggest how the world might look from Allah's vantage point by showing several angles of a building in the same picture or imagining how the earth might look from the heavens.

The Role of Slaves

Islam's dramatic expansion made it very difficult for the Abbasid Caliphate to maintain control over its vast territory. Although the Abbasid Caliphate fits the definition of an empire, Abbasid rule lasted little more than a century. Subjects far away from Baghdad questioned the value of the central government, and the Abbasids even had trouble controlling their own heartland in Mesopotamia and Persia. Tensions arose between Sunni and Shii Muslims, judicial and legislative groups, and Persian administrators and Turkish military forces. In addition, governors who were often independent rulers controlled the provinces.

The increasing use of slaves weakened Abbasid control. Muslims called white slaves *Mamluk*, an Arabic word for "owned," and black slaves *'abd*, which came to mean any black person. Muslims were prohibited from enslaving fellow Muslims or People of the Book (Jews, Christians, and Zoroastrians). Many slaves were bought, but most were prisoners of war or captured in raids. Muslims often fought to get slaves, not converts.

The revolt of Zanj slaves from eastern Africa in the late ninth century is a dramatic example of how slaves were treated. The Abbasid Caliphate brought slaves from Zanj to work removing the crust of salt that had collected on the land near Basra (in lower Mesopotamia) so that it could be cultivated again. Wealthy Muslims wanted to reclaim the land, basing their right to do so on a hadith stating that the person who rejuvenates a dead land becomes its proprietor.

The Zanj slaves lived under inhuman conditions. As many as five thousand workers were packed together, and their only food was a few handfuls of flour, semolina, and dates. Many of them had converted to Islam, but their owners ignored their claim that as Muslims they ought to be freed. Their hardships, coupled with the general weakness of the central government and discontent in the provinces, led them in 879 to revolt in an effort to get more food and acquire weapons. Initially they were successful, but their fourteen year struggle eventually failed. By the time the conflict was over, somewhere between five hundred thousand and two million had died. The Mesopotamian lowlands were abandoned, and the few surviving Zanj slaves were enrolled in the Abbasid army.

The Abbasids had difficulty recruiting troops, in part because they often were not paid. Military leaders thought that using slaves rather than local recruits had several distinct advantages. For one thing, officers could rely on their prompt and unquestioning obedience. Newly recruited slaves had no families, land, or other loyalties and were removed from any local disputes. Additionally, men from nomadic societies were trained to fight, and new slaves had not lost their fighting skills or been softened by urban life. However, letting Mamluks

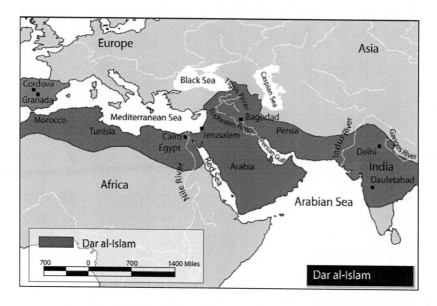

serve as officials and military officers and filling the majority of the fighting forces with them actually weakened Abbasid rule even though Islam prospered and spread.

Dar al-Islam

Dar al-Islam (all under Islam) refers to areas that share a common Muslim culture, either because the people are Muslim or because they are living under Muslim rule. The concept can be likened to "Christendom," because it refers to a community of faith rather than a centralized political control. By the middle of the ninth century Abbasid political authority became more symbolic than real. By then, much of the Abbasid caliphate's territory had been broken up into smaller states. However, this did not mean a lessening of Muslim power, because new lands were becoming part of Dar al-Islam

A group of Shi'ite Muslims, who traced their lineage back to Muhammad's daughter, conquered the Nile Valley in 969 and garrisoned their troops near the delta. They transformed the garrison al-Fustat into Cairo, which became their capital. As Cairo became a major entrepôt, trade through the Red Sea increased significantly. Its al-Azhar mosque was a major center of Muslim scholarship.

Islam made significant inroads in other parts of Africa as well.

Under leaders such as Sunjata and Mansa Musa, Mali, in West Africa, had become a Muslim state. A strong Muslim presence continued in the Swahili city-state along Africa's eastern coast as well as in North Africa.

LIFE IN AL-ANDALUS

In 711 Arab and Muslim-Berber forces had crossed the Strait of Gibraltar and established a Muslim presence in the Iberian Peninsula. It was known as al-Andalus (from *Vandalusia*, "the land of the Vandals"), and Moors (Muslim Berbers) settled there. Within a few months they had reached Toledo in the center of the peninsula and even made several forays across the Pyrenees into Frankish territory, including what they considered a minor skirmish at Tours in 732. After that defeat, they saw little point in pressing farther into territory the Franks held, as most of it was not only sparsely settled, but also undeveloped and would yield little plunder. (The Franks, on the other hand, viewed this battle as a major victory.) A series of governors sent out from Damascus administered al-Andalus for the Umayyads, collecting taxes and sending some of their resources back to Damascus, the Umayyad capital.

Almost from the start, Muslim Arab and Berber culture began to mix with the traditions of the local society. Because few women had accompanied the invaders, the Arabs and Moors soon began to marry local women. Umayyad governors worked hard to reduce ethnic, social, religious, and cultural tensions, and Jews and Christians were left relatively free to trade and

Great Mosque at Cordoba

practice their own beliefs. Jews were generally better off than their counterparts in the rest of Europe.

When the Abbasids came to power in 750, a young Umayyad prince who had survived the takeover fled to the Iberian Peninsula and established his Umayyad dynasty there. He and his successors ruled al-Andalus from Cordoba, their capital, until 1030. As Abbasid power weakened, Abd al-Rahman III (r. 912–61) challenged the legitimacy of the Abbasid Caliphate by taking the title caliph, and he attempted to give Cordoba the same status as Baghdad and Constantinople had. Some called the Great Mosque, built during his reign, the "ka'ba of the West." Its courtyard could hold the whole population of Cordoba when the faithful gathered there to pray.

Women played an active role in the society. Many were famous copyists, especially of the Qur'an. Others became teachers, lawyers, doctors, and librarians. At the same time women living under the Abbasids were increasingly required to wear veils, conceal their bodies, and accept a higher degree of seclusion, especially in the cities, perhaps as a result of Persian influences. Many were expected to stay in the women's quarters and not venture out into the public sphere that was the domain of men.

Al-Andalus became an impressive center of commerce and learning. Ibn Rushd, who came from Cordoba, studied Muslim texts and manuscripts from the Greco-Roman world at the universities at Toledo and Cordoba. Farmers devised new techniques for irrigation, raised grain, rice, olives, and grapes, and cultivated silkworms. Artisans produced fine textiles, dyed wool, silks, felts, and linens that merchants exported throughout the Muslim world. Artisans also worked ivory that they got from West Africa. Commerce benefited from trade in slaves from Scandinavia and Slavic areas who were sold in Christian markets to the north.

In the tenth century al-Andalus was one of the most cosmopolitan areas of the world, and Muslims, Jews, and Christians were involved in the lively hemispheric trade, not only carrying consumer goods but also spreading knowledge about Islamic culture, especially to Western Europe. Cordoba, the largest city in the world in 1000, was home to about half a million people. As one scholar has written: "From the point of view of the rough and cold Christian north, it was

Hall of the Ambassadors

a haven of warmth, sophistication, and refinement in every aspect of life—from the clothes that were worn to the buildings that were built to the ideas that were created and the knowledge that was pursued."

North Africa, another area that broke free of Abbasid control but continued to be a strong Muslim state, was taken over in the early eleventh century by two different groups of conservative Muslim Berbers. The first group ruled not only North Africa but al-Andalus as well. The second group ruled North Africa, the southern part of al-Andalus, and the western Sudan, significantly weakening Ghana in the process. Under its rule Arabic and literacy spread throughout the area, and trade across the Sahara increased. Two-thirds of the gold circulating in Europe and North Africa in the fourteenth century came from the western Sudan.

The last Muslim dynasty to rule in al-Andalus built the Alhambra (started in 1333), a series of palaces on a hilltop in Granada. The outside walls are made of plain red brick, but the interior courtyards and rooms are richly decorated with inlaid wood and carved ceilings. In the Hall of the Ambassadors, where the ruler met visiting dignitaries, the carved ceiling resembles the night sky. The Court of the Lions has one hundred twenty-eight marble pillars. The exquisite plaster ceiling of the Hall of the Two Sisters, constructed like a honeycomb, appears to float in space. The palaces had plumbing and many water fountains, canals, pools, and baths.

SELJUKS MAKE INROADS IN ANATOLIA

Near the end of the first millennium, various groups of Turks started migrating out of the inner Asian steppes and moving south. They came very gradually but so continuously that people in the settled areas hardly realized that these newcomers might pose a danger, and so initially they did not try to resist them. Some Muslim leaders hired them as mercenaries or enslaved them and forced them to serve as Mamluks in their armies.

Gradually it became apparent that some of the Turkish tribes were a threat. The Seljuks, a branch of Western Turks, had been grazing their animals for several hundred years on the grasslands that stretch between the Altai Mountains and the Caspian Sea. Islamic traders, Buddhist missionaries, Nestorian Christians, and countless other travelers and traders passed through this area. When an army of Arab Muslims invaded their region in the eighth century, some Seljuks converted to Islam, although few fully understood or carefully followed the dictates of the faith.

When the Seljuks invaded Abbasid territory, they met little resistance from the caliphate and were able to capture Baghdad in 1055. They now faced the question of what to do about the caliph. Would their position be stronger if they got rid of the caliphate altogether and created their own government or let him remain? They decided to leave the caliph as the spiritual authority, but install a Seljuk as sultan, or secular monarch, who had the political authority. The caliph was reduced to little more than a figurehead, but the Seljuks believed his blessing would give some legitimacy to their rule.

Augmenting their forces with other Turkish mercenaries and Mamluks, the Seljuks defeated the Byzantines at the Battle of Manzikert in 1071 and took control of much of Anatolia. This victory, which brought Anatolia into Dar al-Islam, significantly weakened Byzantium. Seljuk military officers, many of whom acted as though no central Seljuk authority existed, ruled over the newly conquered territory. They did not realize they would soon face European crusaders eager to defend Constantinople against additional Turkish conquests.

Qtib Minar

AFGHAN TURKS PENETRATE NORTH INDIA

Dar al-Islam also extended into the India subcontinent. Although Umayyad forces had created a province in Sind (in northwestern India) in the seventh century, most people living in the subcontinent were unaware of Islam's enormous power until Muslim Turkish nomads in Afghanistan started a series of raids in the tenth century. The lure of India's wealth probably motivated their attacks, and they looted cities of their gold, jewels, and women. In the process, they destroyed many Hindu temples. However, after looting they returned to their homeland and used the spoils to support their kingdoms..

Towards the end of the twelfth century another series of Afghan attacks commenced, but this time the invaders wanted to annex land as well as plunder. When the Afghan/Turkish forces captured Delhi, they left a Mamluk general to govern the area. He oversaw the construction of the first mosque built in India, using stones taken from twenty-six nearby Hindu temples that his men had destroyed. He then ordered the building of a massive minaret—the Qutb Minar—to symbolize Islam's power in the subcontinent. This was the start of the first of five dynasties known as the Delhi Sultanates. They ruled North India from Delhi from 1206 to 1526.

Perhaps the most colorful, if cruel, sultanate leader was Muhammad Tughlak (r. 1325–51), who kept trying to conquer territory south of the Deccan. In an effort to effectively supervise his southern conquests, he ordered the building of an entirely new capital on the Deccan plateau at Daulatabad, almost one thousand miles from Delhi, and summarily forced most of his administration, as well as crafts-men and other artisans, to move there. But ruling from Daulatabad left the north vulnerable to attack, so his successor just as precipi-tously returned everyone to Delhi.

During the period that followed, when no strong sultan emerged, Timur, another central Asian Turko-Mongol leader, invaded the sub-continent. Because a battle wound had left him with a limp, Timur was called "the Lame," and he became known as Tamerlane. Perhaps the most brutal of all the nomadic leaders, Tamerlane's armies devas-tated vast areas, and he even ordered his men to construct towers out of the decapitated heads of his enemies. In 1398 his forces sacked Delhi, massacring most of its inhabitants, except for artisans and women whom they carried back as slaves to Samarkand, his capital. The Delhi Sultanate continued to rule North India after the fires of Tamerlane's devastation cooled, but it never regained significant power.

Although Seljuk Turks significantly weakened the Abbasid Caliphate, the Seljuks extended and strengthened Muslim rule in ter-ritory formerly under Byzantine control, and Afghan Turks extended Muslim rule in North India. Not everyone thought the arrival of the Turks was a bad thing. Some believed they brought a new kind of energy and sense of purpose to Islam (not unlike the Germanic invaders whom some thought had revived a dying Rome). Ibn Khaldun (1332–1406), the great Arab historian whom many consider the first world historian, saw the coming of the Turks as

> proof of God's continuing concern for the welfare of Islam and the Muslims. At the time when the Muslim Caliphate had become weak and degenerate, incapable of resisting its enemies, God in his wisdom and benevolence had brought new rulers and defend-ers, from among the great and numerous tribes of the Turks, to revive the dying breath of Islam and restore the unity of the Muslims.

Muslim political power had moved from the Arab-dominated Umayyad Caliphate to the much larger Persian-dominated Abbasid

Caliphate, but by the tenth century Abbasid control had weaken. In its place a collection of smaller Muslim states under the broader umbrella of Dar al-Islam thrived. Dar al-Islam stretched from the Iberian Peninsula to the Indian subcontinent and included significant areas in Africa. Within it, Muslim merchants, relying on a common set of rules and support, made new contacts and contracts; scholars, using Arabic as their common language, studied with learned men in a wide variety of cultures; and average men and women, following the Qur'an, hadith, and the traditions of the community, sensed they were a part of a vast brotherhood that stretched far beyond their immediate communities and their local rulers.

A brief list of some common English words that derive from Arabic, selected from hundreds of examples, is one small example of the enormous influence of Islamic culture in Europe and the wider world. Tariff, check, magazine, alcohol, alfalfa, sugar, syrup, admiral, algebra, amalgam, alkali, soda, and almanac are just a few of the terms that have entered the English language. These words suggest the intricate system of exchanges and influences taking place after the tenth century, and they direct us to consider the significant influence Islam had in the intellectual expansion of Europe as it grew from a sparsely settled, backward area to an increasingly urban and literate society. It is to the development of Europe that we now turn.

SCENE FOUR

EUROPE UNDER CHRISTENDOM

Setting the Scene

The Xiongnu—mounted horsemen from Inner Asia who threatened China—and Germanic migrations into the Roman Empire were part of a hemispheric movement of peoples that occurred at the start of the common era. The Romans identified the largest contingent of newcomers as *Germani*. Their gradual migration into Europe was accelerated by the appearance in Europe of the Xiongnu, whom both Germanic groups and Romans called "Huns." China had established a relative truce with the Xiongnu during the Early Han (206–9 B.C.E.), but at the start of the common era the Xiongnu launched new raids into China and also headed west. By the fourth century C.E. they had pushed several Germanic groups into Roman territory. In 441 invaders attacked Rome, and by the end of the century the Western Roman Empire no longer existed.

Compared to their Byzantine, Chinese, and Islamic neighbors, Western Europeans in the centuries after 500 C.E. were quite backward. Most were illiterate, innocent of science and technology, and crude in their lifestyles. As one scholar put it, "Material conditions throughout this period were so primitive that we can almost speak of five centuries of camping out." To their more sophisticated neighbors, these settlers must have seemed like uncouth barbarians. The contrast with the world of Islam is especially dramatic if we remember that when Charlemagne (768–814) came to power, there were no major cities in Europe, except Rome, while the Abbasid capital of Baghdad, founded in 756, was already one of the world's major intellectual and commercial centers.

When the Frankish leader Clovis (481–511) accepted Christianity, the Church gained an important foothold in western Europe. Frankish soldiers, using saddles and stirrups, were the best horsemen in Europe and soon defeated their rivals, enabling Clovis to establish the first real military kingdom in Western Europe. Over three hundred years later, Charlemagne led the Franks to control even more area, but his kingdom lasted only through his own lifetime.

Decentralized Europe

Following Charlemagne's death his son Louis kept the kingdom together for a time, but his heirs could not contain the nobles. After bitter fighting, Louis's sons divided the kingdom into three territories that became the rough outlines of modern France, Germany, and parts of Spain and Italy, but these kingdoms lasted less than a hundred years. After that, western Europe took a step backward. Without even the semblance of central control to keep order and maintain roads and bridges, the vast majority of the population depended almost entirely on subsistence farming.

Counts assumed direct ownership of the land they had been administering during Charlemagne's rule. In turn they gave parts of their land to loyal lesser nobles who became their vassals. These vassals then gave some of their land to loyal followers who became their vassals, and so on down the line to the peasants. Prosperous counts built elaborate, even luxurious, houses on their estates along with outbuildings that often included kitchens, bakeries, wineries and breweries, carpentry shops, stables and cowsheds, pigsties, and hay barns. These estates were called manors, and over the centuries they grew in size and complexity. The early manors were usually surrounded by low earthen walls or hedges.

After the collapse of the Carolingian state, owners of manors experimented with different ways to find laborers, including using both tenant farmers and paid workers. The peasants who worked the fields lived outside the manor walls in simple one- or two-room thatched huts and often shared their small living space with animals. Sometimes farmers negotiated contracts with owners and were paid accordingly. Other peasants worked for an owner for a specific number of hours per week; after that, they could till their own land.

A peasant woman's life was harsh and difficult. Besides giving birth and raising children, she ground the grain, baked bread, kept the fires going, looked for wood, cared for animals, and planted and maintained small gardens. In her spare time she might spin flax and wool, dye cloth or patch worn-out clothes. Men tended to specialize in farming the fields of grain and looking after the larger animals, especially horses. There was almost no trade with outside areas and little money to purchase luxury items, and most people led spartan lives.

Vikings and Magyars

Woman with child

The Vikings, also known as Norse, were Germanic nomads who settled in present-day Norway, Sweden, and Denmark. Viking sailors were the best European seamen of their time, and they raided Europe's Atlantic coast as well as along its major interior rivers, terrifying many groups. Danish Vikings occupied Britain and carved out an enclave in northern France at Normandy. Norwegian Vikings invaded Britain and settled in Ireland and western Britain. Swedish Vikings entered what is now Russia and sailed to the Black and Caspian seas. Some even reached Greenland and Newfoundland.

Many of the early scraps of information about the Vikings were written by Europeans whom they terrified. Prayers such as "From the fury of the Northmen, O Lord deliver us," suggest they considered the Vikings violent and barbaric. For nearly two hundred years, people in the settled communities thought they intended to carry off everything of worth, including people they sold as slaves.

No doubt the Vikings were fierce warriors, but they were not much different from other Europeans of the time. Like most people, they were loyal to their families. They lived in small farming communities governed by a common set of values. However, they did supplement their farm production by making seasonal raids into Europe, where they sacked towns, leaving destruction in their wake.

The Magyars, who came from the Asian steppes, were non–Indo-European speaking people like the Finns. By the end of the ninth century, they were living in what is now Hungary. From there they launched raids deep into Europe and for about sixty years stormed into the heartland of the former Carolingian kingdom. Similar to the Vikings and equally dreaded, they survived by looting and kidnapping rich nobles and holding them for ransom. By 955 the princes of Europe managed to unite and defeat them. The Magyars then returned to Hungary and tried their hand at an agricultural way of life.

The Growth of Manors

The absence of any semblance of central authority and the relative peace and security it usually provides convinced large numbers of peasants to seek protection by becoming serfs on neighboring estates. Many must have felt that trying to fend for themselves would result in death or enslavement. Serfs had the right to till a portion of land and pass that right on to their children, but they could not leave the manors nor bargain for better conditions. They were allowed to keep a portion of what they grew, but the major share belonged to the lord of the estate.

Slowly these estates were transformed into large walled manors. Because roads were in poor repair and travel and trade were unsafe, each manor strove to be self-sufficient. Artisans seeking safety also flocked to the protection of the manors, which grew to include workshops and usually at least one mill and a church. To provide the promised protection, each manor raised its own private army consisting of armor-clad men called knights who fought on horseback. It was very expensive to support the heavy horses and knights. As the manors began to raise herds of horses, lords diverted land normally used for growing food to grazing horses and growing alfalfa and hay to feed the horses. Serfs had to support even greater numbers of specialized groups, especially knights, and they watched their already meager standard of living decline still further.

Initially knights were often crude and boorish men who loved to fight, drink, and satisfy their other appetites. Armor, stirrup, lance, and large horses transformed them into a highly effective fighting force. Standing with their feet in the stirrups, they could ride at full speed and use their lances to knock their adversaries off their horses. Knights began to live with their women and children near the manor's watchtowers and were supposed to be ready at all times to defend the manor or go to war.

Gradually the manorial system, with a permanent class of serfs, became a major way of life in several parts of Europe. Many historians refer to this arrangement as a "feudal system" because land (feud) was its centerpiece. The manor was the source of food and security and provided the only protection and control that existed.

European-Style Feudalism

Successful lords gave their vassals parcels of land. Vassals swore allegiance to their lord, and every noble was a vassal of a higher noble. The most important bond was between the lord and his vassal, but vassals were not always loyal to their lords, and they might change sides depending on which lord had the most land or the best chance for victory. By 1000, various levels of lords and vassals had become increasingly frustrated because they could not count on anyone's loyalty. As a result, they began to formalize these relationships with oaths and contracts.

Vassals' responsibilities included fighting for a specific period, usually forty days per year, and providing hospitality should the lord visit their manors. Vassals were also expected to furnish additional knights for their lords in time of war. Vassals, in turn, were lords of their own manors and their knights were their vassals; they also controlled their artisans and serfs.

Lords were also expected to give advice on personal matters, to protect their vassals in law courts, to come to the aid of their vassals if attacked, and generally to treat them with fairness. Nobles could be both lords of their own land and vassals to other lords. Lords lived relatively comfortable lives, sleeping on mattresses and eating from dishes, but owing to their often rapidly shifting fortunes, their lives were also insecure. (The system of large land-based estates that supported knights can be compared with the triumph in Japan of the daimyo and regional units based on samurai military might.)

European feudalism was tightly hierarchical and became increasingly formalized. A thirteenth-century poet wrote rather idealistically about the system:

> One toils in the fields, one prays, and one defends.
> In the fields, in the town, in the Church,
> These three help each other
> Through their skills, in a nicely regulated scheme.

After the tenth century, the majority of farm laborers throughout northern Europe served as serfs, even though large pockets of free labor existed. Serfs' lives were harsh, and they had almost no prospect of achieving their freedom or bettering themselves, except in heaven after death. Lords were the only source of justice, and serfs had no recourse except the will of their superiors. Lords routinely tried to force their serfs to produce more and to work maintaining waterways, roads, walls, and mills. Actual descriptions of the lives of serfs were not so idealistic. Even when they were no longer serfs but

Twelve months of work

were free (villains), they still had to cultivate a certain parcel of land and give dues and services to its owner:

> In June the peasants must cut and pile the hay and carry it to the manor house. In August they must reap and carry in the convent's grain; their own grain lies exposed to wind and rain . . . On the Nativity of the Virgin, the villein owes one pig in eight, at St. Denis's day the manorial dues; at Christmas the fowl, fine and good, and thereafter the grain due of two measures of barley and three quarters of wheat; on Palm Sunday the sheep due; at Easter he must plough, sow and harrow. When there is building the tenant must bring stone and serve the mason; he must also haul the convent's wood for two deniers a say.

No wonder it was said: "This unhappy class owns nothing which in not bought by hard toil."

Church officials and clergy made up the third major group in European feudalism. Serving as a church official, priest, or bishop opened up many jobs that, in theory, any man could perform. In fact the Church offered the best means of social mobility. By 1000, monasteries were being integrated into the economic development of Europe. Monks from monasteries that were under the same set of rules, such as the Benedictines, could communicate with one another across the continent.

A woman's social class determined her place in the feudal hierarchy. Female serfs labored in the fields along with the men and cared for their children as well. Often there was little food to prepare. The average diet consisted largely of porridge, beer, bread and butter, and some pork. The lord and knights of the manor frequently made female serfs serve as their mistresses. Noblewomen had more power, especially when their husbands were off fighting. They could inherit land if they were widowed or had no sons. Because land was so important, these women were ardently sought after. Marriage was a key to political power, and estates were enlarged and kingdoms built by arranging marriage alliances.

Nunneries provided an important outlet for women and were the only way they could escape from their traditional duties as wives and mothers. Several women serving in religious orders made significant literary contributions. Hildegard of Bingen, who lived from 1098 to 1179, wrote on a wide variety of subjects, including science. Popes honored her mystic visions, and her musical scores were widely known. She is now regarded as one of the most original medical writers of the twelfth century. Christine de Pisan (1365–1430) was a professional writer and supported her family by writing.

As manors expanded, lords sought better fortifications. Wooden watchtowers were added to the earthen walls, ditches, and the dirt mounds that served as a lookout site. Gradually moats and higher watchtowers were built. By the late eleventh century, craftsmen learned from the Muslims how to build stone castles. Four-storied buildings with walls that might be as much as fourteen feet thick were bordered by several stone towers and gatehouses with iron gratings; gradually, huge walls were built around them. The lords lived in and ruled from their castles in which serfs could seek refuge in case of attack. The growth of large castles was a major factor in stemming the rise of centralized states throughout western Europe from the tenth to the thirteenth centuries.

Chivalry

In an effort to reduce fighting, popes and bishops began to introduce the idea of holy days to commemorate saints or important religious events. On these holidays, fighting was prohibited, and games and feasts were held instead.

Beginning in the twelfth century, the nobility developed a code of conduct called chivalry to temper the militaristic nature of the feudal system, not unlike the Code of Bushido in Japan. This informal system was a synthesis of Germanic customs, Roman practice, and Christian morality. Its values included honesty, modesty, loyalty, and duty. A knight was bound to obey his lord, protect the virtue of women, help the weak, honor his commitments, and wage war against the infidel (Muslims). Chivalry also entailed rituals, heraldry, titles, and prescribed ways of talking and thinking. Christianity and chivalry formed the core values of later feudal society and culture for the

A troubador sings to the ladies

nobility and knights.

Decreasing military threats and a lessening of tribal conflicts may help explain why chivalry became associated with courtly romance. Knights tried to impress lovely ladies with songs and gallant gestures instead of performing valiant deeds on the battlefield. European troubadours (court poets) glorified romantic, unrequited, love. For example:

> Alas! How much I thought I knew
> About love, and how little I know!
> For I can't keep myself from loving
> Her who'll give me nothing in return.

It is intriguing to speculate the extent to which troubadours might have been influenced by Muslim poets in al-Andalus. Both used love as a metaphor: Muslim poets celebrated love of Allah, while troubadours idealized sensual love.

With diminished warfare and the rise of chivalry, many knights began to make a living as sportsmen in large tournaments. These heroes, like today's rock stars and athletes, were popular with young ladies who often gave these weekend warriors colorful pieces of cloth to carry when they jousted. Although the Church officially con-

demned these tournaments along with the crowd violence, binge
drinking, and free sexual activities they fostered, their popularity continued to grow and the clergy could do little to stop them.

Tensions between Secular and Sacred Values

Devout Christians frequently preached against the Church for failing
to implement its own spiritual values as well as for the countless contradictions between its lofty beliefs and actual practices. By the thirteenth century, the Church controlled nearly one-third of the land in
Europe and wielded enormous economic and political power. Because
land was the main basis of power in Europe from 500 to 1200, the
Church wanted as much land as it could get. Church holdings were
supposed to support its work conducting schools, running hospitals,
looking after the poor, supervising the clergy, and managing the network of churches and cathedrals. However, the Church often managed
these large segments of land as if they were secular estates. Church
officials maintained serfs and knights and tried to maximize their own
power and profits.

Critics of the Church's worldliness leveled their severest censure
against the pope, claiming he was living like a Roman emperor, in a
splendid palace surrounded by some of the world's great art treasures,
and protected by Swiss guards and attended by numerous cardinals
and bishops. Popes who seemed to enjoy an excessive amount of
worldly pleasures were subject to especially harsh criticism.

In response the Church vacillated between attacking reform groups
as heretics and acknowledging their concerns had merit. By the early
thirteenth century, some of the more spiritual protests could not be
ignored, especially those expressed by two monastic orders, the
Franciscans and Dominicans. St. Francis (1182-1226) was born into a
wealthy merchant family but renounced all his worldly goods and
adopted a life of poverty and prayer. Penniless, he wandered around
serving the poor, preaching about the interrelationship of nature, and
calling all creatures his "brothers" and "sisters." Francis attracted a
large number of followers and finally won approval from the pope for
his monastic way of life. He also organized an order for women and a
lay fraternity.

Dominic of Spain (ca. 1170-1221) founded the Order of Friars

A Giotto fresco: St. Francis renounces his earthly possessions

Preachers. (They are mendicant monks who survive on the alms they receive.) He devoted much of his time preaching to those the Church believed were following corrupt forms of Christianity. Both groups took vows of poverty, chastity, and obedience, and friars from both groups traveled throughout Europe and even to Asia.

New Farming Technologies Support More People

Western European farmers and serfs were slowly developing new crops and farming methods in what some scholars have called a mini-agricultural revolution. Between the eighth and tenth centuries, Muslims brought many Indian and Chinese crops to West Asia, and they gradually spread to Europe and Africa. Major Asian crops

An iron plow

included wheat, rice, sugarcane, bananas, oranges, lemons, mangos, watermelons, coconut palms, spinach, artichokes, and eggplant, as well as cotton. Muslims also introduced important new irrigation and other farming techniques.

In the ninth century, European craftsmen had constructed a heavy wheeled iron plow, adapted from earlier moldboard plows first used in China. The new plow sliced like a knife through the thick European sod, turning the soil over, burying sod and weeds, and readying the dirt for harrowing and planting. It also created a series of furrows and embankments that allowed waterlogged soil to drain. Most peasants used several teams of oxen to pull the plow because horses were very expensive. As feudal wars decreased, more large horses became available. Concurrently, metal horseshoes that protected the horses' hooves from the moist northern soils were developed. The introduction of metal-based, water-driven saws, grinding mills, and windmills also expanded agricultural yields.

Between 1000 and 1300, arable farmland in Europe increased three hundred percent, especially in the highly fertile northern plain stretching into Germany. One innovation, the three-field system, enabled farmers to increase their production by fifty percent. The technique, adapted from a similar pattern developed in ancient China, set aside one field to be left fallow while another was planted with rye or winter wheat, and the third with oats, barley, or vegetables.

Towns and Trade Develop

Higher farm production resulted in larger food surpluses that, in turn, supported more people and fostered the development of towns. New towns usually emerged around river crossings, seaports, and where trade routes crossed. They led to increased commerce, enhanced industrial production, and ushered in a new spirit of cosmopolitanism. Artisans, merchants, moneylenders, traders, and other professionals began to develop a market economy. By 1300 Europe's major river valleys had been cleared, and navigation along the major water routes such as the Rhine, Danube, and Po rivers was becoming increasingly common. Towns along these rivers began to grow into cities.

Knights with little or no land, lords seeking greater autonomy, and artisans who wanted to go into business for themselves all welcomed the increased trade and new towns. Because towns fostered a growing sense of equality and freedom, serfs who could leave the manors also flocked to the towns, hoping to lose their semislave status.

The periods of peace that the Church imposed facilitated trade and the flow of information. The Church, however, was not enthusiastic about the rise of commercialism. The clergy insisted that buying and selling, and especially borrowing and lending money, violated the will of God. As a result, Jewish merchants controlled much of the commerce prior to the thirteenth century. As more Christians than Jews became involved in business, European Christian businessmen began to persecute Jews and expel them from Western Europe.

The number of merchants proliferated as demand for luxury goods, such as silk, spices, jewelry, fine cotton, and porcelain from Asia, rose. Venetian and Genoese merchants soon found themselves in the enviable position of supplying consumer goods to the rest of Europe. Each year they took goods from Asia and their own products to large gatherings called fairs, such as those at Champagne in northeastern France. Large periodic trade fairs also developed in major towns along the Rhine River and linked the rising European trade with the more prosperous Mediterranean commercial centers.

Traders also promoted confederations that gave them control over commerce. One of the most important was the Hanseatic League, which organized and regulated trade from London all the way to Novgorod (in present-day Belarus). As many as a hundred towns

A merchant at home

joined the league, and it controlled trade in furs, fish, hemp, wax, flax, grain, and timber across northern Europe, on the Rhine River, and on the coasts of the Baltic and North seas.

Merchants developed standard weights and measures and a crude pricing system for their goods. They also adapted systems of credit Muslim merchants were already using. They bonded together into guilds and developed common commercial rules and ways to enforce them. Merchant guilds even established monopolies over certain trade routes and locations.

Because the nobility, and to some extent the Church, wanted luxury items, nobles began to offer merchants permanent grants of land where they could live together in relative peace and promote their businesses. They also offered artisans rent-free shops if they would move to certain towns; sometimes they provided them with tools and lent them money to start businesses. Many of the land grants turned into towns and later cities. Merchants with feudal loyalties to the lords who had granted them land soon had money to pay off their obligations. Nobles who wanted cash were more than happy to make financial settlements.

To meet the need for a dependable supply of raw materials, businessmen invested in activities that fostered greater production. They encouraged cotton growing in areas nearer Europe. Wool merchants often signed long-term contracts with herders to assure the supply of raw wool. As the cotton and wool industries grew, specialized workers including carders, spinners, weavers, fullers, and dyers developed.

Artisans, like merchants, also began to organize their crafts into guilds and regulate both the supply of materials and the laborers who made the products. Each guild met regularly in its own hall and established rules and guidelines for how its members should act. Guilds served as a major political interest group to limit competition and regulate the number of licensed craftsmen. Sometimes craft guilds openly fought with one another and with merchant guilds.

Members of craft guilds clustered in specific quarters of towns similar to communities in Muslim cities. Their members socialized together, established common charities, and sponsored common religious festivals. Guilds elected their own leaders to protect their rights and privileges. By 1300 Paris, Europe's largest city at that time with a population of perhaps 80,000, was home to a hundred craft and merchant guilds.

Artisans, traders, merchants, and middlemen involved in commerce were growing into a new class called the bourgeoisie, or middle class. (*Bourg,* or burgh, as in *Pittsburgh,* referred to a town, and *bourgeoisie* meant people who lived in towns.) The bourgeoisie stood between the nobility and peasants and were a major threat to the feudal system. As the bourgeoisie grew and prospered, it began to demand more say in politics and became a potential source of support for those who wanted to rule.

City-States Become Prosperous

New cities and a class of merchants were gradually bringing Europeans into the complex hemispheric trading system. Dramatic changes were taking place in the northern part of the Italian peninsula, particularly in Genoa and Venice. Venice had started as a province and ally of the Byzantine Empire. In 1082 the Byzantine emperor exempted the city from the duties its territories normally paid and guaranteed its merchants free transit throughout the empire. Venice soon became Europe's major port for West Asian products as well as luxury items from India, China, and North Africa. It was active in the southern trade route through the Red and Arabian seas and the Indian Ocean. Across the Italian peninsula Genoa grew into a major Mediterranean port. Merchants from Genoa also dominated the northern route through Constantinople and the Black Sea.

City of Good Government

City-states in northern Italy were becoming powerful and prosperous. By the twelfth century Florence had become a great banking center, and its emerging middle class was creating an independent systems of government. Merchants imported large quantities of wool from farther north, and the city was a major producer of woolen textiles. Florentine leaders had to deal with the divisive impact of competing factions, one supported by the Church and the other by the emperor. This wealthy city could boast of some of the most creative men of the age, including Dante, Giotto, and Brunelleschi, the architect of Florence's famous landmark, the cathedral.

Meanwhile, other small European towns and cities were also thriving. The textile-producing region of Flanders, in northern Europe, with the city of Bruges as its commercial and financial capital, sent goods throughout Europe and beyond. Many port cities began to engage in commerce and long-distance trade. Scandinavians, descendants of the Vikings, who were familiar with sailing and trading, dominated trade from the North Sea to Kiev. They bartered fish, furs, and timber for cloth, grain, and wine and established close commercial ties with both the Muslim and Byzantine empires.

Outside Influences, Universities, and Scholasticism

Thanks to the proximity of the Byzantine and Islamic civilizations, Europeans gained access to the best, most up-to-date scholarship in the world, and Muslim scholars had significant influence on European development. For example, by 770, scholars had brought the Indian concept of place numbers and zero to Baghdad and from there the radically new number system traveled first to al-Andalus and later to the rest of Europe.

Muslims' advances in mathematics, the work of scholars such as Ibn Rushd (Averroes), whose work reintroduced Greek learning to Europe, and al-Razi's insights in medicine, as well as his many other contributions, had a profound impact in European scholars. Scholars studied translations of Aristotle along with Ibn Rushd's commentaries and took special interest in his argument that there was no conflict between scientific study and religious beliefs. All these influences contributed to the rapid growth of formal education and a new intellectual vitality in Europe.

Many factors hastened the development of universities in Europe: the development of cities and a wealthy merchant class, a more complex church organization, and the need to be able to recruit educated officials.

By the tenth century large cathedrals began supporting schools that anyone who could meet the admission requirements and had the leisure time needed for study could attend. These schools offered instruction in literature, history, theology, mathematics, and astronomy as well Arabic, Greek, and Latin. Besides works of law, students studied centuries-old Greek and Roman texts that Muslim, Jewish, and Byzantine scholars had preserved, copied, and annotated. They also provided access to Islamic scientific and mathematical scholarship.

Bologna, the first real university in Europe, was established in Italy in the middle of the twelfth century. Bolognese scholars were in demand because they had successfully mastered both Church and commercial law and were able to identify contradictions between them, and students flocked to the city to study with these masters. However, these students did not have any legal rights because they were not citizens of the city. To make matters worse, Bologna's legal residents thought the young men were rowdy, boisterous delinquents, more interested in drinking and picking up women than in studying.

To protect themselves, the students banded together in a *universitas* that was something like a large guild. Its members paid dues and elected rectors who ran its day-to-day affairs. The students hired masters (professors), for whom they established guidelines, and whom they expected would explain course objectives and organization. Students fined masters for being even a minute late for classes or exceeding the allotted time. By 1350 the city had the right to appoint masters and had established dormitories where students lived and could be supervised. It also monitored and maintained higher professional standards for masters.

While students were instrumental in creating the university at Bologna, in Paris it was the masters who organized a universitas. By 1200 the faculty had earned the right to certify all candidates for degrees and to govern itself. It elected a rector to administer the university and oversee all the departments, each with its own dean. The curriculum included theology, medicine, law, and philosophy.

From the thirteenth to the fifteenth centuries many of the world's famous universities were established in Europe, including those of Oxford, Cambridge, and Paris. Students were indeed a privileged group in these increasingly complex European urbanizing societies. Universities attracted students from all over Europe, and they studied a common core of texts taught by a fairly standard method. Moreover, they mingled socially, discussed similar academic interests, and helped create a common European culture, at least among the intellectual elite.

THE DEVELOPMENT OF SCHOLASTICISM
New ideas and translations, particularly of Aristotle's works, and the exciting exchange of ideas among new generations of European students led to a movement called scholasticism. It began with Peter Abelard (1079–1144) and culminated with Thomas Aquinas (1225–74). A dashing, brilliant student in Paris, Abelard often intimidated his teachers with his learning and debating ability. He fell in love with Héloïse, one of his students, and they had a child out of wedlock. Héloïse's uncle was so angry that he had the young Abelard

castrated. Abelard then retired to a monastery, and Héloïse became a nun. Even so, they corresponded until Héloïse died.

Abelard was perhaps the first genuine intellectual that Christian Europe produced. In discussing sin, he emphasized what a person intended to do rather than what one actually did, and he updated Augustine's doctrine of grace. By stressing human reason as a guide to morality, he contradicted many of the Church leaders of his time.

Thomas Aquinas, making good use of the knowledge of Aristotle that Ibn Rushd and other Arab scholars had provided, constructed a modern system of theology. In his most famous work, *Summa Theologica*, Aquinas argued that faith must be supplemented by reason and that the study of the natural world is a legitimate way to understand God's will. He also emphasized that good works in addition to faith were an important means of achieving salvation. Gradually the Church adopted Aquinas's philosophy as the core of its teachings and practices. His emphasis on good works prepared the Church to deal with more complex political and social realities and to accept the expanding values of merchants and traders.

The faith/reason question, as well as Muslim influence, is dramatically illustrated in the fourteenth-century fresco *Triumph of St. Thomas* on the wall of the Spanish Chapel in the Church of Santa Maria Novella in Florence. Thomas Aquinas is surrounded by seven religious virtues, several evangelists and prophets, and female figures representing the theological sciences and liberal arts. Under his feet are three images: two shadowy figures of Christian heretics—Arius and Sabellius—flank Ibn Rushd who thoughtfully looks out from the whole scene. We can speculate as to whether Ibn Rushd is the third heretic or whether the fresco suggest that St. Thomas is building on his scholarship.

The transition from the Augustinian worldview based on faith and love, which had shaped and supported the Church's early success, to Aquinas, who championed good works as the means to salvation, demonstrates the fundamental changes that had taken place in European society between 500 and 1200. Augustine had lived during the demise of the Roman Empire; his world was capricious, disorderly, and harsh, so it is little wonder that his theology stressed faith and a better world in heaven, a "city of God.". By the time of

The Triumph of St. Thomas

Aquinas, Europeans were building towns and enjoying the fruits of a cosmopolitan world. Aquinas's emphasis on good government, justice, order, and the use of reason and personal responsibility were values well suited to the new age.

New Ways to Represent the Christian Message
After 1000, European growth spawned a new vitality in the arts. Authors were writing not only in Latin but in a number of emerging regional languages such as French, German, and English. Romantic poets drew on regional languages for their inspiration, and some writers composed parodies about the Church and even of the Gospels. A growing sense of ethnic pride resulted in Scandinavian, German, French, and English literature celebrating heroic origins and traditions. European bards were similar to the jelis from West Africa. The most famous of these works were the French *Song of Roland*, the Spanish *El Cid*, and the German *Song of the Nibelungs*. Later the German Wolfram produced the classic *Parzival*, and by the end of the fourteenth century, Dante, an Italian writer, had written his masterpiece, *The Divine Comedy*. It is an allegory of the author's journey through hell, purgatory, and heaven, where he meets the blessed and

damned, many of whom were his fellow citizens of Florence. (A recent Pakistani textbook claims that Dante's description of hell, purgatory, and heaven "is basically a replica of the famous Spanish Muslim sufi writer Ibn-I-Arabi's description of *Mairaj* [Muhammad's visitation to heaven].")

One of the most enduring artistic legacies of Europe during the twelfth and thirteenth centuries was the development of Gothic architecture, which inspired some of the greatest Christian buildings. The Gothic style featured lofty, graceful spires, the pointed arch, and ribbed vaulting. Church ceilings and steeples seemed to soar because flying buttresses, a major engineering innovation, could contain the enormous downward and outward pressures that the towers and roofs exerted. Pointed arches supported far greater weight than the earlier round arches could. The Gothic style also accommodated very large

The Epiphany by Giotto

windows filled with intricate and beautiful stained glass.

At this same time sculptors and painters were discovering new ways to express their Christian faith. Greek and Roman monuments and sculptures unearthed in Italy conveyed emotional themes in amazingly realistic forms. They inspired painters such as Giotto (1256–1336) to achieve greater realism in their works. Giotto's Madonnas began to have a three-dimensional quality, and his religious scenes seemed to be set in physical rather than sacred space. His subtle shadings of dark and light, which invested his paintings with depth and perspective, represented a major break with earlier Christian art.

Two Paths to State Development

Concern with expressing one's values in a worldly setting was also manifest in new political developments. In addition to the numerous city-states that were emerging, Europe took two other paths to state-building. One followed the example of traditional empires, and the other moved toward developing a collection of small independent states.

Charlemagne, who had attempted to build the first state in post-Roman Europe, knew that he had to have the support of the Church. The pope's endorsement could attract reluctant followers and give his rule legitimacy. In turn, the Church needed strong political leaders to ensure its survival. It also needed money and often had to accept the help of rich merchants. As a result, both Church and state wanted to appear to support and flatter one another while at the same time they were vigorously competing for supremacy. This uneasy balance between political and religious leaders led to the creation of the Holy Roman Empire, which, over its long history, was always more of an ideal than anything like a genuine empire. This concept combined Church and State in a pale copy of the Byzantine Empire without granting the emperor superiority over the Church.

Roman Catholic Church leaders very much wanted a single state in Europe. The Church's organization had copied the Roman Empire, and Church leaders found it easier to deal with one source of power rather than with many competing groups. In an effort to exert the Church's authority and appoint political leaders, in 800 the pope had crowned Charlemagne emperor, although no actual empire existed at that time. After the Carolingian kingdom disintegrated into a number of small areas controlled by nobles, some leaders sought to unite large segments of Europe into the Holy Roman Empire. In 933 the Pope granted Otto I of Germany the title of Holy Roman Emperor, and successive popes continued to confer the title on various leaders.

A major rift between Church and State developed under Henry IV, the Holy Roman Emperor who ruled from 1056 to 1106. With the elevation of Pope Gregory VII in 1073, the Church aggressively moved to ensure its supremacy over the political governments. The new pope proclaimed, "The pope can be judged by no one; the pope alone can depose and restore bishops; he can depose emperors and all princes should kiss his feet."

Henry ignored the Pope's claim of supremacy and appointed church officials. Gregory retaliated by proclaiming that Henry's actions violated the will of God and stipulated that he had no right to appoint priests and other clergy. Ignoring the Pope, Henry continued to appoint church officials who were loyal to him. Gregory ruled that Henry's clerical appointments were illegitimate. Henry replied that Gregory was not really the pope but a "false monk" and insisted that he resign. In turn, Gregory excommunicated Henry, who soon lost the support of the nobility and painfully discovered just how powerful the pope and Church were. The Pope prevailed and as an act of penance, Henry had to stand barefooted in the snow and ask the Pope to absolve him of his many sins, the worst of which was having challenged the Church's authority. Henry was forgiven, but upon resuming his throne, he hardly changed his earlier behavior.

The Holy Roman Empire continued as a political fiction for centuries, but, as a French philosopher would later state, it was "neither holy, nor Roman, nor an empire." Even so, the vision of empire is very strong even today and the ideal of establishing large empires such as the Roman Empire may have slowed the development of smaller states in the area that eventually became Italy and Germany.

NEW STATES

Creating small states was the other path to state-building. During feudal times Europe was a shifting jigsaw puzzle of small, temporarily united areas. Various counts, dukes, and lesser lords and their vassals, who owned large tracts of land, often united in temporary alliances. In military emergencies, they sometimes elected one of their colleagues, usually a count or duke, to serve as "king" and to coordinate the strategy during a military crisis. The king was supposed to be one among equals and in theory was dependent on the will of the nobility who controlled most of the land.

Some of these leaders did not want to relinquish power at the end of a military crisis. They realized that if they could secure the loyalty of other dukes by promising them certain benefits, they could remain in power and sometimes pass down the office of king to one of their sons. After 1000, several kings claimed to rule areas in Europe and they were the symbolic heads of relatively large regions, even though most of the actual power still lay with the nobility. Although these political arrangements were unstable, they established the foundation for Europe's first nation-states. France and England led the way in this move toward European monarchies, and England's early efforts at state-building were by far the most successful.

"This gives my confidence a real boost."

FRANCE

In the late tenth century, six nobles who controlled most of what is now France chose Hugh Capet, a duke, as their king. Capet proclaimed himself king of a territory about the size of Vermont, although other counts and dukes were actually independent governors of most of that territory and several wielded more real power than Capet did. France was slow to unify around a king, even though produce from the rich farmland could be used to support the state. The French population was quite diverse, and the central government, despite having the pope's blessing, faced strong regional challenges to its authority.

Philip, who held the title of king from 1180 to 1223, really established the French monarchy and defined the boundaries of the country. By deftly playing the game of divide-and-rule with his vassals, he managed to keep them fighting one another rather than challenging his authority. He was also one of the first European monarchs to ally himself openly with the growing middle class, which welcomed his efforts to codify commercial and civil law.

By the fourteenth century France had established a monarchy and an infant state. Philip IV (r. 1285–1314) summoned the first meeting of a parliament (from the French *parle*, "to talk"), which was called the "Estates General." The representative body included three interest groups called "estates": the clergy, the nobility, and the bourgeoisie. Even though peasants and craftsmen—the vast majority—were not represented, the outlines of a system of kingship guided by merchants, churchmen, and nobles was beginning to take shape.

ENGLAND

In the ninth century a group of Viking settlers called Normans (Northmen) established a stronghold in French territory. In 1066 William, one of its strongest leaders, successfully invaded England and defeated King Harold's Angles and Saxons, two Germanic groups that had settled there in the fifth century. William ordered stone castles built and established the feudal hierarchy of nobles and vassals. He also demanded that all nobles swear allegiance to him as king.

The Norman kings continued to strengthen the state under a strong monarchy. They organized a great council of tenants-in-chief that included the major landholders. They also took a census and began collecting taxes. These revenues enabled them to hire mercenary soldiers and construct roads and bridges and other public works. By the reign of Henry II (1154–89) royal courts had been established, and the standardized fines they collected strengthened the monarchy. Henry controlled England and half of France and subdued Scotland and Ireland as well. He extended the role of juries in trials and further codified the law while increasing the role of the court. Henry also increased state power by fighting the Church and fiercely contesting his own archbishop, Thomas Becket, and finally having him assassinated.

Great Council of Parliament

The steps toward a strong central state continued under King John (r. 1199–1216) who made additional attempts to strengthen the king's power at the expense of the nobility. But this time the nobles, believing they were losing much of their former power to the king, fought back. In 1215 they forced John to sign the Magna Carta (Great Charter). This charter officially made the king superior to all nobles, a major step toward a real monarchy, but it also wrote into law many specific rights of the nobility and the Church.

Edward I (r. 1272–1307) took another major step in state development when he recognized the legitimate interests of both the landed aristocrats and the rising middle class. He summoned the Great Council of Parliament in 1254, inviting two knights from each county to attend the council, and later including members of the bourgeoisie as well. This English institution was one of the first representative governing groups and the beginning of a new type of governing body. By the fourteenth century, England, perhaps an unlikely candidate to create a successful and centralized state, was slowly building the first real nation-state in Europe.

By the twelfth century, in addition to these two major new states, people in Italy were building both prosperous city-states, such as Bologna, Florence, Venice, and Genoa, and a number of regional states as well. All these areas challenged the weak authority of the Holy Roman Empire. Farther south, Christian forces were challenging Muslim power in al-Andalus.

Will Infidels Capture the Holy Land?

By the start of the eleventh century, with the exception of Christians in the Iberian Peninsula, western Europeans no longer looked upon the Muslims as a major threat. Muslim advances in Europe had been stopped at the Battle of Tours in 732, and the Muslims seemed satisfied with what they already controlled in al-Andalus, North Africa, and on several islands in the Mediterranean. In spite of what Christians said about Muslims, it appeared that Muslims respected People of the Book. Rumors of impressive Muslim scholarship drifted into Europe. Pilgrimages were a long-established tradition for both Christians and Muslims, and Muslims protected European Jews and Christians, as well as pilgrims from Ethiopia and Nubia, who visited Jerusalem and other sites in the Holy Land.

In spite of these peaceful signs, most European Christians, espe-cially those that lived near the Iberian Peninsula, had a dim view of Muslims. Starting in the mid-eleventh century, Christian forces began efforts to regain al-Andalus from the Muslims. With the enthusiasm that perhaps only religious fervor can motivate, Spanish Christians mounted an all-out holy war against the "infidels:, which they called the *reconquista*. By 1150 they had established four small kingdoms in the north. By 1300 the Muslims controlled only Granada in the south. Christians in Europe hoped that soon the whole peninsula would be under Christian control.

A perceived Muslim threat was never far away from the minds of many who lived in Byzantium, and the Seljuk victory in the battle of Manzikert in 1071 had spread fear through many Christians in that area. Byzantine rulers had long suspected that European forces had their eye on Constantinople, but obviously the Seljuk Turks now posed a much more immediate threat. Only twenty-four years later, in 1095, the Byzantine emperor and his fellow Christians asked Pope Urban to send military forces to help them contain the Muslims and regain the Holy Land for Christendom.

The emperor had expected a few thousand mercenaries to respond to his call. Imagine his surprise when a huge corps of about 100,000 volunteers set out on a crusade to "free" Jerusalem from the Turkish infidels. Crusaders had heard that the Turks were less tolerant of non-Muslims than the Abbasids had been, and pilgrimages to the Holy Land were becoming dangerous. Undoubtedly, many crusaders believed they would receive special grace from God for their efforts against the Muslims. The Pope had promised that the sins of all cru-saders would be forgiven. Instead of being punished in purgatory, they would go directly to heaven.

There were also more practical reasons for joining the crusades. Participation in this adventure offered leaders of the newly emerging nation-states a way to demonstrate the unity and power of their coun-tries as well as an opportunity to expand their land base. The popula-tion of Europe was rapidly growing, and arable land was getting scarce. Because of the practice of primogeniture, the oldest son inher-ited all the family land, and younger brothers had to find other opportunities. If land could be acquired in the East, why not go? It would be a grand adventure in which men could display their military skills and, if things went well, they might get land and other spoils.

Who Are the Infidels?

The Seljuks and other Muslims recognized that many of the people they controlled in Anatolia were Christians who might, if given the chance, be tempted to join the crusaders. Even so, their internal power struggles initially distracted them from fully appreciating the threat the crusaders posed. The numerous small kingdoms were practically independent, and the men who ruled them were preoccupied with their own dynastic struggles and efforts to expand. Sunni opposed Shii, and their common allegiance to Islam masked deep hostilities toward one another. Calls for a jihad made little impression on the various rulers unless they thought they would gain personally from fighting. In addition, they did not take the first crusaders seriously: the far more sophisticated residents of West Asia must have

The conquest of Jerusalem

thought that the European knights and the scrawny soldiers and camp followers that constituted the first wave of crusaders were uncouth nomads or some wretched tribe that had been evicted from its land.

As a result, the crusaders captured Antioch and most of Syria fairly easily. They divided the land they conquered into feudal states and claimed all the goods they seized as booty. Word about crusader atrocities began to spread. It was reported that when crusaders reduced the Syrian city of Ma'arra to ruins, famine spread, and crusaders "boiled the pagan adults in cooking pots; they impaled children on spits and devoured them grilled." A contemporary Arab chronicler wrote:

> All those who are well-informed about the Franj [crusaders] saw them as beasts superior in courage and fighting ardour but in nothing else, just as animals are superior in strength and aggression.

In 1099 the crusaders seized Jerusalem. They took few prisoners killing any Muslims they could find, including women and children. As one crusader wrote in a letter home, "In Solomon's Porch and in his temple our men rode in the blood of the Saracens [Muslims] up to the knees of their horses." The crusaders' religious fervor also resulted in the region's first real wave of anti-Semitism as these "soldiers of God" also slaughtered many Jews living in Jerusalem.

What Was Saladin's Role?

The slaughter, reported atrocities, and mounting losses enraged the Muslims. They realized they needed to set aside their internal conflicts in order to be able to oppose the Franjs more effectively. Recognized for his military skills, Saladin—whose father was a Kurd and who had apprenticed with his uncle, an important Turkish general who was the vizier in Cairo—was given command of the Syrian troops in Egypt. When his uncle died, Saladin became vizier and in 1174 he became sultan of Egypt. He showed his military skill in numerous campaigns to enlarge his territory and against the crusaders. By this time the Muslims were eager to respond to his call and in 1187 Saladin's force retook Jerusalem.

During his victory march into the city, Saladin would not allow his soldiers to kill the inhabitants of the city, loot the defeated crusaders, or set fire to Christian homes and churches. As part of the agreement of surrender, Christians could buy back their freedom. Saladin freed older people and the very young who could not afford to buy back their freedom, and he saw to it that goods from his own treasury were used to help crusader widows and orphans.

Alarmed by the loss of Jerusalem, the crusaders launched a third crusade in 1189. King Richard of England, known as the Richard the Lionhearted, led the crusaders toward Jerusalem. His men and Saladin's forces clashed several times as they headed south, but the exchanges were inconclusive. Although many diplomatic exchanges passed between these two rulers, they never met. Eventually, in 1194, the Peace of Ramla was signed: the crusaders were to control the coastal area while the Muslims controlled the rest. Saladin died the next year.

What Were the Legacies of the Crusades?

Europeans gained no lasting military or political advantage from the crusades. Instead of strengthening Christendom, these campaigns weakened its influence in the eastern Mediterranean. In 1204, Pope Innocent III, vowing to return Jerusalem to the Christian fold, called for a fourth crusade. This crusading army negotiated with Venice to provide ships to transport the crusaders. In return the crusaders agreed to further Venetian interests in Byzantium, a possible reason they went via Constantinople and not directly to the Holy Land.

At first, the relieved residents of Constantinople welcomed their fellow Christians. The crusaders installed what was considered a legitimate ruler over the city and, in return, demanded rewards from the city, in part to pay off their Venetian debt. Protesting the payments, the residents assassinated the new emperor. Shortly thereafter the crusaders sacked and looted the city and established Latin rule over Byzantium that lasted until 1261.

Historians debate the reasons why the crusaders attached Constantinople. Some argue that the Venetians were behind the actions, citing the fact that the Venetians wanted a more sympathetic emperor on the throne. Others, pointing to the deep-seated animosities between Byzantium and Western Europe and between the Eastern

Orthodox Church and the Roman Catholic Church, suggest that the crusaders had planned to attack and install their own emperor from the start. Some even suggest that the sacking of the city was spontaneous Whatever the causes, this unexpected assault on Christendom's greatest city weakened the Byzantine Empire and seriously reduced its ability to withstand subsequent Muslim threats.

On the other hand, direct contact with Muslim and Byzantine areas probably accelerated Europe's economic development. Although Europe's main contact with Muslim culture came from al-Andalus and islands in the Mediterranean, returning crusaders must have talked about what they had seen, and undoubtedly their enthusiasm stimulated greater interest in the wider world as well as an enhanced desire for luxury goods. Venice and Genoa were two big winners. As commerce increased, they became wealthier and more powerful.

The crusades greatly legitimized European leaders' use of violence in support of an ideal. This was unlike the violence that had characterized European society from 500 to 1000, which essentially had been motivated by the struggle for survival or to acquire more land. Now European Christians were employing violence in the name of their faith, even though the founder of Christianity had preached non-violence and turning the other cheek. (Buddhism also espoused nonviolence, but both Chinese and Korean leaders used Buddhism to support their military campaigns.)

The crusades stimulated Muslims in West Asia to unite. Saladin established a new dynasty in Egypt. His worked to make sure his subjects were united and that Cairo was protected by strong walls and impregnable defenses but not to spend resources on building palaces. Internally, he wanted to foster commerce and cultural freedom. Saladin had justly eared his reputation as a skilled warrior, chivalrous knight, and enlightened ruler.

The crusades appeared to have had little lasting effect on the Muslims of West Asia as they learned little from the crusading soldiers. Because the jihad was a long-standing tradition in Islam, using violence in support of an ideal was not new. Soon after Saladin's death, the Mamluks took control of Egypt and in 1261 they re-established the Abbasid Dynasty that the Mongols had destroyed in 1258. The Mamluk dynasty's strength came from trade via the Red Sea and

Nile Valley. Cairo emerged as the greatest city in the Eastern Mediterranean. European travelers in the fourteenth century could cite no European city whose wealth and population came anywhere near that of Cairo.

However, in retrospect it is possible to discern that the crusades left Muslim in that area with a residue of distrust of people from Europe in general and Christians in particular.

Besides the impressive empires that flourished in the first millennium, many small states came into being during this period. Competing regional kingdoms were the norm in India. The power and stability of states such as Srivijaya in Southeast Asia and Ghana and Mali in West Africa depended on control of trade routes. The glory of the Khmer kingdom in Southeast Asia grew out of the surplus rice and fish the flooded land provided. Many important city-states along the Swahili coast in East Africa and Northern Italy also grew in importance.

Increased cross-cultural contact and commerce played an important role in the development of all these areas. Cross-cultural contacts intensified in the second millennium C.E., as the crusades dramatically demonstrate.

In other areas there was no single source of authority. Some areas in Africa maintained stability by cooperating and sharing authority but no single leader emerged with absolute power over the community. In both Japan and Western Europe, a feudal-type arrangement emerged as a way to furnish the security a central government usually provides. In both cases symbolic leaders existed — the emperor in Japan and kings in Europe — but in reality they exercised little or no power. In the Muslim world Dar al-Islam was composed of many different states rather than any single centralized area.

In the next act we will follow the proliferation of cross-cultural interactions and exchanges that is creating a single hemispheric network of contact and exchange. In addition, we will examine again what happens when both large and small new groups of nomadic and settled people come into contact.

ACT FOUR – NEW STATES EMERGE IN AFRO-EURASIA

Setting the Stage

1. What is a heterarchy and how does it differ from a centralized state? What are some of the advantages and disadvantages of each type of political organization?

2. Describe the various forms of forced labor and identify the characteristics of each. What were the sources of slaves? What kinds of jobs did slaves perform?

3. Describe the monsoon. How did the monsoon affect cross-cultural contacts in the Indian Ocean? Why did diaspora communities form?

4. Why did the camel become the dominant form of transportation between 300 and 1300 C.E.? What are the advantages to using camels and camel caravans instead of horses and wheeled vehicles for long distance overland travel?

SCENE ONE
Extension of Indian, Byzantine, and Chinese Influences

1. How did rulers presented in this scene react to religious influences? Why did Vladimir decide to convert to Christianity? Why did the kings of the South Indian kingdoms patronize Hinduism and make land grants to Brahmins?

2. What aspects of a theater state did the Southeast Asian kingdoms exhibit? How does the layout of their cities and temple complexes symbolize the Hindu worldview? How did these complexes enhance the ruler's power?

3. What aspects of Hinduism does the Nataraja symbolize?

4. How did increased trade facilitate Indian influence in Southeast Asia?

5. What evidence is there that the Vietnamese tried to build an independent state? Explain why the Vietnamese adopted some Chinese cultural ideas.

6. How did the Koreans react to Indian and Chinese influences, particularly Buddhist and Confucian ideas? What aspects of Chinese culture did Korea adapt? How did Koreans modify Chinese culture to fit their own beliefs

7. What aspects of Chinese culture did the Japanese appropriated? Which forms seemed to work well and which ones failed to take root in the new setting? How did the Confucian values change the role of women in Japan?

8. What accounts for the expansion of Indian, Byzantine, and Chinese culture?

SCENE TWO
City-States and Empires in Africa

1. Describe the important geographic features of Africa. How did people take advantage of these features? What challenges did Africa's geography and climate present? How did people meet these challenges?
2. Evaluate the reliability of the sources about Africa's past including archaeological evidence and oral sources. What were jelis expected to do? What were Ibn Battuta's impressions of Mali and Kilwa?
3. What were the causes and effects of the Bantu migrations? What role did iron play in Bantu settlements?
4. Describe the political organization of Jenne-Jeno. How does it fit the definition of a heterarchy?
5. Identify the role and importance of trade in West Africa. What were the major products exchanged in this trading system? What role did Muslim traders play?
6. Identify how East Africa was integrated into the Indian Ocean trading system.
7. How did Sunjata gain control of Mali? What was his relationship with neighboring leaders?
8. How did Ethiopia adapt Christianity to its own needs?
9. Why was Great Zimbabwe successful in developing a centralized state?
10. What roles did family ties and age sets play in creating a sense of community in many African groups? How were slaves integrated into these societies?
11. What was the basic worldview of many African people? In what ways might it be compatible with the teachings of Islam?
12. Identify the importance of Islam in Africa. Why would political leaders support this faith? How could it be integrated with existing beliefs?

SCENE THREE
From the Abbasid Caliphate to Dar al-Islam

1. How did conversion to Islam help weaken the Umayyad Caliphate?
2. Why did the Abbasids build Baghdad? What are the city's characteristics? In what ways was it as it a cosmic city? a sacred city? a political or economic center?
3. In what ways did Persian society influence the Abbasid Caliphate?
4. What were some of the achievements of Muslim scholars? Explain the role and importance of the House of Wisdom in Baghdad.
5. Describe the relationship among Islamic scholars and scholars from other

areas. What impact did they have on the development of Europe?
6. What role did slavery play in Islamic civilization?
7. Explain the concept of Dar al-Islam. How was that different from the Abbasid Caliphate or an Islamic empire? What areas were included in Dar al-Islam by the fourteenth century? If you could live in one of those areas, which would you choose and why?
8. How did Seljuk Turks challenge the Abbasid caliphate? What did they decide to do about the caliph? Why?
9. What was the significance of the Battle of Manzikert? How would the Seljuk Turks have viewed this battle? How would the Byzantines have viewed this battle?
10. Initially, why did Afghan Turks invade the Indian subcontinent? Who ruled during the Delhi Sultanate? What was the sultanate's attitude toward Hinduism?
11. Did the coming of the Turks weaken or strengthen Islam? Explain the reasons for your answer.

SCENE FOUR
Europe Under Christendom

1. What evidence is there to support the statement that life in Western Europe from 500 to 1000 was "five centuries of camping out"?
2. Why were the Vikings and Magyars able to carry out so many successful raids against other Europeans? What were the consequences of their raids?
3. Why were independent peasants willing to become serfs on manors? Why did manors seek to be self-sufficient?
4. How did feudalism develop out of the manorial system? What were the major characteristics of European feudalism?
5. What was the class system in European feudalism? What social mobility existed?
6. What were the reasons for the rise of chivalry after the eleventh century? Compare European feudalism and chivalry with the Japanese feudal system and the Code of Bushido.
7. What did the Church hope to get from alliance with political powers? What did rulers hope to get from Church support? Who supported the Holy Roman Empire and why? What are some examples of the continuing struggle between the Christian Church and emerging states in Europe?
8. Explain the reasons for the rise of towns. How did increased trade and growing numbers of towns change the character of European culture?
9. What were the two approaches to the creation of states? What issues were involved in the tension between nobles and kings?

Summing Up

1. Discuss the role cross-cultural contact played in the development of new states during this act. How do these examples compare with the role of cross-cultural contacts in the development of earlier empires?

2. Describe interactions between political and religious leaders during this act. What did each group hope to get from the other? Are these reasons similar to ones we saw in earlier periods? If not, what new issues emerged?

3. What caused political leaders to persecute religious institutions? Which reasons for persecution are found in more than one area? Are these reasons similar to ones we saw in earlier periods? If not, what new issues emerged?

4. identify the process of cross-cultural encounters, adoption, and adaptation in any two of the following areas: Indian influences in Southeast Asia; Buddhist influences in East Asia; Muslim influences in West and East Africa; and Muslims influences in the development of Europe. What role did syncretism play? What generalizations can you make about how ideas travel?

5. Briefly identify the major changes that took place in the development of one of the universal religions. Identify what you think were the causes of these changes. To what extent were these causes the same for all the universal religions? Which were unique? Support your answer with specific examples.

6. Briefly review the characteristics of a land-based kingdom and a theater state. Identify examples of each. Identify examples of a state that combines both characteristics.

7. Compare and contrast a city-state such as one of the Swahili states with several other kinds of states we have examined in this act, or contrast and compare any two states from the following list: Khmer kingdom; Nam Viet; Silla kingdom; Ghana or Mali; Swahili city-states; Abbasid Caliphate; Delhi Sultanate; and al-Andalus. Compare one or more of these areas with one of the major empires of this millennium.

8. Compare the concept of Christendom with Dar al-Islam. In what ways were they similar? How were they different?

ACT FIVE

Hemispheric Interaction (1100 to 1450)

SETTING THE STAGE

The movement and exchange of people, goods, technology, germs, and worldviews had become widespread throughout the Afro-Eurasian world by 1000. Some people met as enemies in war and conquest; many more met as traders seeking profits, pilgrims in search of spiritual nourishment, travelers looking for adventure and knowledge, scholars and philosophers searching for new insights and longing to teach their own, and refugees seeking a better way of life for themselves and their children. Even those who never left home felt the effects of cross-cultural interaction, and new challenges came to them whether they sought them or not.

The Japanese are often singled out for adopting much of their culture from China and Korea, but England borrowed just as much from the continent and early Mediterranean cultures. Both Europeans, who thought of themselves primarily as Teutonic peoples, and the Byzantines had built their civilization on a Greco-Roman-Christian foundation. Kievan Rus, in turn, borrowed heavily from Byzantium.

Interaction and exchanges have occurred in very diverse areas throughout history. Mesoamerican city-states built on the original Olmec culture. Teotihuacan's influence went far beyond the territories it claimed to control. China served as example and inspiration, whether entirely voluntarily or not, for much of East Asia. Southeast Asia was receptive to influences and trade with both South and East Asia, and Indian influences can be found from Christendom to the Pacific. Merchants eagerly sought African resources, and Africans adapted aspects of both Christianity and Islam. Crusaders were strongly influenced by the Muslim communities they encountered. European scholars borrowed heavily from their Muslim neighbors, who, in turn, had access to Greco-Roman learning and had adapted such things as Indian numerals, crops, and the mariner's compass.

Cross-cultural interaction tends to blur political borders, and economic and trading networks have their own kind of boundaries that do not necessarily coincide with the ones usually found on world maps. The Muslim world cut across many different borders in Inner Asia, North India, West Asia, and the Mediterranean, and Muslim scholars who wanted to know more about the world were encouraged to travel. Christendom comprised several states, including Byzantium, a crossroads of trade and human exchange, and ports bordering the Mediterranean Sea and Indian Ocean provided meeting places for ships and merchants from many societies.

Nomadic-Settled Interaction

Interaction between nomads and settled peoples has been a recurring example of cross-cultural contact since the second millennium B.C.E. Almost every time nomads move into settled areas, they adapt many characteristics from the area into which they go. At the same time, the nomadic presence challenges settled people. When peoples interact, both groups change, even though their reactions and adaptations vary.

Some may think it is "progress" when nomads adopt the culture of settled complex societies. After all, nomads are transforming themselves from "uncivilized" tribal societies to sophisticated urbanized, centralized states. But groups may not want to change their way of life even when they are perfectly able to do so, because the culture they have developed for themselves seems to work very well as is.

HOW DID THE AZTECS ADAPT?

The early history of the Toltecs and Aztecs in Mesoamerica offers a chance to review the process of interaction and adaptation that nomadic and settled groups go through. In the years after the destruction of the sacred buildings at Teotihuacan and the disintegration of many Maya centers, nomads from the northern deserts called "dog people" [Chichimecs] migrated into the relative power vacuum in the Valley of Mexico. Two of these groups were Toltecs and Aztecs (Culhua Mexica).

The Toltecs settled north of Teotihuacan and created Tula, their capital. Building on the existing trade network, Tula seems to have quickly become the center of a vast network of trade and exchange. Eventually Toltec influence may have reached north as far as the present-day southwestern United States. These skilled and ruthless warriors sacrificed countless humans in an effort to provide the blood they believed the sun god needed to sustain its journey in the underworld and defeat the powers of darkness. They instituted sacred wars in order to capture slaves and victims for sacrifice and to increase their power and wealth. But in spite of their military skills, by 1187 they had lost their political power.

The Aztecs, who followed them into the Valley of Mexico in the thirteenth century, were looked on as uncouth, violent nomads who survived by eating snakes or whatever else they could find. More than fifty Indian groups were competing for supremacy in that area at that time. It seemed most improbable that the Aztecs, who seemed only skilled at slaughtering people, would one day prove to be the most successful group.

Seeking a way to attain legitimacy, the Aztecs decided to copy the Toltecs, whom they thought were heroic warriors. The Aztecs became successful mercenaries for neighboring groups, earning a reputation as ferocious fighters. They also arranged a marriage between one of the Aztec warriors and a neighboring princess who claimed descent from the Toltecs. When the princess's father arrived at the wedding celebration, he discovered a priest dressed in his daughter's skin and learned she had been sacrificed according to Aztec custom. Such behavior did not enhance their status among other groups.

Banished again, in 1325 the Aztecs finally settled on a low, swampy, bug-ridden island in Lake Taxcoco. The island proved easy to defend. They adapting local farming techniques and their rich, fertile, well-watered chinampas produced surplus food and allowed them to trade. They continued to adapt Toltec ways, including offering human blood to the gods, and they soon developed a stratified society and a centralized state and were in a position to make alliances with two powerful neighbors. By 1425 they had become a significant power in the area. Their initial success came not only from their skill as warriors but also their willingness to adapt characteristics of Toltec culture.

WHAT HAPPENED TO THE VIKINGS IN GREENLAND?

The story of the Viking settlement in Greenland offers a different example of the interaction between settled and nomadic people. Starting about 600 the Vikings began raiding, trading, and settling in land along the northern coasts of Europe, the British Isles, and Ireland. In the late ninth century they established a society of perhaps two thousand people in Greenland.

The Vikings who settled Greenland had become farmers. Their status and wealth depended on how much land they owned, and they wanted to find new land, not to change the way they lived. When they reached Greenland, they looked for ways to support the way of life they had maintained in Norway and Iceland, and they imported cattle, sheep, goats, and pigs, the same animals they had raised at home. They expected to graze these animals during the summers and during the winters feed them the hay they had grown and harvested. They ate little fish but supplemented their diet with caribou and seal, although the religious and political leaders severely restricted hunting. They were devout Christians and built numerous stone churches.

Their survival was precarious. Their animals, especially the sheep, soon overgrazed the land, making life all the more uncertain and preventing them from building up a surplus. Around 1250, the temperature grew colder and the winters longer. In order to survive, they would have to adapt their lifestyle to meet the harsher conditions.

About the same time that the Vikings were establishing their farming settlements, a nomadic hunting and gathering people called the Inuit (Eskimo) were gradually migrating east from Alaska and some reached the Norse hunting areas in northern Greenland. These nomadic newcomers, who survived by hunting and fishing, gradually moved down the west coast to the outskirts of the Norse settlements.

The nomadic Inuit dressed in animal skins; they hunted and fished, using harpoon-hunting and ice-fishing techniques that they had developed in order to survive in very harsh environments.

The Vikings and Inuit were in direct contact as the climate got colder, and off and on the two groups fought. The Vikings considered the Inuit "heathen wretches," and it may never have occurred to them to "revert" to the hunting and fishing way of life that the Inuit followed. Instead, the Vikings continued raise cattle and sheep, which were overgrazing the land, causing the fragile top soil to blow away. The Viking survival strategy also included building more churches and giving church leaders additional authority. As a result, by the end of the fourteenth century, the Viking community in Greenland was gone. The last record of it describes a Christian marriage held in one of the churches and explains how a man was burned at the stake for practicing witchcraft.

Why were the Vikings unable to survive? There is no evidence that they were killed in a battle or taken away as slaves. More likely, they perished because they were unwilling to give up their more "civilized" way of life as farmers and follow the lead of "uncivilized" Inuit hunters. Going from farming to hunting/gathering may have seemed like going backward, against "progress." How could they possibly do that? Unable to give up their familiar way of life, they could not recognize the value of what their neighbors had to offer.

In this act we examine examples of the increased pace of interaction during the first half of the second millennium. Examples proliferate: the Mongol conquest, the "super bowl" of encounters between nomadic invaders and settled peoples; the spread of disease; and the observations of two hemispheric travelers whose reports inspire increased cultural interaction. We shall consider how different groups adapt to changing circumstances and new ideas and what they think of one another. We shall examine again to what extent and in what ways individuals and groups are willing to learn from strangers as well as what their new neighbors learn from them. Finally, this act focuses on the vibrant Indian Ocean trade, the contacts it fostered among so many different people from across the hemisphere, and how these interactions helped change the direction of the human drama.

SCENE ONE

THE MONGOLS: THE LAST NOMADIC EMPIRE

Setting the Stage

Even though the Song capital at Kaifeng fell to invading nomads in 1126, the Southern Song continued to prosper and became a leading producer of iron and steel and the largest exporter of silk and porcelain. Hangzhou, their major trading center, grew into one of the world's largest cities. Its examination-based meritocracy ensured that talented men became officials. To the southwest, subjects in the Khmer Kingdom were enjoying the many rituals and festivals their god-kings sponsored. To the east, Korea was flourishing under the Koryo dynasty where Buddhism's influence was strong and its celadon pottery was much in demand. Japan, under both the emperor in Kyoto and shoguns in Kamakura, was perfecting its aesthetic traditions and its warrior code.

In West Asia, the Abbasid Caliphate was still the nominal ruler, although Seljuk sultans had the real power. The Mamluks, having defeated Saladin's dynasty in Egypt, turned Cairo, their capital, into a vibrant trading center. Dar al-Islam, embracing areas all across Eurasia, formed a huge cultural system that fostered trade and exchange. But the creative civilizations in all these areas are about to face an unexpected threat that will challenge their stability. The new challenge is coming from the Mongols, a small tribe that lived in Mongolia on the fringes of urban civilization.

Mongol Life

The following is a Mongolian poet's description of his homeland.

> As a great yurt are the heavens
> Covering the steppe in all directions . . .

Blue, blue is the sky
Vast, vast is the steppe
Here the grass bends with the breeze
Here are the cattle and sheep.

Existence for the Mongols who lived in the central Asian steppes revolved around five principal animals: sheep, goats, yaks, camels, and horses. Yaks provided food, clothing, shelter, and fuel; camels were useful for transporting goods and trading across desert areas; and horses provided mobility. The Mongol diet consisted mainly of meat, and they drank fermented mare's milk called *kumis*. They lived in yurts, wooden frame tents covered with animal skins, which they could move relatively easily. They regularly dismantled small yurts and set them up again at new sites. Larger yurts stayed on large wagons that they dragged from site to site.

Mongol society was organized on bloodlines: members of a given lineage shared a common ancestor and gave one another absolute loyalty. A chief, the strongest and bravest man who could fight and ride a horse better than others, led his clans. If a younger man successfully challenged him, he became the new leader. If threatened or in order to conquer new lands, tribes, composed of a number of clans, might join

Hauling a large yurt

Nomadic Encampment: Women's Activities

together under a single leader called a "khan". Usually these alliances were unstable because they depended on the charismatic leadership of someone who could inspire loyalty among men from different, often feuding, tribes and clans.

Although we may associate nomadic life with lone cowboys on the plains, in reality men and women in nomadic society may live closer together than they do in agricultural communities. Because there is little surplus, nomadic society may also be more egalitarian than agrarian societies: everyone shares the same pressures and fate. Mongol women, along with the men, shared jobs such as breaking up camp and selecting and setting up a new site. Both men and women milked the animals. Although men were trained to hunt and fight, women also fought to protect their campsites, sometimes on horseback.

Campsites were divided between women's and men's areas, not between public space (for men) and private space (for women) as is the case in most settled societies. Women worked together preparing food, tanning skins, and making clothes and containers for wool and

Nomadic Encampment: Men's Activities

skins, activities they performed in the shared areas between yurts. Following the herds, especially in search of water, often took men far afield, leaving women to care for everyone who remained at the campsite. The Mongols practiced polygamy, and grooms paid a bride price rather than the bride's family giving a dowry. Women had a significant amount of political power. The khan's wife, his queen or *khatun*, served as co-ruler, and after her husband died, she ruled until the community selected a new khan, which could take up to two years. She also suggested successors.

Why Were the Mongols So Successful?

The Mongols were one of several large ethnic groups, such as the Turks and Huns (Xiongnu), who lived on the central Asian steppes. They rose to power in the twelfth century when a charismatic leader, Temujin (1162–1227), succeeded in uniting several tribes. Temujin was the son of a minor clan chieftain of a powerful tribe living in eastern Mongolia. A rival chieftain poisoned his father when Temujin was only nine years old, and for several years he and his mother fled for their lives. At one point, he was captured and almost killed, but he escaped by floating down a river. Repeatedly proving his strength and bravery, Temujin won the loyalty of several Mongol tribes. In 1206 the tribal assembly proclaimed him Chinggis Khan or Universal Ruler.

Historians speculate why Chinggis Khan was able to unite the Mongols and why they decided to expand. Climate change may help explain the expansion. A sharp decline in the mean annual temperature of Mongolia caused less and shorter grass to grow. This shortage seriously endangered the animals and forced the Mongols to either trade or raid.

A major reason for Chinggis Khan's success in uniting the Mongols was that he replaced clan-based loyalty with loyalty to new "tribes" that included members from many clans. He also broke up groups his troops had defeated and scattered their members among the tribes. He appointed officers to be in charge of such things as food supply, looking after sheep herds and horses, and guarding his person, rather than using clan leaders. As a result, tribes were no longer self-sufficient but had to work together.

Whether or not Chinggis Khan instituted a law code, loyalty was the Mongols' highest value, and the Mongols punished disloyalty with exile or death. For lesser crimes, they favored fines rather than harsh punishments, perhaps reflecting Buddhist influence. They did not want to spill the blood of princes or kings, so they killed guilty leaders by strangling, crushing, or exposing them to the elements.

MILITARY STRENGTH AND SUPERIOR STRATEGIES

Military superiority was the main reason for Mongol success. Mongol cavalry had great mobility and offered no fixed lines that the enemy could attack. Hunts for wild animals, involving massive numbers of men, provided good training for warfare. In a hunt, groups of warriors, stationed over a very wide area, gradually moved in toward each other, eventually trapping the animals in the center. These campaigns taught the warriors timing, how to communicate over vast distances, and how to coordinate attacks from different directions. Individual hunts sharpened their skills as riders and archers and taught them to "read" the terrain well.

Chinggis Khan could count on total mobilization in times of war. Every male from age 15 to 70, even an only son, had to serve in the army without pay. Sharing captured goods was their reward. Each man also had to present a certain number of horses, felts (fabric made by matting wool, fur, or hair), and services. Fighting units were organized into groups of 10: 10 households, 100 households, then 1,000, each with its own commander and with a super-official in charge of 1,000 households. Troops were well disciplined. In battle, if two or three in a household fled, all ten were reputedly killed; if all ten fled, all one hundred were killed; if two or three threw themselves into battle, those who did not follow were put to death.

Soldiers were equipped with bows, arrows, and axes. Each man came equipped with several horses, a small tent, a pot, a leather bag in which to carry liquids, and a small and large needle so he could repair his clothes. Soldiers wore leather helmets and leather jackets. Sometime they wore silk under their armor. When an arrow struck a warrior's armor, it pushed the silk in but usually did not tear the silk, so it was possible to pull the arrow out. Borrowing from the Song, they regularly filled bamboo sticks with gunpowder to blow open city gates. Herds of animals that followed the troops were a source of food.

The Mongols used clever military strategy, and much of their success was based on surprise and deception. They would feign an attack or appear to retreat, and then suddenly turn on the enemy. To make it look as if they had more men than they actually had, they stuffed extra clothes with grass and tied these dummies to the backs of their spare horses during an attack. Spies brought information about the enemy's strengths and weaknesses so they could attack weak points. The Mongols would often bypass strongholds and attack the weaker countryside or cut off the supplies of the best-defended areas. They attacked when least expected, such as when herds were weak after winter. Moreover, their intimate knowledge of the seasons and terrain made them much more successful on land than on the unfamiliar sea, where they could not read the signs of impending violent storms.

The Mongols also attacked the morale of the enemy, creating so much fear that the opposition was often defeated before the battle started. Chinggis Khan would send "orders of submission," announcing he was going to attack but he would be lenient if the area would submit and acknowledge his authority. If it submitted, he often left the leadership in place. If it did not, Chinggis would often order his men to destroy the area completely and brutally kill everyone. This tactic had a profound psychological effect, making areas fearful of resisting because of the potentially lethal consequences. On the other hand, the Mongols were experts in forming alliances and they were tolerant of all religions: In some areas where minority groups suffered persecution, Mongol armies sometimes seemed to come as liberators!

Mongol Advances

Internal weaknesses helped Chinggis Khan in his campaigns against China. The Jurched, who had driven out the Song and ruled north China, were not popular with the Chinese people. When a great flood in 1194 damaged food production in the north and dramatically changed the course of the Yellow River from the north to the south of the Shantung Peninsula, the Chinese were sure that this disaster indicated that the Jurched had lost the Mandate of Heaven. In 1215 the

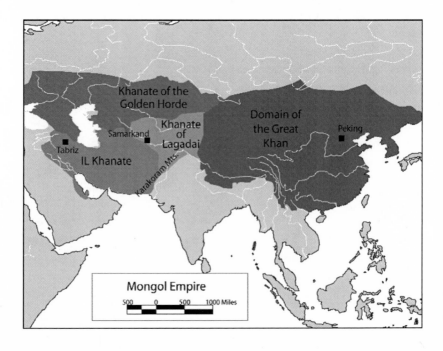

Mongols destroyed the Jurched capital at present-day Beijing and let it burn for a month. They then moved on to Central Asia.

As the Mongols conquered areas north and west of the Tian Shan Mountains, they recruited Turkish troops for their armies. Turkish-Mongol forces invaded Persia, where they destroyed the city of Merv and slaughtered perhaps 700,000 of its inhabitants. They went on and destroyed Nishapur, killing its residents, and other cities that refused to surrender suffered a similar fate. The numbers killed or driven from their homes is staggering, and it is hard to imagine the terror many experienced as the Mongols advanced.

Chinggis Khan supervised the building of Karakorum, his capital, in the nomadic heartland. Without adequate sources of food nearby enormous quantities of food and other supplies had to be carried overland to support the city's population. This helps explain why the Mongols treated merchants so well. Horses pulled as many as five hundred carts loaded with merchandise into Karakorum every day.

Who Should Be the Great Khan?

By 1227 the Mongols had defeated large areas in Central and West Asia and northern China. However, before Chinggis Khan could return to his planned campaigns further into China, he died. The Mongols met together at a *khuriltai* where they selected Ogodei to be the next Great Khan. Following Mongol custom, Chinggis's empire was divided among his four sons: Ogodei became the Great Khan, Chaghadai got Central Asia, Batu got the westernmost lands that would include Russia, and Tolui got North China.

Ogodei continued the policy of expansions. By 1237 Mongol commanders were leading troops into Russia, and in 1241 they conquered Poland. Ogodei's forces got 60 miles from Vienna, but in the winter of 1241, quite suddenly, he died. His officers had to return to Karakorum for another *khuriltai*, so the rest of eastern Europe was spared a Mongol invasion.

Ogodei's son became the next Great Khan in 1246, but he only ruled for two years. After he died, fierce competition broke out among Chinggis's surviving sons. Although Tolui, who ruled North China, was weak, his wife Sorghaghtani Beki was an exceptional person. When Tolui died in 1232, she had refused to remarry and concentrated instead on promoting the fortunes of her four sons and ensuring that their land in North China was ruled well. She encouraged tolerance of all religions and supported farming rather than letting the Mongols convert the farmlands to pastures for their animals.

In 1251, Sorghaghtani Beki's eldest son Mongke was chosen Great Khan, but his legitimacy was always in question. So was the legitimacy of his brother Khubilai, who became Great Khan in 1260. Khubilai's forces defeated the Southern Song in 1279 and united China for the first time under foreign rule. He had to establish his authority not only as Great Khan but also as the legitimate emperor of China.

Was the Yuan Dynasty a Chinese Empire or a Nomadic Kingdom?

Khubilai Khan named his new Chinese dynasty "Yuan," which means "origin of the universe." Faced with the monumental task of ruling such a vast area, he had to decide whether to adapt the Chinese method of ruling or impose the type of leadership the Mongols recognized. Other decisions involved whether to establish a capital along the border or in the steppes, whether or not to support agriculture, how to treat Chinese subjects, whether to use Chinese bureaucrats in his government, and to what extent to adapt Chinese values and way of life.

FARMING OR GRAZING?

Because the Mongols disdained the agricultural way of life, many Mongols advised Khubilai Khan to turn the farmland into pasture for horses. Chabi, his wisest and most influential wife, was among those who objected to that plan, pointing out that he would get much more revenue from taxing peasants than from raising horses. Khubilai followed Chabi's counsel and issued an edict prohibiting horses from roaming on farmland. He also created an Office for Stimulation of Agriculture and ordered the creation of storage areas for grain that could be distributed in case of famines, especially in the north where fighting had damaged farm land. The Mongol capital had 58 granaries that stored more than 48 million pounds of grain. Marco Polo said the Great Khan fed 30,000 poor people every day in the capital.

The Yuan organized the farmers into groups called *she*. Each *she* was composed of 50 families. They were encouraged to plant trees, work on irrigation and flood control projects, stock rivers and lakes with fish, and promote silk production. They were supposed to supervise their own members, rewarding those who worked well and punishing those who were lazy. The she system was intended to promote better agricultural techniques and basic literacy, and it made it easier for the government censor to watch over the Chinese.

WHERE SHOULD THE CAPITAL BE?

Khubilai Khan faced the problem of deciding where to place the capital of his dynasty. Chinggis Khan had not been interested in a settled way of life even though he had ordered Karakorum built; he preferred to rule from the saddle of his horse. Khubilai Khan ended up building two capitals: Shangdu, the "Upper Capital," 125 miles from Peking, and the "Central Capital," slightly northeast of the old Jin capital. Shangdu had a large hunting preserve and garden where Mongol warriors felt at home. It was a welcome relief for Khubilai Khan, who never lost his fascination with hunting and horseback riding.

TAXATION AND CORVÉE

Khubilai Khan organized a fixed, regular tax payment that went directly to the central government. He demanded a great deal of corvée from peasants, especially working on extensions of the Grand Canal so as to ensure that a regular grain supply reached the Central Capital. Many laborers also worked on the construction of palaces and Buddhist temples. At the same time he issued edicts forbidding overseers from being oppressive or from demanding corvée labor that took farmers away from their land so it could become pasture for horses, and artisans did not have to perform corvée.

COMMUNICATION AND TRADE

The Mongol communication system was based on relays of horses that made it possible to send a message from Peking to Vienna, a distance of about 5,000 miles, in only twenty days. At first the system was used mainly for official news, but merchants used it as well. By the end of Khubilai Khan's reign, there were about 1,400 postal stations, which used up to 50,000 horses, 8,400 oxen, 6,700 mules, 4,000 carts, 6,000 boats, 200 dogs, and 1,150 sheep. Rest stops provided travelers with hostels that had kitchens, halls, and areas for animals and grain storage. Rider-messengers could cover 250 miles in one day

Under Yuan rulers both overland and maritime trade flourished. Mongols were not involved directly in the caravan trade, but they welcomed merchants and other foreigners, including Russians, Arabs, Jews, and Venetians. Marco Polo claimed he received a warm welcome from the Great Khan, who gave him a job as a minor official. Merchants felt secure and had relatively high status in Yuan China, and Khubilai Khan gathered lots of intelligence from them. He was the first Chinese ruler to put paper currency into use throughout the country. Merchants converted foreign currency into paper money when they crossed into China.

ATTITUDE TOWARD THE CHINESE

Khubilai Khan ordered a census of the population. He divided the people into four categories: Mongols; miscellaneous aliens including West Asian Muslims who performed important services for the Mongols; North Chinese, called "Han" people, who had been part of the Jin kingdom; and finally Southern Chinese, subjects of the Southern Song, whom the Mongols considered the least trustworthy.

Khubilai Khan was not sure he could trust any of the Chinese. As a result, he preferred to employ foreigners rather than Chinese in his bureaucracy because he thought they would be more reliable. Confucianism seemed anti-foreign and he abolished the civil service exams. Mongols and Chinese obeyed different laws. However, the Mongols soon realized it was not good policy to alienate the vast majority of the population, and they could not rule the country without employing some

Mongol ruler with an Arab scribe

Chinese bureaucrats and advisors.

By 1279, Khubilai Khan had established himself as an intellectual as well as a warrior and he tried to rule as a traditional Chinese sage-emperor. He enjoyed the company of scholars and philosophers and worked out a new script with them. He was tolerant of various religious groups. Because he thought Confucianism was biased against foreigners and was also too complex with too many social restrictions, he promoted Buddhism. He knew the importance of fair laws rather than using force or bribes. In order to impress upon his fellow Mongols that he was indeed ruler of the world, he encouraged diplomats and traders like Marco Polo from the Far West to kowtow in his presence.

In spite of his policies of tolerance and his use of some Chinese in the government, the Mongols did not want to become like the Chinese. As much as possible, they kept separate from the men and women they ruled, clinging to their own values and way of life, celebrating their traditional festivals, and enjoying their feasts. The women did not adapt the Chinese custom of footbinding, which the Chinese considered a sign of high status, and they continued to dress in their own clothing. In fact, during Mongol times there was an increasing focus on a woman's chastity, and a widow was not to remarry but remain faithful to her dead husband and serve his family.

Effects of Mongol Rule across Asia

The Yuan dynasty was just one of the four Khanates that made up the Mongol Empire, which eventually covered eight thousand miles from east to west and nearly two thousand miles from north to south. It was the largest empire in world history. In each area the Mongols ruled, they used local bureaucrats to institute efficient administrative systems, adapting much from both the Muslim system of governing and Chinese-style bureaucracy. Since most Mongols were illiterate and inexperienced in public administration, they employed Persian, Turkic, and Chinese bureaucrats to assist in determining taxes, collecting revenues, and administering the various regions. Civil servants and merchants played a major role as well, even though court life was dominated by traditional Mongol nomadic values.

Hulegu, one of Chinggis Khan's grandsons, ruled the Il-Khanate of

Persia that included present-day Iran, Iraq, Syria, and Anatolia. In 1258 his forces sacked Baghdad, killed the last Abbasid caliph, and ended the caliphate. The Mongols had little interest in farming and did nothing to support agriculture. The fighting destroyed many *qanats,* underground water channels used for irrigation, or, even worse, left the qanats in disrepair. Without this irrigation system, farmers could not grow anything on the land.

On the positive side, the Il-Khanate unified a large area and facilitated travel. Because its capital was at the western end of the Iranian plateau, contact between West and East Asia increased. The fourth Il-Khan forbade fighting and taking goods from local farmers. In 1295 he converted to Islam. Many Mongol and Turkic people who settled in that area became Muslim as a result, and their culture mixed with that of the people they had conquered.

Another of Chinggis Khan's sons ruled the Chaghadai Khanate of Central Asia that the Mongols controlled until the 1370s. The relative peace the Mongols imposed allowed trade to flow through this area.

The part of Chinggis Khan's conquests that encompasses present-day Russia was known as the Golden Horde (*ordu,* horde, means headquarters or camp). Batu, one of Chinggis's grandsons, was the first to rule there. The invading Mongols had terrified the countryside, but Batu supported trade, allowed various missionaries to visit, and encouraged people to accept Islam. The Golden Horde officially accepted Islam around 1300.

Mongol rule separated Russia from Kievan Rus. During the 250 years of Mongol control, the Russian Church was relatively isolated and developed into the Russian Orthodox Church. Taxes on the peasants were heavy, but Russian bureaucrats collected them, suggesting that the bureaucrats may have been partly responsible for some of the hardships the Russian people endured.

Mongol rule has sometimes been called the *Pax Mongolica,* and the Mongols made travel relatively safe. The postal system facilitated communication. Merchants had been accustomed to paying tariffs and buying protection from bandits along the way. The Mongols reduced these costs because they made efforts to eliminate banditry and tariffs.

Unlike the Chinese, nomadic groups cannot survive without trade. The Mongols respected artisans and merchants and encouraged trade.

In fact, according to Morris Rossabi, the foremost authority on Central Asia and the Mongols, the Mongols started merchant associations that financed caravan trips and shared the risks (not unlike limited liability in modern corporations). These innovations facilitated commerce, enabling interaction along the Silk Roads to reach its greatest heights. Merchants, caravan drivers, missionaries, and adventurers gained intimate knowledge of diverse languages, cultural groups, and business opportunities, and participated in a lively exchange of people and ideas across the immense expanse of Eurasia.

Like other nomads, most Mongols had no interest in farming and considered peasants who worked the soil the dregs of society; horses were far more valuable. They thought nothing of killing peasants and destroying farmland. On the other hand, they valued artisans and transported vast numbers of them to cities in Inner Asia that they had conquered. They believed that the people living in areas nominally under the Abbasid Caliphate, whom the Chinese called "Persians", were very advanced. To take advantage of their knowledge and skills, they sent Persians into Central Asia and China. Persian medicine, particularly many herbal remedies, reached China in the thirteenth century, and Persians set up the first astronomical observatory in Peking in 1267. At this time the Chinese regarded Persian civilization as the most advanced of any they knew.

Decline of the Mongols

Despite the dramatic Mongol military victories in many parts of Eurasia, the various Khanates that were carved out of the world's largest empire did not last. When the leader of the Il-Khanate died in 1335 without leaving an heir, the Il-Khanate in Persia came to an end, and about thirty years later Tamerlane invaded that area. Ineffective leadership and raids by Tamerlane's forces weakened the Golden Horde. Mongol control there was over by the end of the fifteenth century.

Khubilai Khan's rule in China slowly deteriorated. For one thing, although he already ruled a vast empire, he wanted to enhance his right to be the Great Khan by conquering Japan. The Mongols had already captured the Koryo capital and occupied much of the Korean peninsula. Members of the Koryo court escaped to an island off the coast, and Koreans on the peninsula resisted adapting Mongol culture and never gave up their opposition to Mongol occupation.

Under Khubilai Khan's direction, the Mongols forced the Koreans to help build nine hundred ships and supply crews and food for two Mongol invasions of Japan. On 1274 he sent a great naval force of 25,000 men, including 9,000 Koreans, against Japan. A devastating typhoon (which the Japanese called *kami kazi* or "the divine wind") destroyed the fleet. In 1281, he launched another naval invasion, this time sending 140,000 men. From the Japanese perspective, their gods protected them again, for another kami kazi destroyed this fleet. That defeat broke the Mongol image of invincibility, and when Khubilai Khan mounted campaigns in Southeast Asia, he failed there as well. Mongol expansion was over.

The attempted invasions of Japan proved very costly. In addition, to counter widespread inflation, the Mongols devaluated currency and increased demands for corvée, which they used to built Shangdu, a new city, and to extend the Grand Canal. Khubilai Khan began to issue anti-Muslim legislation, such as forbidding the slaughter of animals according to Muslim law. His support of Buddhism further separated the Mongols from the Chinese intellectuals who had already turned away from Buddhism. His efforts, towards the end of his life, to promote better relations with the Chinese people by letting Chinese serve in lower-level government positions had little effect.

After 1294, when Khubilai Khan died, succession became a problem. In the period between 1308 and 1333 there were eight emperors: two were assassinated and all died young. Without a strong leader who could command their loyalty, military leaders began using troops to farm their land rather than to fight, which undermined the morale of the troops who thought farming was distinctly unmanly.

The Yuan end came "by expulsion and not by absorption." Overtaxation, a burdensome corvée system, unsuccessful military campaigns, and general insecurity, especially after Khubilai's death, increased peasant unrest. The Chinese always considered the Mongols foreigners who were unfit to rule their homeland and eventually revolted and drove them out. A Chinese peasant soldier who gave up banditry to become a Buddhist monk led the revolt and founded the Ming dynasty in 1368.

The Mongols brought major changes to the people of the Eurasian steppes. Many characteristics of settled agricultural life were introduced there, including private ownership of land, cities, the rise of a merchant class, and the beliefs and practices of one or more of the universal religions, particularly Islam and Buddhism. In Europe there was a growing interest in Asia, and many Europeans sensed startling contrasts between their world and societies further to the east. As fear of Mongol advances lessened, Europeans began to react with awe at what they were learning about the wealth of the Mongol courts and the riches of China and India. We shall look more closely at what travelers and merchants were experiencing and some of the consequences of the expanding hemispheric interconnections in the next scene.

SCENE TWO

TRAVELERS, GERMS, AND IDEAS ON THE MOVE

Setting the Stage

The Pax Mongolica was not the first period of intensive Eurasian trade. Stability created by the Roman-Parthian-Kushan-Han period (from about 100 B.C.E. to 200 C.E.) greatly facilitated overland communication and exchanges across the Silk Roads of Eurasia and into the Mediterranean basin. Again, with the reunification of China under the Tang (618), coupled with the spread of Islam starting in 622, a second period of cross-hemispheric trade began. It encompassed both overland and maritime commerce and included merchants and goods from West African kingdoms and Swahili city-states on Africa's east coast. Camel caravans also crossed the Sahara carrying gold, ivory, and slaves north. Muslim traders were welcome in cities in Ghana and Mali, and contact with Muslim merchants helped Islam spread in both West and East Africa.

The relative stability in the thirteenth century, enhanced by Mongol presence along the Silk Roads, stimulated a third period of intensive Afro-Eurasian interaction and exchange. By 1300 long-distance trade was brisk, and a hemispheric trading system that stretched from western Europe all the way to China had developed. This network included Africa, Europe, and Asia, and goods moved over both land and sea. Dar al-Islam was making it possible for Muslims to "seek knowledge, even in China" as well as for adventurous individuals to travel widely and bring back firsthand accounts of what they had seen. Christian missionaries began to travel east in hopes of making converts.

Marco Polo and Ibn Battuta were two famous thirteenth- and four-teenth-century travelers. Both men gave compelling accounts and fascinating details about their experiences. To get a sense of the world they encountered, we might note several events that took place in 1325, one year after Marco Polo died and the year Ibn Battuta started

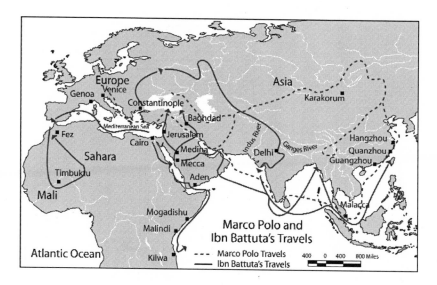

Marco Polo and Ibn Battuta's Travels
- - - Marco Polo Travels
——— Ibn Battuta's Travels

on his travels. In 1325 Mansa Musa of Mali started his hajj. He distributed so much gold that its price in Cairo was depressed for years. The Aztecs are said to have ended their wanderings and settled on the small island in Lake Texcoco in 1325, the same year that Muhammad Tughluq took over the sultanate in Delhi. Osman, the Turkish leader, lay dying, but in 1326 his followers, the Osmanli, captured Bursa and continued to expand their control in Anatolia. That same year the first extant picture of a gunpowder weapon appeared in Europe. Dante had been dead for four years, but Giotto, who would not die until 1340, was busy painting his form-filled frescos. Ivan I captured Moscow in 1325 and began to collect tribute for the Mongols who ruled the Golden Horde. And the Mongol army reported its first case of the plague.

World Travelers: Marco Polo

Marco Polo set out with his father and uncle in 1271 to make good on an invitation to visit China that they had received from Khubilai Khan, the Mongol emperor. They made their way from Italy overland across Central Asia to Peking, the Yuan capital. Marco lived in China for seventeen years, and most scholars now believe he probably served in a minor government position under Khubilai Khan .

Khubilai Khan impressed him immensely. He notes with approval

Marco Polo leaves for China

the Great Khan's tolerance and concern for his subjects. He wrote that if bad weather or a plague hurt the farmers, he reduced taxes, and he did not collect anything from shippers whose cargo had been lost at sea. He reported that the Khan distributed grain and animals to those in need so that those he governed "may be enabled to live by their labor and improve their substance."

Marco Polo was amazed at Hangzhou, the Southern Song capital that had just fallen to the Mongols. He praised its "grandeur and beauty" as well as "its abundant delights, which may lead an inhabitant to imagine himself in paradise." He described the city's twelve thousand bridges, wide boulevards, baths, and dwellings, and mentioned artisans' workshops, innumerable stores, and ten principal markets, each four miles apart. "Three days a week there is an assemblage there of from forty to fifty thousand persons," selling everything one could desire. He claims that more than 10,000 pounds of pepper were brought to the city daily.

Honoring the emperior's request, on their return trip the Polos took a Chinese princess to her new husband, the ruler of the Il-Khanate in Persia. When the Polos reached Italy, Genoese sailors captured Marco and put him in jail. While he was in jail, he dictated the story of his travels to a fellow prisoner, who happened to be a writer of popular romances.

Ibn Battuta

No doubt Ibn Battuta was unaware of the events happening around the world as he left Tangier in 1325 to make the hajj. Unlike Marco Polo, a merchant, Ibn Battuta was a Muslim on a pilgrimage, a devotee seeking wisdom from venerable holy men, a judicial scholar seeking fellow scholars living in some of Afro-Eurasia's great urban centers, and an adventurer looking for hospitality, honor, and good employment. World historian Ross Dunn, an authority on Ibn Battuta, reports that in the course of his travels, he visited territories equivalent to about forty-four modern countries and covered approximately 73,000 miles.

Ibn Battuta noted the large number of trading centers across Eurasia and described the wealth of both the Delhi Sultanate and the Mongol Empire. He noted that in traveling, the *khatun* or wife of the ruler of the Il-Khanate of Persia, had ten or fifteen Greek and Indian pages.

> dressed in robes of silk gilt, encrusted with jewels, and each of whom carried in his hand a mace of gold or silver, or maybe of wood veneered with them. Behind the khatun's wagon there are about a hundred wagons, in each of which there are four slave girls full-grown and young . . . Behind these wagons there [again] are about three hundred wagons, drawn by camels and oxen, carrying the khatun's chests, moneys, roves, furnishings and food.

Mosque at Daulatabad Fort

He arrived in the Indian subcontinent in 1334, shortly after Sultan Tughluq had decided to create Daulatabad, a new capital on the barren Deccan plateau. Ibn Battuta reported that the mass exodus from Delhi that the Sultan ordered left the city "empty and unpopulated" of all the government officials and much of the population.

Many times Ibn Battuta barely escaped death. He was caught in a snowstorm in Anatolia and would have died if a friend had not rescued him. After being robbed, stripped, and left to die in Arabia, he was miraculously saved. Sultan Tughluq alternated between praising him and threatening to kill him. Finally, the sultan asked him to head a diplomatic mission to China. When the ships carrying the rest of the mission left the port, he was still on shore, looking for a lady friend. The next day the ship capsized in a storm, and everyone on board was lost. After another series of adventures, he finally reached southern China, and he reported on Peking, the capital, as well.

Several years after returning to Morocco, Ibn Battuta set out again, this time for West Africa. He was impressed with the thriving Muslim communities he visited and with the understanding and commitment men and women in Mali had for Islam. As his travels came to an end, the sultan of Morocco commissioned a literary scholar from al-Andalus to write a *rihla*, or travel book, about all Ibn Battuta had done.

TWO TRAVELERS, TWO DIFFERENT WORLDS

It is instructive to compare the experiences of these two men. Marco Polo came from a commercial family in Venice, a major cosmopolitan trading center on the Adriatic Sea, so he focused a lot of his attention on markets, shipping, and available products. *The Travels* are filled with details Marco Polo observed or read about but little about himself. He saw things from a European perspective, and never met people who shared his own culture, nor did he visit familiar surroundings. He was a stranger everywhere.

Ibn Battuta, on the other hand, felt at home in the world in which he traveled. He found people who could speak Arabic and shared common laws, values and a similar cosmopolitan Islamic worldview almost everywhere he went. In spite of the dangers he encountered, he never seemed surprised when friends turned up in the most out-of-the-way places. He was out of his own cultural context only in China, and some scholars believe he got only as far as its southern coastal region. Even in West Africa, where he was critical of what he viewed as the stinginess of the leaders, and a bit shocked at the way women dressed and the freedom they enjoyed, he found many fellow Muslims and a thriving Muslim community.

Marco Polo's book was published and circulated, but at first people were reluctant to believe what they read. How could a city have twelve thousand bridges? How could stones (coal) and liquids (oil) burn? How could a man travel 250 miles a day on horseback? *The Travels* revealed a world unknown to Europeans, who were enthralled with descriptions of such things as explosives and pieces of paper being used as money. His details about Chinese life and the impressive quality and diversity of Chinese goods and commerce made many Europeans anxious for more contact with that prosperous land.

By contrast, Ibn Battuta's *rihla* circulated among learned people in North and West Africa and Egypt but was unknown outside Islamic countries. Dar al-Islam, which this work described, was already a reality to its readers, so the work did little to change their perceptions. But as we read now about his travels, we may be amazed at the scope and wealth of fourteenth-century Islamic societies.

Silent Travelers

Not the least of Ibn Battuta's brushes with disaster was the Black Death. During the time he was traveling, bubonic plague, a different kind of invader, was also on the move, a silent and all but invisible voyager that accompanied animals, people, and goods. Infected fleas hiding in the fur of rodents brought this terrifying new disease to Europe. They moved easily from rodents to camels and other pack animals traveling overland, and ships transported them with their cargo. A second form of plague was transmitted directly from one human to another.

Bubonic plague probably originated in the central Asian steppes sometime around the middle of the thirteenth century. Initial symptoms included fever and boils on the arms and groin. Within a day or two the boils turned black, so people called it the "Black Death." Infected victims vomited blood and usually died within three days. By 1331 the epidemic had killed nine-tenths of the population of Hopei province in China and spread to eight other provinces.

The plague first broke out in Europe in 1346 in the Crimea. Mongol troops had laid siege to Caffe, and as part of their terror tactics, they catapulted infected bodies over its walls, causing an outbreak of the disease in the city. Several fleeing Genoese merchants carried the disease with them to Sicily. Within a year the plague had spread to Italy, Spain, and France, and by 1348 traders had taken it to Germany. Two thousand people a day were dying in Damascus when Ibn Battuta visited there, but he did not contract the illness. A year later it reached England and Scandinavia.

LIVING AND DYING WITH THE PLAGUE

The plague was the worst natural calamity known in Europe's history. Normal life was completely disrupted. Men and women deserted the sick. Parents abandoned their children and wives their husbands. City dwellers tried to escape to the country, where they thought they would be safer. The smell of decaying corpses was everywhere, and there was no one to bury the dead. Crops were left standing in the fields, and trade was severely curtailed. Living with the constant threat of sudden and inexplicable death hovered like a long shadow over almost everyone.

The triumph of death

The sweep of the plague was devastating not only in the actual
deaths but in other ways as well. "What is causing us to get sick and
die?" people asked. "Why are we suffering so? What could God have
in mind?" Men and women frantically tried to figure out how to protect themselves. Frenzied residents of cities crowded into temples,
churches, and mosques to pray for an end to the disaster, unaware
that close contact made it easier for germs to spread. Many carried
bunches of herbs to ward off the evil spirit of the plague. This practice, together with the fact that infected people developed rose-col-
ored rings on their bodies, led to the nursery rhyme:

> Ring around the rosies,
> A pocketful of posies [flowers believed to repel the plague]
> Achoo! Achoo!, [sneeze]
> We all fall down. [dead]

WHY IS THIS HAPPENING TO US?

God is just, so he must be punishing us for our sins, some Christians reasoned, and they began stabbing themselves with spikes and beating themselves with clubs. Sometimes hundreds of these "flagellants" traveled from town to town, wounding themselves as they went. One witness explained, "They . . . scourged themselves with whips of hard knotted leather with little iron spikes. Some made themselves bleed very badly . . . and some foolish women had cloths ready to catch the blood and smear it on their eyes, saying it was miraculous blood." Muslims do not believe in original sin—the belief that all humans are flawed because Adam disobeyed God in the Garden of Eden—so they tried to accept the plague as a manifestation of Allah's unknowable plan for his creation. Muslims were advised, among other things, to spend their nights in the mosques begging for Allah's mercy.

Perhaps God is angry at nonbelievers, some Christians argued, and they singled out Jews as the culprits: as a result anti-Semitism swept through Europe along with the disease. Christians accused Jews of poisoning the water supply and practicing witchcraft. At least sixty Jewish communities were destroyed in Germany. Angry mobs murdered the entire Jewish community in Mainz. Pope Clement VI issued two bulls (laws) against the plunder and slaughter of Jews, but the butchery continued. In Strasbourg in 1349 more than a thousand Jews were burned in the town square; another thousand were spared because they accepted baptism. One observer speculated that money was the reason Jews were killed. "If they had been poor, and if the feudal lords had not been in debt to them, they would not have been burnt." Once the creditor was dead, the debts were canceled.

Long-Term Consequences of the Black Death

There had been plagues before the Black Death, but this was the most devastating one, affecting people throughout Eurasia and North Africa. Poorly trained priests replaced those who had died, and the Church seemed helpless to alleviate the suffering. Religious holidays, pilgrimages, and the sale of indulgences to ensure the believer entered heaven proliferated. Conversely, many rejected the Church and looked for human solutions or lived for the moment. Others turned to individual mysticism or direct communion with demons, spirits and God.

The population throughout Eurasia fell dramatically. Although population figures are approximate, it is estimated that in 1000 Europe had 38 million people; by 1200 there were 59 million. In 1347, on the eve of the Black Death, there may have been 75 million people. Five years later, in 1352, there were only 50 million. Twenty-five million people had died in just five years. England on the eve of the Black Death had a population of approximately 3.7 million. In 1377 it had fallen to about 2.2 million. In large cities, such as Florence, Italy, as much as sixty percent of the population perished. Although scholars debate the impact of the plague in Asia, China's population dropped from 123 million in 1200 to only 65 million in 1368, and India also suffered from outbreaks of disease at this time.

Industrial production and trade also declined dramatically. Manufacturers in Florence who had probably produced 80,000 pieces of cloth in 1338 were turning out only 24,000 in 1378. But the consequences were not all bad. On the whole European towns fared better than agricultural estates, and the plague led to improved public hygiene.

The plague was also a major factor in eroding European serfdom and feudalism. The poor died in great numbers, and laborers and peasants who had survived were in great demand. The labor shortage gave peasants more bargaining power, and they demanded that landlords reduce rents and begin to pay cash wages to keep them on the land, or they would leave. Wages increased the mobility of poor peasants, and some became tenants rather than serfs. Cities grew, weakening the power of the nobility and increasing the potential power of kings who could provide protection.

The plague caused some Christians to question the teachings of the Church and turn to other sources of meaning. As religious skepticism deepened, various humanistic movements developed that began to produce art and literature that focused on more worldly activities. Ironically, even though the Church lost some followers, it became wealthier by taking over tracts of land that had belonged to plague victims.

The number of artisans in Muslim communities in West Asia waned as did trade moving through that area. For example, Alexandria had approximately 13,000 weavers in 1394 and only 800 in 1434. The plague had long-term consequences in East Asia as well. A significant decline in population and confidence in government played an important role at the end of China's Yuan dynasty.

Other Cross-Cultural Exchanges

Countless items crossed political and geographic boundaries during the millennium 500 to 1450. Besides travelers and germs, we have noted how universal religions and the many Chinese and Indian ideas and crops traveled far from the places they originated. We have considered the importance of Islam and some of the Muslim scholars whose insights were important in the development of Europe, as well as the interaction of Muslim scholars and traders in various areas in Africa. Here are a few more examples of cross-cultural exchanges.

PAPER

Although our word paper comes from Egyptian papyrus, which the ancient Egyptians made out of strips of the papyrus plant, and many other groups wrote on parchment that is made from animal hides, paper was invented in China. Initially the Chinese wrote on strips of

wood or bamboo, which may help explain why their writing runs vertically rather than horizontally, and then on pieces of cloth. Their early books were scrolls of woven cloth that had been trimmed.

Chinese sources credit Ts-ai Lun, a eunuch in the Han court, with inventing paper in 105 C.E. He made sheets of paper from fiber by beating discarded cloth, hemp (the plant now used to make burlap), and the bark of trees. Knowledge of how to make paper had reached Korea by 600, and Dokyo, a Korean Buddhist

Ts'ai Lun, Dokyo, and Mochizuki who established papermaking in Japan in 1572.

monk, brought the new information to Japan. The Japanese first made paper in 610 and were soon producing it in nine provinces. Papermaking spread into Central Asia and Persia along the Silk Roads. It appeared in Mecca in 707.

In 751, during the Battle of Talas in Central Asia, the Arab army captured several Chinese soldiers who were skilled papermakers, and they taught Muslims how to make paper. By 760 Samarkand had a paper factory and was exporting high-quality paper. Papermaking soon spread to Baghdad, where a paper factory opened in 795. The earliest paper manuscript found in Cairo was dated 878–9. A visitor in Cairo in 1035 saw goods in the market being wrapped in paper.

Paper must have reached Constantinople before 947 because a Byzantine ambassador who visited Muslims in Cordoba carried a letter written "on sky-blue paper." In 985 a Muslim geographer told Berber merchants they should not be writing on leather when Andalusians were experts at making paper. In 1284 the Christian king Alfonso X initiated paper manufacturing in Castile. Papermaking technology crossed the Pyrenees Mountains in 1270.

Paper was first made in Morocco in 1100 and in France by 1189. It may have reached Italy in the mid-twelfth century, and the first paper mill in Italy was established in 1276. Papermaking reached England in 1309.

PRINTING

The Chinese also developed the first printing, initially with seals and later with single blocks. The earliest extant example of printing, made by rubbing stone inscriptions, is dated 627. Soon Chinese craftsmen were making multiple copies of images from rubbings, blocks, and stencils. The world's first block printing on paper took place in Japan in the eighth century. During the reign of a Japanese empress who ruled in Nara from 749 to 769, a serious smallpox epidemic broke out. In an effort to drive out the demons causing the epidemic, the empress ordered the printing of a million prayer papers using Chinese techniques. The prayers were then placed in hundreds of small, carved wooden pagodas, the East Asian term for a stupa. (We can speculate whether she knew about how Emperor Ashoka and the Sui emperor had distributed Buddhist relics in stupas in India and China.)

In 868 Chinese printers completed the Diamond Sutra, the first printed book in history. (A copy is in the British Museum.)

In about 1041 the Chinese invented movable type made of clay, but because Chinese characters do not lend themselves to this technology, they made little use of it. By 1250 Egyptians had mastered Chinese block printing. Marco Polo was fascinated that the Chinese used paper for money, but he failed to mention that it was printed. In the mid-thirteenth century Korean monks carved wood blocks to print the Tripitaka. The earliest known Korean example of a book printed from movable type was published in 1409. Korean printers used sand casting, which involved making molds of letters in sand and then pouring a lead alloy into the molds to create letters. After that, they began mass-producing books.

About thirty years later, in about 1450, a young metalworker named Johannes Gutenberg noted the demand for copies of indulgences (written statements forgiving certain sins that the Church issued). He probably first used sand-casting to print them, instead of uniform metal molds. Finally, in 1457, the date given for the arrival of printing in Europe, he produced his 42-line Bible. It is interesting that the initial motivation for printing in China, Japan, Korea, and Europe was the desire to have copies of religious documents.

INCARNATIONS OF THE PANCHATANTRA

Long before the printing press or the Internet, Indian animal and folktales were traveling from India to "Greek academies, Chinese monasteries, Persian courts, Indonesian temples, Jewish rabbinates, and virtually every European household." One of the best-known sets of animal tales is the Indian *Panchatantra*, which was written sometime after the beginning of the common era but before the sixth century. A court Brahmin is said to have composed them to try and teach the subtleties of statecraft to several dull-witted princes. The first book, "The Loss of Friends," tells how a lion king's friendship with an ox makes his jackal advisors jealous. Fearing the ox will replace them in the lion's affection, they steadily and artfully sow distrust between the two friends until the duped lion kills the ox, without having any idea that the jackals had set him up to it. The princes, hearing these tales, were supposed to learn how to rule: in these examples they learned to be wary of both friends and advisors. Other *Panchatantra* stories illustrate such things as how to achieve one's ends by playing on the pride and arrogance of one's adversaries but some also stress the value of friendship and cooperation.

Stories from the *Panchatantra* traveled to Nepal, Kashmir, and South India. The *Panchatantra* reached Persia in the sixth century C.E. and was translated into Persian as *Kalila and Dimna,* the names of the two jackals. Instead of offering amoral advice on statecraft, however, this version adds a moral dimension, and ends with the scheming jackal being thrown in jail for misleading the Lion King.

The Persian version reached al-Mansur, the second Abbasid caliph, who had commissioned the building of Baghdad. He ordered it translated into Arabic and the result—*Kalilah wa Dimnah*—also included a few of the translator's own tales. Some claim it soon became second only to the Qur'an in popularity.

German crusaders had a copy of the work translated into German, and it was then translated into Latin, Italian, and Hebrew. A copy may have been available to Machiavelli when he wrote *The Prince,* another amoral treatise on statecraft that uses animals in several of its episodes to illustrate a point. A Persian copy of the German text was translated into French, and at least eleven *Panchatantra* tales are included in the work of La Fontaine.

It is even possible that some of the stories reached Africa and that enslaved Africans brought them to the Americas. Several Uncle Remus stories, including the one about a rabbit that tricks a lion into jumping in a well, are identical to *Panchatantra* tales, and so are some of the fables attributed to Aesop. Young people in the United States today are familiar with Walt Disney's renditions of some of the same tales.

SUGAR

Sugarcane and sugar beet are the principal sources of sugar. According to Sidney Mintz, in *Sweetness and Power,* his fascinating study of sugar in modern history, sugarcane was first domesticated in New Guinea as early as 8000 B.C.E. Two thousand years later it had reached the Philippines, India and possibly Indonesia. The Indians, who were the first to figure out the difficult process of crystallizing sugar from a liquid, mentioned its use in documents from the fifth century B.C.E. After the cane was chopped, ground, pressed, pounded, soaked, boiled, and carefully cooled, molasses resulted. One of Alexander of Macedonia's generals mentions a reed from India that produces honey without the help of bees. Sugar, produced in India, was known in Rome during the first century C.E.

A Hindu religious document dated about 500 describes making a taffy-like brittle substance. A Byzantine emperor reported finding this "Indian luxury" in a Persian palace near Baghdad. Arab Muslims learned about making sugar from the Egyptians, and they soon introduced the cultivation of sugarcane and how to make granulated sugar, and they also created a demand for it in the Mediterranean Basin. In fact, sugar "followed the Qur'an." Wherever Arab Muslims went, Mintz tells us, they spread information about making sugar. By the eighth century sugar was being consumed in southern Europe, but it was not known in northern Europe until about 1000. By then sugarcane was being grown throughout North Africa, Sicily, and Spain.

Growing and processing sugar requires a great deal of hard labor, so as the "sweet tooth" spreads around the world, it will have far-reaching consequences, not least of which will be the search for new labor supplies such as slavery and indentured labor and the displacement of farm land to grow it as a commercial crop. In our our day, the seemingly benign addiction to sugar is contributing to obesity, a major health problem.

These are only a few examples of the many products, ideas, and technological and scientific knowledge that spread in many directions across Eurasia. Other examples range all the way from games like chess, dominoes, and playing cards to complex weapons, inventions, and religious worldviews and rituals. It is intriguing to try to figure out the many ways people over the ages have built on one another's insights. It seems that the more original we think we are, the more we realize how much we have adapted from others who may have lived centuries ago and thousands of miles away.

SCENE THREE

SEAS OF CHANGE IN THE INDIAN OCEAN

Setting the Stage

The Indian Ocean trading network extends from West Asia through the Red Sea and Persian Gulf to the Arabian Sea, around the coast of India to the Bay of Bengal, then down the Malay Peninsula and through the Strait of Malacca to the South China Sea. These bodies of water connected Christian, Muslim, Buddhist, and Hindu religious worlds, as well as the Byzantine, Abbasid, Turkish, Srivijaya, Chola, and Chinese kingdoms and empires, Swahili city-states, and Southeast Asian trading ports. Exchanges taking place over these waters touched the lives of the people living along more than six thousand miles of coastlines, and they indirectly affected countless other lives as well.

The monsoon system determined how and when ships and travelers could cross the seas. Several major diaspora communities — including Jewish, Arab, Armenian, Chinese, and Indian — developed

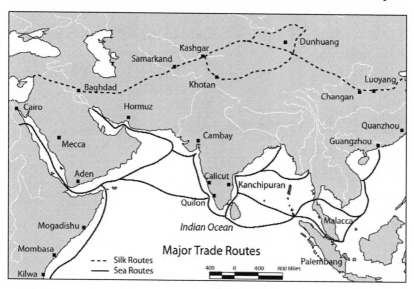

Major Trade Routes

- - - Silk Routes
——— Sea Routes

because merchants had to wait for the reverse monsoon to return home. These communities not only provided a home away from home for various trading groups but served as a means of bringing technical and cultural insights to new areas.

Products from China and India dominated the trade in the early centuries of the second millennium. Indian jewelry, cotton, Chinese porcelain ceramics and, to a lesser extent, Chinese silk textiles were the major items of exchange. Indians also traded iron and steel products, glass, spices, rice, wheat, and animals, such as elephants and monkeys, and birds. Other exports from China included tea, medicines, copper, and iron products. High value goods, such as silk, moved overland across the network of Silk Roads from China and India to the Mediterranean Sea. Bulk goods, such as Chinese porcelains, food, timber, metals, and heavy manufactured goods usually traveled by sea.

The Indian Subcontinent

The Indian subcontinent juts into the center of the Indian Ocean, and Indian merchants from the subcontinent's west coast played an important role in the circuit of trade in the Arabian Sea. After the Delhi Sultanate captured Gujarat in 1303–4, its prosperous trading ports came under Islamic control, and the sultanate collected the custom revenues. In the aftermath of Tamerlane's raids into north India in the 1390s, Gujarat declared its independence. Exporting cloth created a favorable trade balance with Europe and states in West Asia. Gujarat's magnificent mosques and impressive palaces attest to that wealth. Businessmen envied its merchants, known as *bania*.

Bengal, in northeast India, became rich from Indian Ocean trade that went from the Bay of Bengal to Southeast Asia. Known for their very fine cotton cloth called "muslin", Bengali traders found ready markets for this attractive product. Further south, the Cholas were trading from ports on both the subcontinent's east and west coasts. The island kingdom of Sri Lanka also figured prominently in the Indian zone of contact and exchange.

The Importance of the Strait of Malacca

When ships started sailing through the Strait of Malacca, Srivijaya became the most important kingdom in that area. Palembang, its capital, served as the major port for ships on their way to and from China and the meeting point for goods from both China and India. Many Chinese Buddhist pilgrims and missionaries visited Palembang on their way to and from India and China.

The Tang government granted privileged status to merchants coming from Srivijaya, in large part because the Srivijayan merchants were willing to pretend that their commercial activities were tribute. Srivijaya sent tribute missions to the Tang court from 670 to 742 and to the Song from 960 into the eleventh century.

Muslim Merchants Play a Major Role

From its inception Islam was sympathetic to trade. The hajj promoted travel and encouraged the development of support networks for travelers. Islam was the main stimulus of contact between different cultures. The Qur'an stated:

A dhow under sail off the coast of East Africa

> And of His signs is this: He sendeth herald winds to
> make you taste His mercy, and that the ships may sail
> at his command, and that ye may seek His grace, and
> that haply ye may be thankful. (Qur'an 30: 46)

Adopting the Chinese mariner's compass and Indian lateen sails, Muslim sailors soon dominated trade in the Indian Ocean. Instead of Hindu and Buddhist Indians carrying most of the goods, Arabs, Persians, and Muslim Indians began to dominate commerce. An authority on world trade concluded: "Islam was the central civilization for the whole of the old world. Not only was it the most dramatic and creative of Rome's and Persia's successors; it was also the principal agency for contact between the discrete cultures of this period."

The thirty to forty independent Swahili city-states on the east coast of Africa played an important role in the Indian Ocean trade. Swahili merchants carried on an extensive cross-cultural trade, and Muslims dominated that commerce as well.

The Islamic world, knit together by a common religious faith, proved a fertile ground for the exchange of ideas, technologies, and crops. Muslim businessmen were among the first to establish large-scale banking institutions that not only lent money but also provided currency exchanges and helped arrange investments. They introduced letters of credit called *sakk*, from which we take our practice of using checks. They also formed joint ventures, sharing both risks and profits. Muslims introduced rice, oranges, sugarcane, cotton, apricots, and peaches to Europe and the Mediterranean region. Their skill as salesmen was well documented. For example, a story circulated about an Arab merchant in Medina who sold all his stock of veils except the black ones. To help sell the remaining veils, his friend wrote a short song that may well be the first singing commercial.

> Go ask the lovely one in the black veil
> What have you done to a devout monk?
> He had already dressed for his prayers
> Until you appeared to him by the door of the mosque.

Soon, they said, every lady in Medina wanted to own a black veil.

"God Has Given the Seas in Common"

Traders from many different areas participated freely in the thriving Indian Ocean trading network. Although Muslim merchants were the most numerous, ships came from many different places. However, no European ships were part of the Indian Ocean system until 1498. European traders who wanted to reach Asian ports had to travel on Asian or Muslim ships.

No single area or state controlled which merchants could trade in the Indian Ocean. No matter who was transporting the goods, ships could come and go as they wished, and all were welcome. An Indonesian ruler stated as late as 1615, "God has made the earth and the seas, has divided the earth among mankind, and given the seas in common. It is a thing unheard of that anyone should be forbidden to sail the seas."

China's Role in Trade

China, whose population had probably reached 125 million by 1400, anchored the eastern end of the whole Eurasian trading system. Chinese merchants sent their goods along both the Silk Roads and the maritime routes. Tang naval engineers developed ships called junks that could safely make very long journeys. Song sailors had invented the "north-pointing needle" (the magnetic compass) by at least 1119. After 1250 the shipment of heavy goods increased, mainly because Chinese junks improved. Chinese traders dominated trade from the China Sea to the Spice Islands in Southeast Asia. In the mid-fourteenth century, Ibn Battuta reported that the thirteen Chinese junks he saw in Cambay, in western India, dwarfed all the other vessels. These large junks could carry bulk goods fairly cheaply.

When the Mongols took control of northern China in 1279, they had little knowledge of the sea. In order to defeat the Song, which had an impressive navy and controlled the south, they captured 140 Song ships and developed their own naval force. Their merchant fleet traded at ports in Sri Lanka, the Malay Peninsula, and Java. However, Khubilai Khan's naval campaigns against Japan and ports in Southeast Asia were unsuccessful. These defeats, which damaged Yuan prestige and weakened the government, coupled with the devastation brought on by disease and famine, encouraged the Chinese to revolt and drive out the foreign rulers.

The Ming Policy in the Indian Ocean

The Chinese expelled the Mongols in 1368, and the Ming, an indigenous Chinese dynasty, claimed the Mandate of Heaven (the legitimate
right to rule). Ming leaders immediately set about trying to erase the
humiliation of foreign rule. In an effort to reestablish the tributary
relationship among his neighbors, the first Ming emperor sought to
restrict all trade coming to China to tribute missions. He also tried to
discourage contact between his subjects and foreigners.

But private Chinese merchants had grown rich on overseas trade,
and they were reluctant to give it up. Realizing many merchants were
defying the directive to limit trade, the third Ming emperor ordered
shipbuilders to alter Chinese oceangoing ships so they could no longer
be used on the high seas. In their place, he wanted to let the Ming fleet
support the tribute trade. He hoped the fleet would also demonstrate
the Ming's wealth and power and increase tribute missions.

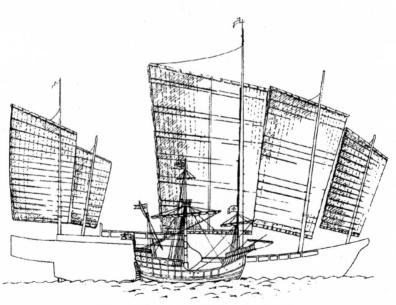

*Zheng He's treasure ship (four hundred feet)
and Columbus's St. Maria (eighty-five feet).*

ZHENG HE COMMANDS THE FLEET

The Ming fleet's initial voyage in 1405 had 317 ships, almost twenty-eight thousand men, and large supplies of arms, food, and other necessities. It also included several massive "treasure ships" that were approximately 400 feet long and 160 feet wide. The emperor hoped their grandeur would awe the leaders around the Indian Ocean. During the voyages, the sailors were also to gather information about lands surrounding the ocean and bring back a unicorn if they could find one. The commander of this fantastic fleet was Zheng He, known as the "Three-Jeweled Eunuch." He was a Muslim, and he probably hoped that on at least one of the trips he and his fellow Muslim sailors could make the hajj.

SECURING MALACCA

The fleet made seven voyages between 1405 and 1433. The main objective of the third voyage (1409–11) was to curb piracy and make sure that whoever controlled the Malay Straits acknowledged China's authority. Srivijaya was the most powerful kingdom in the region at that time, but no area completely dominated it.

In the struggle for power in the Malay Straits, Parameshvara, a Hindu prince who claimed he was related to the Srivijaya royal family, fled to a small fishing village at the strait's southern end. The village, which he named Malacca, had an excellent harbor and was strategically located to control the strait, and he hoped to attract merchants to his port. If the Ming wanted to control trade in the strait, Malacca was critical. So when the Ming fleet stopped at Malacca, Zheng He named Parameshvara the legitimate ruler and gave him a tablet declaring that Malacca was a vassal state of China.

The next Ming voyage, which lasted from 1414 to 1415, went to Champa, Sumatra, and Java. One part of the fleet continued on to Bengal, where they found a giraffe for the emperor because it looked something like a unicorn. Zheng He and the rest of the fleet continued to Ceylon, the Maldives, the Indian coast, and Hormuz on the Arabian Peninsula, and he and the other Muslim sailors may have made the hajj. This voyage marked the height of Chinese influence in the Indian Ocean.

SHOULD WE CONTINUE THE VOYAGES?

Many of the emperor's advisors were already arguing that the voyages were expensive and wasteful. Memories of the Mongols were fresh in people's minds, as well as the recent news that Tamerlane had sacked Delhi. It was clear to them that the northern barbarians were the real menace. No invaders had ever threatened China from the sea, and it seemed ill-advised to waste government resources on a fleet that would mainly be used to protect self-serving merchants from pirates. The Ming leaders believed they should be building up their defense against the tribes on the northern border who had recently kidnapped the young emperor and posed a growing threat to China. Resources would be better spent constructing the "Great Wall" to prected against possible invasions. Further, they insisted, China was self-sufficient and did not need foreign trade. Let foreigners come to China with tribute if they wished. Wasting resources on the fleet would overtax the peasants and cause discontent. And since the initial voyages had reestablished China's authority, why keep them up?

In 1433, after three more trips, the Ming emperor decided to end the voyages and withdraw the fleet. He ordered it dismantled and instructed his officials to destroy all records of the voyages. The government let the fleet rot, and soon no one remembered how to build the magnificent treasure ships. Future Ming emperors tried hard to close China's seaports to foreign visitors and prohibit Chinese merchants from trading in overseas ports.

WHAT WAS HAPPENING IN MALACCA?

At first it seemed that Malacca would profit from Zheng He's visit. But Parameshvara quickly realized that his special relationship with the Ming court did not give him a monopoly on trade with China. In spite of the band, Chinese merchants were now trading in all the ports the fleet had visited, and they had no particular incentive to stop at Malacca. That meant Muslim merchants could get Chinese goods from ports with Muslim rulers at the northern end of the strait and on Java. Those rulers were making fellow Muslims feel especially welcome.

When the Ming suddenly announced it was ending the voyages and withdrawing the fleet, the ruler of Malacca realized that his city would be ruined without trade with the Chinese fleet. His only hope was to attract Muslims to his port. It was not long before he revealed that the prophet Muhammad had appeared to him in a dream. As a result he became a Muslim and took the name Muhammad Shah.

Certainly part of his motivation must have been to attract Muslim merchants and make Malacca part of the lucrative Muslim Indian Ocean network. His conversion also underscored the growing importance of Islam in the islands of Southeast Asia and the Indian Ocean network in general. By the sixteenth century a Portuguese explorer would declare: "Whoever is lord of Malacca has his hands on the throat of Venice."

The Situation in 1450

Countries bordering the Indian Ocean experienced many political changes in the early fifteenth century. But political realignment did not significantly slow the brisk commerce across the Indian Ocean nor end land-based trade. Political stability is certainly an important factor in facilitating trade, but the fall of kingdoms and empires does not necessarily mean the end of long-distance commerce. This was especially true in the Indian Ocean where no state had a monopoly on trade and commerce was not identified with particular states.

The Thais on mainland Southeast Asia were becoming more powerful. In 1350 they founded the kingdom of Ayuttaya (named after Aydohya, Rama's Indian kingdom) and made repeated attacks on their Khmer neighbors. By 1400 they had defeated the Khmer kingdom, and within a few years the Angkor cities were deserted.

Changes were taking place in the Indian subcontinent as well. Vijayanagar had become a powerful South Indian kingdom, and by 1400 it was the third-largest city in the world. Vijayanagar, a self-sufficient, land-based kingdom far from the sea, was not especially interested in overseas trade. Even so, South Indian merchants continued their long-established trading patterns. Bengal in northeastern India and Gujarat on the northwestern coast remained two of the major exporters of fine cloth throughout the hemisphere.

By the start of the fifteenth century, the agrarian economy in Egypt had slumped, and the Mamluk dynasty that had succeeded Saladin needed new sources of revenue. Its capital, Cairo, was a good vantage point from which to control trade through the Red Sea into the Indian Ocean. Their more active role in the maratime trade made it increasingly difficult for Venice to participate in that route.

Even though Ming China had withdrawn its fleet, independent Chinese sailors continued their lucrative trading activities. Hundreds of ships plying the Indian Ocean also stopped at Chinese ports. China was much too large an economic power—as well as the most important source of silk and porcelain—to be isolated from the hemispheric trading network.

Ottoman Turks Enter the Drama

One of the most significant events of the mid-fifteenth century occurred in Byzantium. It involved a group of Turks from Inner Asia initially commanded by Osman. Under Osman's leadership they began to challenge Seljuk power. Osman's forces, the Osmanlis (or Ottomans as they came to be called), converted to Islam and became loyal believers. Although Osman died in 1325, his forces continued to expand, and they established small enclaves of power in Anatolia, west of the main Seljuk strongholds. Over the next two hundred years the Osmanlis launched repeated attacks against Byzantium and captured territory both east and west of Constantinople.

For centuries feudal Europeans, as well as Muslims, Byzantines, Japanese, and Indians, had built walls and castles to protect themselves from attackers. From behind strong defenses, they could fire arrows and pour hot oil and other liquids onto the unfortunate soldiers who tried to attack. Clearly, the

Rumali Husar

defense had the upper hand. However, after gunpowder—a new technology that came originally from China —became available, and soldiers learned to fire cannonballs and propel balls of fire over the walls, the balance of power gradually shifted to those on the offense.

The Ottomans, armed with gunpowder, turned their sights on Constantinople. Initially Mehmet, the young Ottoman ruler, had sworn friendship with the leadership in Constantinople, but he obviously had other ideas in mind. In 1451, when he was only nineteen, he ordered his men to build a fortress called Rumeli Hisar north of the city at the narrowest portion of the Bosporus, the strait connecting the Sea of Marmara and the Black Sea, so he could control the strait. In 1453 the Ottoman army launched an all-out campaign against the city. Although his troops had access to European-made cannons, gunpowder was not yet very effective, and their initial bombardment of the city walls was unsuccessful. In addition, their ships were unable to circumnavigate the city and enter the Golden Horn, the inlet north of the city, because a defensive chain lying across the mouth of the Bosporus kept boats out.

To get their ships into the Golden Horn, the Turks constructed a road with metal tracks that went from the Sea of Marmara, over the 200-foot hill behind the city walls and to the inlet. They attached iron wheels to wooden cradles large enough to hold the keels of their boats. Secretly, one night, teams of oxen hauled twenty-seven Turkish ships up the hill and then lowered them into the Golden Horn. From there Ottoman soldiers launched a surprise attack against the three and a half miles of the city's northern walls. The Ottomans soon breached the wall and claimed Constantinople. The emperor was killed and his body was never found.

If Muslims had been the most prominent presence in the Indian Ocean trading network before 1453, they certainly increased their position dramatically by taking Constantinople, the "second Rome" and the last great bastion of Christian power in the eastern Mediterranean. Conversion to Islam was on the rise, and Muslims were on the offensive. The Iberian Peninsula was the only place where Muslims were losing ground. Christian forces had conquered much of the Muslim territory, and by 1450 only Granada, on the tip of the peninsula, was still in Muslim hands.

And now what? Will the Turks and other Muslims continue to expand? Will they soon rule Europe? Will more and more Africans convert to Islam? Can any group check Muslim power?

What about the new states in Europe? How will they react to the fall of Constantinople? What will happen to Genoa and Venice and to Europe's growing merchant class now that the Ottomans control that important entrepôt? How will the fledgling European states compete with the older and larger states across the hemisphere? How can their leaders reconcile their strong commitment to Christianity with their desire to increase their political authority? How can European navigators and sailors compete in the profitable Indian Ocean trade?

What about India, Southeast and East Asia? Will they continue their dominance in manufacturing, and will their urban populations continue to grow? What will happen as a result of China's ban on maritime trade? How will the emerging states of Japan and Korea fare against their more powerful neighbors? What changes will gunpowder and other improved weapons make in the balance of power?

And what about the Western Hemisphere? Will the Aztecs continue to expand their power base in Mesoamerica? What other societies and civilizations will come to prominence there? And how long will it be before adventurers begin to cross the Atlantic and Pacific oceans, knitting the whole world together?

Summing Up and an Invitation to Future Acts

Two major themes have emerged from the millennium we have been studying. One is the importance of Asia during this period. From 500 to 1450 the balance of power resided in the zone from Byzantium to China and included South and Southeast Asia. The other overreaching theme is the dramatic and rapid spread of Islam. The new states and empires that embraced the Muslim faith helped make Dar al-Islam, that vast area under Muslim influence and control that stretched from the western coast of Africa to the border of China, a huge zone of communication and trade.

During this millennium, first Gupta India and Byzantium, and then China and the Islamic world, were the most creative and powerful societies in the hemisphere. However, these civilizations did not develop in isolation. Each was built on traditions from their past and major contributions from their neighbors. India took many things from the Greeks, especially mathematics and science. Buddhism and Hinduism may have been influenced by Christianity, and Greek and Roman sculpture inspired Indian images of the Buddha. Zero and place numbers, knowledge of astronomy and medicine, metallurgy, sugar, and cotton textile manufacturing were but a few of India's many exports to the wider world. Buddhism was perhaps its most far-reaching gift.

China drew on its Confucian and Daoist traditions and the Han concept of an administrative system based on merit. It contributed important technology, including paper, printing, gunpowder, and the mariner's compass. Muslim scholars preserved and made commentaries on an extensive body of Greco-Roman knowledge and also made significant advances in many disciplines including mathematics, astronomy, and medicine. Muslim scholarship exposed Europeans to many new ideas as well as to Greek and Roman texts. New crops and technological and scientific innovations from India, China and the Muslim world led to an increase in European agricultural production and resulted in an increase in population. New scholarship and an outburst of creativity followed.

Swahili city-states, part of the Indian Ocean trading network, and West African kingdoms thrived during this period. Ghana and Mali's gold helped fuel European development. In the Western Hemisphere, Teotihuacan and the Maya, building on earlier Olmec culture, were the most highly developed areas of Mesoamerica, sharing a common worldview and many beliefs and practices. Urban life increased, and new cities developed in many areas.

The empires that prospered during this era were similar to their predecessors in many ways. They based their economies on the crops of peasant farmers, and the elite took most of the produce for itself. Kings and emperors governed from lavish courts where they led opulent lives. They fought frequent wars in which conscripted peasants, mercenaries, or slave soldiers were expected to shed their blood on behalf of their sovereigns. Large horses, cavalry, and later gunpowder changed the face of warfare, shaped many economies, and was beginning to usher in new types of empires. Ships became larger, and inventions such as the mariner's compass and more accurate maps and charts encouraged rulers to commission impressive fleets, as well as to develop extensive land-based forces.

Continuing the age-old pattern of empires, wars and taxation often discouraged poor farmers, and many fled to private estates for protection. Most rulers depended on land taxes for revenue, so as estate owners became stronger, the central government often grew weaker. The Tang and Song examination-based civil service was the most innovative attempt to control the landed elites, but all states, including the Song, had difficulty checking their growth and power.

New farming technologies and crops changed agriculture across Afro-Eurasia. Muslim control of much of the heartland of Eurasia facilitated the transfer of crops, especially from India to Europe. These crops included rice, sugarcane, bananas, lemons, watermelons, spinach, eggplant and cotton. In Europe the horse collar, first used in China, together with the iron moldboard plow and new irrigation techniques, made it possible to farm the northern European plains. Water-powered mills and the mobilization of large numbers of workers stimulated production and consumption.

Amid all these changes the majority of people found meaning in their lives and direction for their actions from their religious beliefs, whether they followed one of the three universal religions or another faith. Each religion provided its followers with plausible explanations for life's contradictions and pains as well as incentives for living moral lives and the hope of future rewards. Despite the emerging hemispheric system of exchange, men and women still gave their hearts and allegiance to local areas and beliefs.

As we leave the human drama at about 1450, we can ponder some of the big questions about the course of history. Have we seen evidence of progress? Were average farmers better off in 1450 than they were in 500? Were women? Were leaders more just? Were bureaucrats fairer or more impartial? How did new crops, innovative farming techniques, and new inventions such as printing and gunpowder, affect people's lives? To what will these innovations lead?

Keep in mind that men and women are not destined to act in predetermined ways. At each point in history they face options and make choices. As circumstances change, options change, and people make different decisions. We can ponder and gain insight from the collective choices that people have made in the past. Why were they receptive to new religious insights? What sense did they make of tragedies such as the Black Death or destructive invasions? How did they react to new technology? What did it feel like to use decimals or print books for the first time? How did men and women respond to new crops and more food to eat? What are the new options you and I will face? What choices will we make?

As we end this portion of the human drama, we might wonder what connection exists between events that occurred over a thousand years ago and all of us with our shopping malls and satellite dishes. Do we have anything in common with people who lived so long ago? If we were transported back to Gupta India in 500, Tikal in 700, Constantinople in 1000, or Song China in 1200, would we find many familiar joys and challenges? Like each or us, people before us experienced satisfaction and sorrow, reveled in success and feared failure, laughed at absurdities and tried to make sense of the world. Moreover, their thoughts and insights, the technology they developed, and the art and literature they created are all part of their gift to us and to our lives. It may be that those of us in the twenty-first century will gain greater knowledge, develop more sophisticated technology, discover better ways to control some diseases or see farther into the universe. However, it is important to remember that our insights, discoveries and vision will come in large part because we build on the experiences and accomplishments of people who have gone before us.

ACT FIVE – HEMISPHERIC INTERACTION

Setting the Stage

1. Review the major groups of people that facilitated the exchange of goods and ideas during the period from 300 to 1450.
2. Describe the Aztecs when they first came into the Valley of Mexico. How did they change? Why?
3. How does the Aztec experience compare with earlier periods of nomadic migrations and interaction with settled peoples?
4. Why did some Vikings settle in Greenland? What kind of settlement did they create? What did they do when the climate got colder?
5. Describe the differences between Inuit and Viking ways of life. In what ways were the Inuit more suited to living in Greenland?
6. How did the Vikings view the Inuit? What might be some of the reasons that the Viking community in Greenland did not survive?

SCENE ONE
The Mongols: The Last Nomadic Empire

1. Describe the Mongol way of life. How was Mongol society organized?
2. What effects did geography have on the Mongol way of life?
3. Assess whether Mongol society was more egalitarian that other societies you have studied or than your own society today. Be specific.
4. What were the gender divisions in Mongol society?
5. Why was it often difficult for nomads to organize a large successful empire? How did the Mongols manage to create such a large empire?
6. Why were the Mongols so successful militarily? What kinds of psychological warfare did they use?
7. Cite two examples of how the Yuan Empire combined Mongol and Chinese ways. What Chinese customs did the Yuan maintain? What Chinese customs did they resist? Why?
8. Explain the Mongol system of communication. Why did they welcome merchants?
9. What was the Pax Mongolia? How did it affect trade?
10. Describe the various areas that were part of the Mongol empire. Why did the various parts of the Mongol Empire decline?
11. What were the immediate and long-term effects of Mongol rule?

SCENE TWO
Travelers, Germs, and Ideas on the Move

1. What impressed Marco Polo about China?
2. Compare Ibn Battuta and his journey with Marco Polo and his experience. How were they similar? How were they different?
3. What impact did the travels of Marco Polo and Ibn Battuta have in their societies?
4. How did people explain the reasons for the plague? How did they try to combat it?
5. What were the immediate effects of the plague? What were some of its long-term consequences?
6. What do the examples of the spread of paper, printing, the Panchatantra, and sugar suggest about the way ideas, diseases, inventions, and goods travel?
7. Select another commodity, idea, invention or belief and research the ways it has traveled to new areas. How did it change? Share your findings with the class.
8. What factors seem to facilitate the spread of commodities, idea, inventions, and beliefs? What factors might inhibit their spread?

SCENE THREE
Seas of Change in the Indian Ocean

1. Review how the monsoon system shaped commerce in the Indian Ocean.
2. Why were Malacca and the Straits of Malacca so important in the Indian Ocean trading network?
3. What role did Muslim merchants play in hemispheric exchanges? What was China's role in the Indian Ocean trade?
4. Why did the Ming embark on the voyages of the Treasure ships? What did the voyages accomplish? What were the arguments for and against ending the voyages?
5. Describe the Indian Ocean trading system in 1450. Who controlled the network?
6. What was the significance of the Ottoman victory in 1453? Assess the strength of the Muslims in Afro-Eurasia at that time.

Summing Up

1. Identify the main movements of people between 300 and 1450. What were the most important reasons people moved from one place to another? What were the major results of these movements on both those who moved and on the areas that they entered? How do these migrations and invasions compare with the movement of people in the period before the common era?

2. Identify some of the technological innovations that occurred during the period from 300 to 1450. What old ways did they replace? How did they affect the way humans lived? To what new innovations did they lead?

3. Assess the role of the environment during the period from 300 to 1450. For example, how did the environment affect the movement of people and the creation of new states or the decline of existing ones?

4. What were the major types of political organization that developed during the period from 300 to 1500? What are the similarities and differences between a land-based empire and a theater state? Between city-states, a large centralized state, and a decentralized or heterarchical state?

5. Assess how one of the following groups fared during this period or in different states: aristocrats, religious leaders, peasants, slaves, merchants, warriors, or the poor. Did both women and men perform these roles? If so, were they expected to do the same things and were their rewards the same? If not, how were they different and why?

6. Identify the methods that central governments in various areas used to discourage the development of large landed estates and to prevent them from becoming rival centers of power. Evaluate the effectiveness of these efforts.

7. Identify and compare some of the ways one or more of the universal religions adapted as it spread to new areas.

8. Assess the role of Muslims in the development and spread of agriculture, commercial strategies, scientific knowledge, and religious insights.

9. Into what areas did Indian and Chinese ideas and values spread? Compare and contrast how their insights were adapted in these areas.

10. Compare and contrast the complex civilizations that developed in Mesoamerica with one or more of the states in the Eastern hemisphere. What were some similarities? What were major differences?

11. From the vantage point of 1450, what were the major ways that the spread of universal religions affected and changed people's lives? Were the changes for the better? Explain your answer.

12. If you had a chance to live during this period, where and when would you want to live? What job would you want to have? Would you like to be a man or a woman? Explain the reasons for your choices.

13. Which groups (religious leaders, slaves and serfs, merchants, peasants, large landowners, etc.) were better off and which ones became worse during this epoch? Cite specific reasons for your answer.

14. What factors might lead a person in 1450 to conclude that Islam would become the dominant religion in all of Afro-Eurasia?

15. As a result of your study of history up to 1450, do you see signs of progress? In what ways were people's lives improving or getting worse?

16. What do you think is the major cause of chance over time? Cite specific reasons for your answers.

SOURCES OF ILLUSTRATIONS

Page 14: Art Resource, NY

Page 15: Werner Forman/Art Resource, NY

Page 19: Blanton, Richard E., Kowalewski, Steven A., Feinman, Gary M., and Finsten, Laura M. *Ancient Mesopotamia: A Comparison of Change in Three Regions*, 2nd ed. (Reprinted with the permission of Cambridge University Press.)

Page 20 & 21: Sean Tyrer, Friends Seminary, New York

Page 23: NYT Graphics/NYT Pictures

Page 25: Sigvad Linne, *Archaeological Researches at Teotihuacan*, 1934

Page 29: D. Donne Bryant/Art Resource, NY

Page 31: Jarrod Burks/NYT Pictures. (Permission pending)

Page 33: Top: Werner Forman/Art Resource, NY. Bottom: Erich Lessing/Art Resource, NY

Page 44: © The New Yorker Collection 1982 Edward Koren from cartoonbank.com. All Rights Reserved.)

Page 48: Indian Museum. Archaeological Survey of India, New Delhi. 71/58

Page 53: Courtesy Indonesian Consulate, New York City

Page 57: The Metropolitan Museum of Art, Purchase, Lila Acheson Wallace Gift, 1994. (1994.207)

Page 58: Don Johnson

Page 61: With the kind permission of the Korean Overseas Information Service

Page 68: © The New Yorker Collection 1960 James Stevenson from cartoonbank.com. All Rights Reserved.

Page 70: Reprinted from Mart Williams and Anne Echols, *Between Pit and Pedestal*, Markus Wiener Publishers, Princeton, p 116. Reprinted by permission of the publisher.

Page 74: Reprinted from Spuler, 12

Page 78: Scala/Art Resource, New York

Page 85: Government of India, New Delhi

Page 86: Erich Lessing/Art Resource, NY

Page 88: Copyright © 1991 by Nezar AlSayyad. Reproduced with permission of Greenwood Publishing Group, Inc., Westport, CT

Page 89: Reprinted from Heina Halm, *Shi'a Islam From Religion to Revolution*. Markus Wiener Publishers, Princeton, 1999, p. 10. Reprinted by permission of the publisher.

Page 112: The Metropolitan Museum of Art, Purchase, Diana and Arthur Altschul Gift, 1933 (1933.7)

Page 113: National Museum, New Delhi

Page 115: Archeological Survey of India, New Delhi, India

Page 116: Archaeological Survey of India, New Delhi, India

Page 127: Erich Lessing/Art Resource, NY

Page 129: Lauros-Giraudon/Art Resource, NY

Page 137: The Metropolitan Museum of Art, Fletcher Fund, 1947, The A.W. Bahr Collection. (47.18.93)

Page 138: Edwin O. Reischauer.and John Fairbank, *East Asia: The Great Tradition*. © 1960 by Houghton Mifflin Company. Reprinted with Permission.

Page 140: The Metropolitan Museum of Art, Purchase, Friends of Asian Art Gifts, 1989. (1989.152)

Page 149: Harrison Sacket Elliott

Page 154: The Metropolitan Museum of Art, Rogers Fund, 1929. (30.76.291)

Page 155: Edwin O.Reischauer and John Fairbank, *East Asia: The Great Tradition*. © 1960 by Houghton Mifflin Company. Reprinted with Permission.

Page 168: Harold Loucks

Page 172: Robert Auty, *An Introduction to Russian Art and Architecture*. (series Companion to Russian Studies). Reprinted with the permission of Cambridge University Press.

Page 174: Asia Society, New York: Mr. and Mrs. John D. Rockefeller 3rd Collection, 1979.020. Photography: Lynton Gardner

Page 178: C.M. Bhandari. *Saving Angkor*. Bangkok, White Orchid Press, 1995. Reprinted with Permission.

Page 183: Donald Johnson

Page 185: With the kind permission of the Korean Overseas Information Services

Page 189: With the kind permission of the Korean Overseas Information Services

Page 202: Reprinted from Said Hamdun and Noel King, *Ibn Battuta in Black Africa*, Markus Wiener Publishers, Princeton, 1999, p. 51. Reprinted by permission of the publisher.

Page 204: Reprinted from Hamdun and King, 33. Reprinted by permission of the publisher.

Page 206: Werner Forman Archive/Art Resource, NY

Page 209: Hamdun and King, XXIII. Reprinted by permission of the publisher.

Page 211: Blair Seitz/Art Resource

Page 219: Nezar AlSayyad. *Cities and Caliphs.* © 1991 by Nazar AlSayyad. Reproduced with permission of Greenwood Publishing Group, Inc. Westport CT.

Page 221: Reprinted from Charles Issawi, *The Middle East Economy Decline and Recovery.* Markus Wiener Publishers Princeton, 1995. p. 65. Reprinted by permission of the publisher.

Page 226: Reprinted from Bertold Spuler, *The Age of the Caliphs*, Markus Wiener Publishers Princeton, 1999. p. XVIII. Reprinted by permission of the publisher.

Page 228: Tor Eigeland

Page 230: Jean Johnson

Page 238: Giraudon/Art Resource, NY

Page 241: Art Resource, NY

Page 243: Giotto, St. Francis Basilica, Assisi

Page 244: Giraudon/Art Resource, NY

Page 246: Reprinted from Williams and Echols. Reprinted by permission of the publisher.

Page 248: Scala/Art Resource, NY

Page 252: Triumph of St. Thomas (Spanish Chapel, Church of Santa Maria Novella, Florence, Italy.)

Page 253: The Epiphany by Giotto (The Metropolitan Museum of Art, John Stewart Kennedy Fund, 1911. [11.126.1]

Page 256: © The New Yorker Collection 1983 Edward Koren from cartoonbank.com. All Rights Reserved.

Page 258: Great Council of Parliament. http://images.google.com/

images?q=English+PArliament&hl=en&btnG=Google+Search <www.mal-hatlantica.pt/mediateca/politica1600> Permission pending.

Page 261: Scala/Art Resource, NY

Page 277: Reprinted from Bertold Spuler, *The Mongol Period History of the Muslim World*. Markus Wiener Publishers, Princeton, 1999. Reprinted by permission of the publisher.

Page 278 & 279: From a Khamsa od Nizami by Mir Sayyid' Ali. Harvard University Art Museums. Arthur M. Sackler Museum.

Page 286: Reprinted from Hamdun and King. Reprinted by permission of the publisher.

Page 294: Art Resource, NY

Page 296: Archaeological Survey of India, New Delhi, India

Page 299: Scala/Art Resource, NY

Page 292: Dard Hunter. *Papermaking The History and Technique of an Ancient Craft*. (New York: Alfred A. Knopf, 1943), 250.

Page 309: Reprinted from Hamdin and King. Reprinted by permission of the publisher.

Page 312: Arnold Pacey, *Technology in World History*. (Cambridge, MA: MIT Press, 1990). Illustration by Hazel Cotterell. Reprinted with permission of the publisher.

Page 316: Jean Johnson

SOURCES OF QUOTES

Page 20: Rene Milton, quoted in Richard Blanton, Stephen A. Kowalewski, Gary M. Feinman, and Laura M. Finsten, *Ancient Mesoamerica A Comparison of Change in Three Regions*. (New York: Cambridge University Press, 1993), 128.

Page 46: See Jerry H. Bentley, *Old World Encounters*. (New York: Oxford University Press, 1993)

Page 50: Atasahasrika Prajnaparamita 22.403-3 quoted in Ainslie Embree, *Sources of the Indian Tradition*. Vol. I. (New York: Columbia University Press, 1988), 160

Page 59: Quoted in Arthur F. Wright, *Buddhism in Chinese History*. (Stanford: Stanford University Press, 1959), 67.

Page 60: Ahn Kye-hyon "A Short History of Ancient Korean Buddhism," in Lewis R. Lancaster & C.S. Yu, editors, *Introduction to Buddhism to Korea New Cultural Patterns*. (Berkeley, Ca: Asian Humanities, 1989), 19.

Page 82: The Glorious Qur'an. Text and Explanatory translation by Muhammad M. Pickthall.(Elmhurst, NY: Tahrike Tarsile Qur'an, Inc.,1999), 19. All quotes from the Qur'an are from this source unless otherwise indicated.

Pages 107-8: Adapted from James Legge, *A Record of Buddhist Kingdoms*. (New York: Dover Publications, Inc. 1965), 42-3.

Page 109: *Manu Smriti* IX:3 Quoted in Ainslie Embree, *The Hindu Tradition Reading in Oriental Thought*. (Vintage Books, 1972), 88.

Page 114: Pattuppattu, Tirumuruganarrupadai. 285-90, quoted in A. L. Basham, *The Wonder that was India*. (New Delhi: Rupa & Co, 1994), 333

Page 117: Barbara Stoler Miller, *Theater of Memory The Plays of Kalidasa*. (New York: Columbia University Press, 1984), 130.

Pages 118: Krishnaji Patwardhan, Pateardhan Somashekhara Amrita Naimpally and Shyam Lal Singh, translators, *Lilavati of Bhaskaracarya A Treatise of Mathematic of Vedic Tradition*. (Delhi: Motilal Barnarsidass Publishers, 2001), 58. Answer: 30 pearls

Pages 119: Basham, 67.

Pages 121-2: Procopius. *History of the Wars.*

Page 128: Quoted in John A.Garraty and Peter Gay. *The Columbia History of the World.* (New York: Harper & Row, Publishers, 1983), 424.

Page 128: *Ibid.*

Page 136: Quoted in Ann Paludan, *Chronicle of the Chinese Emperors.* (New York: Thames and Hudson, 1998), 99.

Page 137: Paul Wheatley, *The Pivot of the Four Quarters: a preliminary enquiry into the origins and character of the ancient Chinese city.* (Chicago: Aldine Publishing. Co, 1971), 428.

Page 138: *Wheatley,* 450.

Page 141: Patricia Ebrey, *Cambridge Illustrated History of China.* (New York: Cambridge University Press, 1997). 127.

Page 142: "Quiet Night Thoughts" translated by Arthur Cooper, *Li Bo and Tu Fu.* (Baltimore, MD: Penguin Books, 1973).

Page 142: Rhodes Murphey, *A History of Asia.* (New York: HarperCollins College Publishers, 1996), 109.

Page 142: Bai Juyi, translated by Arthur Waley, *More Translations from the Chinese.* (New York: Knopf, 1919)

Page 143: Waley, 71.

Page 143: A. R. Davis, *Du Fu.* (New York: Twayne Publishers, Inc. 1971) p. 46.

Page 143-4: Rewi Alley, trans., *Tu Fu Selected Poems.* (Beijing Foreign Language Press), 13.

Page 145-46: Han Yu. quoted in Edwin Reischauer, *Ennin's Travels in T'ang China.* (New York: Roland Press, 1955), 221-4.

Page 146: Emperor Tang Wuzong. "Proclamation Ordering the Destruction of the Buddhist Monasteries" quoted in Reischauer, 288.

Page 149: Wang Fungwu "The Rhetoric of a Lesser Empire" quoted in Morris Rossabi, *China Among Equals.* (Berkeley: Univ. of California Press, 1983), 53.

Page 153: Li Qing-zhao, quoted in *Selections from Tang and Song Poetry.* (Boston:Primary Source. info@primarysource.org),

Page 155: Laurence J.C. Ma, quoted in Susan Mann, *East Asia, China, Japan, Korea.* (Washington, D.C.: American Historical Association and the Committee on Women Historians, 1999), 26.

Page 171: Serge A. Zenkovsky, editor, *Medieval Russia's Epics, Chronicles, and Tales.* (New York: Dutton, 1974), 67, 70.

Page 171: Michael Florinsky, *Russia: A History and Interpretation.* (New York, Macmillan, 1953) 128.

Page 175: K. M. Panikkar, *India and the Indian Ocean.* (New York: The Macmillan Company, 1945), 80-81.

Page 177-8: Ploy Prittsangkul, International School in Bangkok. Posted on I*earn, January 25, 2001.

Page 184: Yong Jin Kim Choi, *Korea Lessons for High School Social Studies Courses.* (New York: The Korea Society, 1999), 139.

Page 185: Kichung Kim, *An Introduction to Classical Korean Literature From Hyangga to Pansori.* (Armonk, NY: M.E. Sharpe, 1996), 13-15.

Page 189: W. G. Aston, trans, *Nihongi: Chronicles of Japan from the Earliest Times to A..D. 697,* Vol. 2. (Rutland, Vt: C. E. Tuttle Co.,1972), 128-133.

Page 191: Lady Kasa, quoted in Donald Keene, translator and editor, *The Anthology of Japanese Literature: From The Earliest Era to the Mid-Nineteenth Century.* (New York: Grove Press, 1955), 41.

Page 201: Abu Ubaydallah al-Bakri. *The Book of Routes and Realms* quoted in J. F. P. Hopkins. *Corpus of Early Arabic Sources from West African History.* (Cambridge: Cambridge University Press, 1981), 80-81.

Page 203: D.T. Niane, *Sundiata an Epic of Old Mali.* (Longman Group Ltd, 1965), 75-78, 81.

Page 205: Al-Omari, quoted in Basil Davidson, *A History of West Africa, 1000-1800.* (London: Longman, 1977), 51.

Page 205: Ross Dunn, *The Adventures of Ibn Battuta A Muslim Traveler of the 14th Century.* (Berkeley: University of California Press, 1986), 300, 299-300.

Page 209: Ibn Battuta, quoted in Richard W. Hull, *African Cities and Towns Before the European Conquest.* (New York: W.W. Norton & Company, 1976), 11.

Page 210: *Hull,* 11.

Page 212-3: John S. Mbiti, *African Religions and Philosophy.* (London: Heinemann, 1988), 2, 108-9.

Page 213: G. K. Osei, *The African Philosophy of Life.* (London: African Publication Society, 1970), 11.

Page 213: Richard Olaniyan, *African History and Culture.* (Lagos: Longman Nigeria, 1992), 35.

Page 216: Mbiti, 34-5.

Page 219-20: Lynda Norene Shaffer, *Maritime Southeast Asia to 1500.* (Armonk, NY: M.E. Sharpe, 1996), 40.

Page 220: Cited in Alfred J. Andrea and James H. Overfield, *The Human Record Sources of Global History*, Vol. I. (Boston: Houghton Mifflin Company, 1994), 280.

Page 220: Al-Suyuti, cited in Susan L. Douglass and Karima Alavi, *The Emergence of Renaissance Cultural Interactions Between Europeans and Muslims.* (Fountain Valley, CA: Council on Islamic Education, 1999), 180.

Page 222: *Rubaiyat* of Omar *Khayyam, the Astronomer and Poet of Persia.* trans. (NY: Thomas Y. Crowell Co., 1921)

Page 227-8: Oleg Garbar, "Islamic Spain, the First Four Centuries An Introduction." in Jerrilynn D. Dodds, ed., *Al-Andalus The Art of Islamic Spain.* (New York: The Metropolitan Museum of Art, 1992), 8.

Page 231: Bernard Lewis, quoted in Albert Hourani, *The Ottoman Background of the Modern Middle East.* (London: Longman for the University of Essex, 1970) 3-4

Page 233: Edward Burns, *et al., World Civilizations Their History and Their Culture.* (New York: W. W. Norton & Company, 1982), 386.

Page 238: Adapted from *Miserere,* quoted in Joan Evans, *Life in Medieval France.* (London: Phaidon, 1969), 16.

Page 239: *Conte des Vilains de Verson,* quoted in Evans, 32.

Page 239: Adalberon of Laon, quoted in Evans, 31.

Page 241: Bernart de Ventadorn, quoted in The Metropolitan Museum of Art. *Chivalry Courtly Love and Other Pastime*s. (New York: Macmillan Publishing Co., Inc)

Page 253: Rosser, Yvette C., on H-ASIA, 5/29/01, quoting a Pakistani text translated by Zahar Jaffry. y.r.rani@mail.utexas.edu

Page 255: R. W. Southern, *Western Society and the Church in the Middle Ages.* (Penguin Books, Ltd., 1970), 102.

Page 262: Amin Maalouf, *The Crusades through Arab Eyes.* (New York: Schocken Books, 1984), 39.

Page 276-7: "Song of Ch'ih-le" quoted in Sechin Jagchid and Paul Hyer, *Mongolia's Culture and Society.* (Boulder, CO: Westview Press, 1979), 10.

Page 294-5: *The Travels of Marco Polo.* (New York: The Orion Press, n.d.), 163. 229, 231

Page 281: Dunn, 168-9.

Page 299: Helen Grady, Helen Finken, Mary Price, and Sue Robinson ,

Woodrow Wilson curriculum.

Page 300: Jean Froissart, *Chronicles*, ed. and trans. by Geoffrey Brereton. (Harmondsworth. Baltimore: Penguin Books, 1978 c1968), 111.

Page 300: Konigshofen's history. Quoted in Jewish History Sourcebook. Web www.fordam.edu/halsall/jewish/1348-jewsblackdeath.html)

Page 302-3: See Susan L. Douglass and Karima Alavi, 127 and Dart Hunter, *Papermaking The History and Technique of an Ancient Craft*. (New York: Alfred A. Knopf, 1943).

Page 304: See *Hinduism Today*. September 1992, p. 13

Page 305-6: Sidney Mintz, *Sweetness and Power*. (Elisabeth Sifton Press, Viking Penguin. 1985)

Page 310: Abu'l-Faraj al-Isfahani, Kitab al-Aghani, iii, pp 45-46, quoted in Bernard Lewis, *Islam from the Prophet Muhammad to the capture of Constantinople*, Volume II. (New York: Harper & Row, 1974), 47-48.

INDEX